Top Tips for Online Shoppers

Inside this book, you'll find hundreds of tips, pieces of insider advice, and all-around help for shopping online—as well as lists of the best shopping sites you'll find online. Here are some tips for online shoppers:

➤ **Be sure you buy only from secure sites—and know which sites are secure and which aren't.** A secure site scrambles personal information and your credit card number so hackers can't find them as they get sent out over the Internet.

➤ **When you buy several items from the same site, have them shipped together.** Sometimes the items become available at different times. If you can, wait and have them shipped together; you'll save on shipping costs.

➤ **When buying computer hardware, never pay "restocking fees."** Some buying sites charge you a "restocking fee" if you return a computer—as much as 20%. Avoid these sites.

➤ **Look for hidden costs before buying.** When you tally up the cost of your online buy, figure in shipping costs, taxes, and similar costs.

➤ **Buy from sites that list mailing addresses and phone numbers.** You want to be sure you can contact a site, and that it's a legitimate one.

➤ **Don't buy products or stocks solely on advice you come across on discussion boards or chat areas.** Be wary of anyone heavily promoting a product on the Internet.

➤ **Check out return policies and warranties before you buy.** What kind of warranty does the product carry—and how long do you have to return it?

➤ **Try out software for free before buying it.** Almost any piece of software has a free version you can try for a month or so before buying.

➤ **Be careful how you pay at auction sites.** At many auction sites, you'll buy from individuals whom you might have never met. So be careful how you pay—consider using an escrow service that will hold your money until you receive the goods.

➤ **Use shopping robots (ShopBots) to get the best deal possible.** A number of sites called ShopBots will do your comparison shopping for you and find the best price on anything you might want to buy. Shop there first.

➤ **Use your credit card when buying online.** When you pay with a credit card, you get a variety of consumer protections, so always pay with your credit card when you buy on the Internet.

➤ **Always print out your order and put it in a safe place.** Whenever you buy online, you'll come to a page that confirms your order. Always print out that page and put it in a safe place—it's your confirmation of the order, and you'll need it if you run into trouble with the order.

W9-BEJ-304

Best Shopping Sites Online

Amazon.com
www.amazon.com

Best bookstore on the Internet—buy any book at a great discount. And get CDs and buy at auctions as well.

Edmunds
www.edmunds.com

This site tells you what the dealer paid for the car you want to buy. Armed with that, you can buy the car at your price.

CoolSavings.com
www.coolsavings.com

Save big-time on everything from clothes to food to cruises and more at this coupon site.

eToys
www.etoys.com

You want to buy a toy? You'll find it here at a discount, along with advice on what to buy.

Expedia
www.expedia.com

An all-in-one travel site for checking ticket prices, buying tickets online, and travel tips.

HomeRuns
www.homeruns.com

Never go to the supermarket again—shop at this grocery site and get free delivery.

eBay
www.ebay.com

Buy anything at great discounts at this online auction site.

Internet Fraud Watch
www.fraud.org

Check this site out and you'll never get burned by an Internet scam.

CompareNet
www.comparenet.com

Get side-by-side comparisons of thousands of products at this great consumer advice site.

Fogdog Sports
www.fogdog.com

You'll find anything to do with sports at great discounts.

RocketCash
http://www.rocketcash.com

Set up a shopping account for your kids—and monitor what they buy.

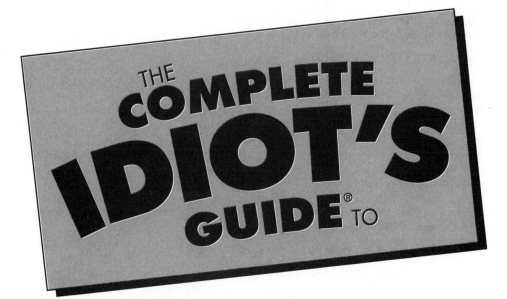

Online Shopping

Second Edition

by Preston Galla

201 W. 103rd Street, Indianapolis, IN 46290

The Complete Idiot's Guide® to Online Shopping, Second Edition

Copyright © 1999 by Que®

International Standard Book Number: 0-7897-2130-9

Library of Congress Catalog Card Number: 99-63010

Printed in the United States of America

First Printing: September 1999

01   00   99   4   3   2   1

Trademarks

Warning and Disclaimer

Publisher
Greg Wiegand

Acquisitions Editor
Stephanie J. McComb

Development Editor
Nicholas Goetz

Managing Editor
Thomas F. Hayes

Project Editor
Tom Stevens

Copy Editors
Kay Hoskin
Ryan Walsh

Indexer
Aamir Burki

Proofreaders
Jeanne Clark
Maribeth Echard

Technical Editor
Nicholas Goetz

Illustrator
Judd Winick

Interior Designer
Nathan Clement

Cover Designer
Michael Freeland

Copy Writer
Eric Borgert

Layout Technician
Brad Lenser

Contents at a Glance

Table of Contents

xi

xiii

About the Author

Preston Gralla is the author of 11 books, including the best-selling *How the Internet Works* and *The Complete Idiot's Guide to Protecting Yourself Online*. He has written about the Internet and computer technology for many magazines and newspapers, including *USA Today, PC Magazine*, the *Los Angeles Times, Boston Magazine*, and *PC/Computing*, and has won several writing and editing awards, including one for the best feature article in a computer magazine from the Computer Press Association. As a well-known Internet expert, he appears frequently on TV and radio shows such as *CBS This Morning, MSNBC,* and ZDTV's *Call for Help*. He is the executive editor of the ZDNet Software Library at www.hotfiles.com, was the founding managing editor of *PC Week*, and was a founding editor of *PC/Computing*. Gralla lives in Cambridge, Massachusetts, with his wife Lydia, children Gabriel and Mia, and a rabbit named Polichinelle. He also writes the free *Gralla's Internet Insider* email newsletter. To subscribe to it free, send email to preston@gralla.com with the words **SUBSCRIBE NETINSIDER** on the subject line.

Dedication

For Lydia, for whom shopping is a calling, not a mere hobby.—Preston

Acknowledgments

Shopping is often a solo experience; writing and publishing a book isn't. My name might be on the cover of this book, but it was the work of many people.

First of all, thanks to John Pierce at Macmillan, who helped hatch this book over the course of a long lunch. And thanks, yet once again, to Renee Wilmeth, editor extraordinaire who helped shape this book from the very beginning and stuck with it through every step. A big thanks to Stephanie McComb, acquisitions editor, not just for this book, but for the many others we've worked together on—and many more to come. And many thanks to development editors Noelle Gasco and Nick Goetz, who slaved over every one of my words and made sure that the text was coherent, on target, and (relatively) on time. And thanks also go to Jamie Barnett, the duke of URL for this book, who tech-checked everything, including the myriad shopping locations. Thanks also to project editors Linda Seifert and Tom Stevens and copy editors June Waldman, Kay Hoskin, and Ryan Walsh.

As always, thanks to my agent, Stuart Krichevsky. And finally, most of all, I have to thank my wife, Lydia, my own personal shopper and shopping consultant. Lydia has bought and returned so many goods in her lifetime that no one on the planet is better equipped to know all the ins and outs of how and what to buy, of return policies, of warranties, and the like. And let's face it, who else would spend 20 minutes ensuring that the colors of shirts and pants match in a screen shot for this book—and all for a book that's being published in black and white?

If there's something Lydia knows, it's shopping. If there's ever going to be a Shopping Hall of Fame, she'll be its first inductee. Without her, there would be no book.

Tell Us What You Think!

As the reader of this book, *you* are our most important critic and commentator. We value your opinion and want to know what we're doing right, what we could do better, what areas you'd like to see us publish in, and any other words of wisdom you're willing to pass our way.

As a Publisher for Que, I welcome your comments. You can fax, email, or write me directly to let me know what you did or didn't like about this book—as well as what we can do to make our books stronger.

Please note that I cannot help you with technical problems related to the topic of this book, and that due to the high volume of mail I receive, I might not be able to reply to every message.

When you write, please be sure to include this book's title and author as well as your name and phone or fax number. I will carefully review your comments and share them with the author and editors who worked on the book.

Fax: 317-581-4666

Email: consumer@mcp.com

Mail: Greg Wiegand, Publisher
          Que
          201 West 103rd Street
          Indianpolis, IN 46290

Introduction

How would you like to find airline tickets at hundreds of dollars less than the advertised prices? How would you like to be able to get discounts of up to 40% on books you buy—and have them delivered straight to your doorstep? How about having the power to buy nearly any CD ever made—and listen to selections before you decide to buy? Do you want to save hundreds or thousands of dollars on your next car? You can if you have insider information about the real price that your dealer paid for it. Do you want to find free stuff and coupons galore—and even get software that you'll never have to pay for? Want to save hundreds or thousands of dollars a year when you trade stocks? How about never having to go to the supermarket again, because all your food is delivered right to your home?

Sounds pretty good, doesn't it? Well, guess what: You can do all that and more just by using this book. What I listed is only a tiny percentage of the benefits you can get by shopping on the Internet—or by using the Internet to do consumer research before you buy. The truth is that anyone who owns a computer and a modem can tap into a wealth of goods online and save big-time in the bargain. The Internet and online services such as America Online have truly become a shopper's paradise. Billions of dollars are already being spent online every year, and many more billions will be spent in the coming years. That's because of the ease of shopping online, the bargains you can find online, and the amazing resources you can find online to help you become a smarter shopper.

This book can help you get the most out of shopping online. It's filled with insider tips; shopping secrets; hands-on advice; lists of the best shopping sites in cyberspace; $350,000 in gold bullion…oh, sorry, I got carried away there, I guess there isn't any bullion in here, or at least there wasn't the last time I checked. But the advice you'll find is certainly as good as gold and worth mucho money as well.

If you haven't yet bought anything on the Internet, I hope this book will at least get you to put your money on the line—on the modem line, that is. It'll teach you everything you need to know before shopping online—how you can be sure that no one will take your credit card information, how to research anything before buying it, the best places to go for buying anything on the Internet, and pretty much everything else you need to know before making the plunge.

If you've already bought something online, this book will help you become a better shopper—you'll learn all the tips and tricks of the trade, and you'll get the best product at the best price.

And whether you have or you haven't yet shopped online, this book will certainly help you become a more cybersavvy shopper.

One thing you should keep in mind when using this book is that the Internet is a great place for getting shopping information and advice, whether or not you actually buy something online or not. So even if you don't buy a car or airplane tickets or other goods over the Internet, you can use the Internet to get shopping information, inside deals, and consumer advice about all kinds of products and services.

So, what are you waiting for? It's time to shop!

How to Use This Book

This book is divided into four parts. It starts with the basics of online shopping, moves on to teaching you how to be a cybersavvy online shopper, clues you in on all the ways to get great bargains online, and finally, teaches you how to buy anything over the Internet or with an online service.

Part 1, "How to Shop 'Til You Drop in Cyberspace," made up of Chapters 1 through 3, covers everything you need to know before embarking on your online shopping expedition. Armed with the information in these chapters, you'll be able to boldly go where many have gone before—to the malls, stores, and shopping sites on the Internet.

In Part 2, "How to Be a Cybersavvy Online Consumer," Chapters 4 through 7, you learn how to be a sharp-eyed online shopper, always getting the best deal possible and ensuring that you don't get burned.

Part 3, "In Search of Bargains Online," Chapters 8 through 11, gives you the lowdown on how to get great deals and freebies online.

The final section of the book, Part 4, "How to Buy Anything in Cyberspace," Chapters 12 through 27, covers just what it says. Here's where to turn when you want to buy anything from cars to CDs, electronics, food, sports equipment, and household goods...well, you get the idea. Each chapter covers a different type of product or service. In each chapter, you'll find hard-core consumer advice, tips on how to buy, what you should know before buying, and a list of the best sites online for buying.

Finally, a glossary titled "Speak Like a Geek: The Complete Archive" defines important computer and technical terms.

Conventions Used in This Book

To help you shop online, this book also gives you inside secrets, tips, and bits of information that will help you get the most out of your money. You'll find them in these boxes:

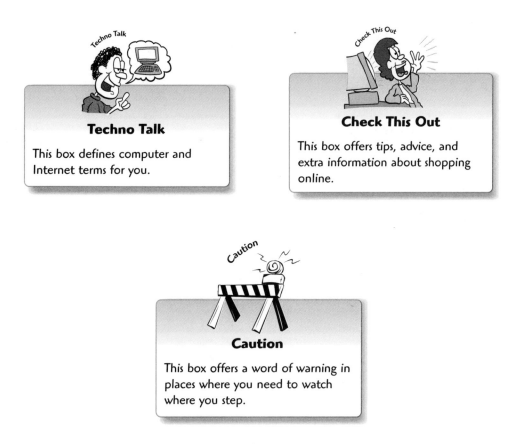

Techno Talk

This box defines computer and Internet terms for you.

Check This Out

This box offers tips, advice, and extra information about shopping online.

Caution

This box offers a word of warning in places where you need to watch where you step.

Part 1

How to Shop 'Til You Drop in Cyberspace

Attention cybershoppers! Big savings, convenience, and more stuff to buy than you ever can imagine is only a modem call away.

Sounds good, you're no doubt thinking. But you're also probably wondering how do you actually shop online? What should you expect to see when you get to a shopping site on the Internet? How do you pay? How can you be sure that no one steals your credit card information? And when you're online, won't you miss the familiar God-like voice calling out over the PA system, "Attention, K-Mart Shoppers"? (Answer: No, you won't miss that voice at all. Believe me on this one.)

Well, you've come to the right place if you're looking to learn how to shop online. This first part teaches you everything you need to know before starting your online shopping expedition. You'll learn how to shop, how to be sure that your credit card information is never stolen, and how to protect your privacy online. You'll find out what kind of stores you can buy from in cyberspace and how to use them all. You'll become a pro at using virtual shopping carts and getting free samples of stuff before you buy. In short, it'll teach you how to become a cyber-shopping pro. So get ready to learn to shop 'til you drop in cyberspace.

Chapter 1

Getting Started on Your Online Shopping Expedition

In This Chapter

➤ How to get started

➤ What you should know before buying

➤ How to use virtual shopping carts

➤ How to research online and buy offline

Okay, so you're raring to go. You've heard all about the great shopping deals you can find on the Internet, and you have a long list of stuff and gadgets you want to buy. You've got your Internet browser fired up, your credit card is jumping and shaking so much, it wants to be used, and you're ready to start shopping.

Well, calm down, Bucky. Before you send your plastic over the line, you'll want to know a few things: for example, exactly how you buy anything online; how to make sure no one steals your credit card number; how to use "virtual" shopping carts; and how to get free samples and coupons. And yes, even how to make sure you don't lose your cookies when you shop online. (Yes, you can lose your cookies on the Internet...strange but true. Check out the section "How Buying Online Works" to find out why and how.)

This chapter covers all the basics of shopping online. So put your credit card away for at least a few minutes and read on. It'll pay off big time when you're ready to start your Internet shopping expedition.

What You Should Know Before Buying

As the man says, the best place to start is at the beginning. So let's start with the basics of what you need to know before you buy online.

To shop on the Web, you need a Web browser, such as Microsoft Internet Explorer or Netscape Navigator. A Web browser is software that lets you get onto the World Wide Web and displays Web sites on your computer. You also need a connection to the Internet through an Internet service provider such as AT&T WorldNet or from an online service such as America Online. Depending on your location, you might also have access to a local Internet service provider. You can connect to the Internet other ways as well, for example, with a cable modem or through your television set with a service such as WebTV.

You need a credit card as well, because most sites require them for a purchase. Visa and MasterCard are the most commonly accepted cards.

How Can TV Work with the Internet?

These days, TV services and the Internet are getting closer together. A cable modem lets you get onto the Internet using your computer and your cable TV service—and it does so at a much higher speed than a normal modem. WebTV is a service that lets you use your TV set to browse the Internet. And DirectPC is a satellite service that lets you get onto the Internet using a satellite dish that can also give you TV reception.

You shop by going to Web sites with your browser. You are able to browse through these online stores by pointing and clicking—and you won't have to put up with annoying sales clerks, fellow shoppers who push you out of the way to finger the merchandise, or bad fluorescent lighting. Just as in the real world, there will be specials on sale (the complete recordings of the Carpenters for only $19.99—how can you pass that one up!) And just as in the real world, you'll have to pay for what you buy as well, usually with your credit card. To pay with your credit card, you type the necessary information into your browser. Don't worry, as I explain in Chapter 2, "Show Me the Money! Paying with Credit Cards and Electronic Wallets," and Chapter 4, "How to Be a Cybersavvy Shopper," you can take precautions to ensure that stealing your credit card numbers is all but impossible.

Typically, you pay a shipping charge and then wait a few days to receive your purchase by mail or a delivery service (unless you've bought a car, of course, which won't fit inside a typical postal sack).

How Buying Online Works

The preceding section describes the basics of what you need to know before buying. But, there's a lot more you should know as well, starting with what exactly happens when you visit a shopping site, and then what happens when you decide to buy.

The Internet is home to several different kinds of buying sites. (For more details on these, head to Chapter 3, "So, Where Should I Shop Online?") The following is a list of just a few of the types of sites you can find on your Internet travels:

➤ You can buy directly from the manufacturer of a product, such as from computer maker Dell at www.dell.com.

➤ You can buy from the online version of a retail store or mail-order outlet, such as Land's End at www.landsend.com.

➤ You can buy from a store that specializes in a specific product and that exists only in cyberspace, such as the online bookseller www.amazon.com.

➤ You can buy from an online mall that sells hundreds of kinds of products, much like a real-life mall, such as at ShopNow.com at www.shopnow.com. (For more on mall shopping, see Chapter 15, "Mall Fever: Department Stores, Malls, Closeouts, and Bargain Hunting.")

➤ And you can buy from online auctions such as at www.ebay.com. (For more information on auctions, see Chapter 11, "Sold American! Buying Through Online Auctions.")

No doubt, you'll find other kinds of places to buy from online, but for now that covers the basics.

So what happens when you get to a site? Well, for one thing, you are usually hit with a sales pitch—the day's specials, one-shot sales, that sort of thing. Sometimes you find good deals there, but sometimes these are just plain dogs that the site is hoping to fob off on unsuspecting shoppers. Be extra wary about these specials. In a real store, you can examine the merchandise and see that perhaps the orange polyester jumpsuit with a lime-green belt isn't quite as flattering as you might hope. Online, you might not have that luxury, depending on whether the site includes photos of the items for sale.

When you finally get beyond the day's specials, you'll find out why online shopping is better in many ways than shopping in real-life malls and stores: It's so much easier to find the merchandise you want to buy. You are almost always able to browse through the site by the category of the item you want to buy, such as shoes or consumer electronics, and you won't have to walk by aisles of closeout specials (doilies embroidered with the likenesses of George and Barbara Bush, anyone?).

An even faster way to find what you're looking for is to search. Most sites include a search box—a box into which you can type a word or words that describe the goods you want to buy. You can type in the name of the product, the manufacturer, the type of product, or any other word or words that describe what you want to buy. After you type in a search term, you'll be shown a list of items that might match what you're looking for, as shown in this figure, which details the search results for the words "Talking Heads" on the CDNow music shopping site at www.cdnow.com. Click any link for more details.

Start making sense: the results of searching the www.cdnow.com music site for Talking Heads.

A word of warning about searching shopping sites: Some of them have terrible technology. Be prepared to wade through lots of irrelevant links. If the first word or words you type in don't get you what you're looking for, keep trying.

So, you've browsed, you've searched, you've been pitched, and now you're primed to buy. What next? Well, now it's time to buy. In general, you're going to pay with your credit card when you buy over the Internet. Don't worry—there are ways to ensure that your card information is safe and isn't stolen by hackers, crackers, or crooks. Chapter 4 explains how to know that you're buying through a secure site and how to protect your credit card number.

Typically, before you buy, you'll be sent to an area that's a "safe site," secure from prying eyes. You'll be asked for your name and address (both postal and email); credit card brand, number, and expiration date; your address; and sometimes verification information such as your mother's maiden name. Some sites also ask for more information, such as your age and family income. It's rare that they require that information, though. And if you feel uncomfortable about giving out that information, no problem: Just make up some numbers! Make yourself as rich as Bill Gates if you like; no one's going to turn down your business just because you didn't provide your exact income. It's not as if you're dealing with the IRS (and if you were, you certainly wouldn't be buying anything).

After you fill in the information, you'll click a button on a link, wait a few seconds while your credit card information is checked (you have paid up this month, haven't you?), and then receive some kind of verification about your purchase. Some sites also send an email verification of your order. A word to the wise: Print out your verification and keep it in a safe place. It's the only printed matter that you'll have if the merchandise doesn't arrive, if you need to return it, or if some other kind of trouble pops up.

Sometimes When You Search a Site for Something to Buy, You Won't Be Able to Find Exactly What You Want

Don't despair: There are ways to quickly find that perfect cappuccino maker you've always been looking for. Many sites allow you to use "Boolean logic" when you search. Despite a nerdy-sounding name, it's not hard to use. Boolean logic lets you combine words together when searching. In its simplest form, you use the words AND and OR. You use AND when you want to narrow a search. When you use AND, you'll find items related to both of the words. So, for example, if you were to type Car AND Sedan into a search box, you'd get a list of all cars that are sedans. You wouldn't be shown any cars that aren't sedans.

You use OR to broaden a search. When you use it, you'll find items related to do either of the terms. So, for example, if you were to type Roth OR Bellow into a search box, you'd find all the books that Phillip Roth wrote and all the books that Saul Bellow wrote. Here's one more tip as well: When you surround your words with quotes, you'll search only for things that contain the exact phrase. So if you type in "How the Internet Works, Fourth Edition," you'd find the book of that name (written by yours truly).

Some sites ask you to specify a delivery method: regular mail, second-day air, or overnight express. To save money, go with the cheapest option (which is usually also the slowest). Although many sites offer discounts when you buy online, that savings can easily be eaten up in delivery costs. So, the book that you bought at a 20% discount could actually end up costing you more money than buying retail.

To make shopping easier for you, most sites let you establish a standing account. In fact, some sites require you to establish an account before shopping there. This feature means that when you visit the site again, you won't have to type in your name, credit card information, and so on—that'll already be on record. And, of course, customer accounts make things easier for the sites as well, because then you'll always be only one or so clicks away from buying something (which does not make things easier on your bank account).

Often, in order to access your account, you'll need to type in a username and password, or possibly just a password. Sometimes the site will create the username and password for you, but more often than not, you'll get to create both. That way, no one can use your credit card because only you know your username and password.

Be careful when creating these names and passwords. Because, believe it or not, many hackers gain access to people's accounts not by some amazing feat of programming mastery, but instead by guessing passwords and usernames. That's right, just plain old guessing. And the reason they can do this is because—well, there's no way to put this politely—because many people are just plain dumb when they create usernames and passwords. For usernames, people often use their last name and first initial of their first name. For passwords, they'll often use their initials or some common word such as, yes, you guessed it, password. Let me give you some advice: Forget cute when you create a username and a password. Think complicated. Think impossible to guess. Think about some hacker getting access to your credit card. Because let's face it— it doesn't take any programming genius to guess the name tsmith, or the password love.

Here are a few more tips about passwords and usernames. Print out a list of them and keep them somewhere safe. If you keep track of them only on your computer and your computer crashes, you'll lose the information. Don't use the same username and password on every site you visit—that way, if someone discovers a username and password on one site, he or she won't be able to use it on other sites. And if you're exceptionally paranoid, change your username and password at each site regularly.

You'll notice that some shopping sites that you've visited know who you are when you visit them again. They might even welcome you back by name. How can they do that? No, they haven't hired the Amazing Kreskin to use his supernatural powers to discern through the Internet wires who you are. Instead, when you visit for the first time, they put something called a "cookie" on your computer. A cookie is a bit of information that identifies you to a site. You'll want to know a lot more about cookies when you shop (no, not whether Mrs. Fields or Famous Amos has the better chocolate chip cookies). See Chapter 2 for more information about cookies and shopping.

Using Virtual Shopping Carts

A lot of times when you're shopping online, you'll want to buy more than one item at a time from a particular merchant. Enter the virtual shopping cart. It lets you collect as many items as you want and then proceed to a virtual "checkout" when you are ready to buy. This feature also gives you a final chance before checkout to decide whether you want to buy all that stuff. (Sure, a wristwatch that beeps on the hour, will work at 300 feet under water, and lets you play Tetris while checking the time sounds pretty appealing, but is it really worth $300 to you?)

This virtual shopping cart works a whole lot like a real-life shopping cart. (What's nice, though, is that the wheels never squeak.) Here's how virtual shopping carts work: As you browse and search, each item has a button or a link, which allows you to put that item into your virtual shopping cart. Clicking that link or button sends you to a page—your shopping cart—where the item you were just looking at will be as well. You'll have a chance to order more than one of the items. After that, you'll be able to go on shopping. When you see another item you're thinking of buying, just click, and that item will go into the cart.

At some point, your cart will be full of whatever you want to buy. This figure shows the virtual shopping cart used by Amazon.com (www.amazon.com) filled with (blush, blush) several of my other books. (Go ahead, buy them, please. My kids are hungry, and my mortgage payment is due.)

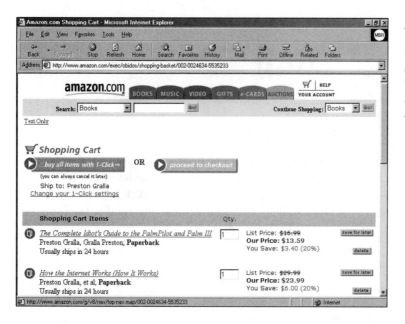

Amazon.com was one of the first Internet sites to use a virtual shopping cart. Here's a cart filled with a few of my other books. Buy them, please. My kids need food!

From your cart, you are able to go to the virtual checkout counter. Here you get a last chance to take goods out of your cart, decide on how you want them shipped to you, and increase or decrease the amount of each item that you want to buy.

Some sites require you to fill in information about yourself, including your credit card information, before you can use a shopping cart. Others ask for that information when you proceed to checkout.

Express Checkout: How to Do One-Click Shopping

Maybe you're someone who likes to do everything fast. You dance double-time. You thrive on takeout food. You can't stand to wait in checkout lines, and always be sure to have fewer than 10 items in your grocery cart to qualify for express checkout. Well, the online shopping world has help for you—sites are starting to create the Internet version of express checkout counters.

Express checkout—called "one-click shopping," or a similar term—works pretty much as you might expect. When you want to buy something, you just click on a button or link on the site to go immediately to a page with all your vital information already filled in, such as name, address, credit card number, and shipping method. Click on a button, and the sale is made. You can also change any information, such as how to ship the goods.

Be Careful When Using One-Click Shopping

One-click shopping is a big timesaver—but it can be a real money-waster as well. When you use one-click shopping, you don't get a chance to review your order as you do when you use a shopping cart, and it's very easy to click blithely away, unaware of the sizable bill you're running up. So be very, very careful before using this service—in fact, consider never using it at all.

To use an express checkout service, you first have to fill out a Web form, including your name, address, phone number, credit card information, and the way you want things shipped to you. After you do that, whenever you do one-click shopping, the site will use that information. At some point, you might want to change that information—such as having items shipped to you the least expensive way rather than via overnight mail. Check with the particular site to see how to make a change.

Nirvana for Cheapskates: How to Get Free Samples Before You Buy

One of the best reasons to shop over the Internet is that you can often try out the goods before deciding whether to buy them. You'll be able to sample CDs, videos, and software for free—and you'll be able to try them as often as you want. In fact, you might get to use complete working versions of software products, often for a month or more. And when it comes to CDs, you'll often be able to listen to sizable portions of every single song on a CD, over the Internet.

So how can this be? Won't you soil the merchandise? What about the "you touch it, you buy it" ethos that prevails in so many retail stores? And how can you get free samples like this over the wires that make up the Internet?

You can get free samples because they're all just a bunch of bits and bytes that are sent from a computer somewhere on the Internet to your own computer. In the case of music and videos, you'll be able to listen to the music and see the videos right on your computer screen—you won't actually pop a CD into your CD player or a tape into your VCR. And in the case of software, you'll run it just like any other software on your PC.

The following sections cover everything that a cybersavvy shopper needs to know to take advantage of these free samples.

Getting Free Music and Video Samples

Many sites sell music CDs and videos on the Internet, such as CDNow (`www.cdnow.com`) and CD Universe (`www.cduniverse.com`). (See Chapter 14, "That's Entertainment: Buying Books, Tapes, Movies, and CDs," for a list of some great music and video sites.) They work like most other shopping sites. You can browse or search for the CD you'd like to buy—anything from megasellers such as Celine Dion to more obscure artists such as Dar Williams, and yes, even to purveyors of muzaklike, pseudo-music such as that of Yanni and John Tesh.

What makes these sites different from many other sites on the Internet is that you can listen to many of the CDs for free. And on sites that sell videos, you are able to watch portions of the videos as well.

So how do you do it? It's pretty simple. All you need is special software that lets you listen to music and watch videos. The most popular software programs by far for this application are RealPlayer and the Windows Media Player, built into Windows. Pretty much any video or audio site that lets you listen to or view free samples will let you use RealPlayer to do that. Head to the RealNetworks site at `www.realnetworks.com` and download a copy. Then just follow the instructions for installing it. It's free; you won't have to pay a penny for the software unless you want a version with some extra bells and whistles. Take my advice, though: You don't need the bells, and you

15

certainly don't need the whistles. Stay with the free versions. The Windows Media Player is free as well and built into most versions of Windows. If it's not built in to yours, head to www.microsoft.com and download it for free.

When you have the software installed, and you're browsing a music or video site, you'll just have to click on the music or video you want to watch. Then, voilà!, in a few seconds you'll be watching and listening. After you check out the samples, you can decide whether to buy. There's a bonus to installing this player, by the way. With it, you can also see the latest news at news sites such as CNN (www.cnn.com), and see the latest music videos at the MTV site (www.mtv.com). In some cases, you might need a special plug-in to view a clip or listen to audio.

What's a Plug-In?

No, it's not a new electrical gadget for your wall outlet. When you're shopping on the Internet, you might come across a site that needs special software in order for you to look at something or do something—to play a game, perhaps, or to see a video or listen to music. That special software you need is called a plug-in, because it plugs in to your Web browser. (These geeky programmers certainly do have a clever way with words, don't they?) RealPlayer is an example of a plug-in. Here are a few more that you might want: The QuickTime plug-in (get it at www.apple.com) lets you view videos, and the ShockWave plug-in lets you view special animations and play games (get it at www.macromedia.com). The Windows Media Player at www.microsoft.com plays a variety of audio and video files as well. Lots of other plug-ins are also available. To get the latest list of up-to-date plug-ins, go to one of the popular download sites on the Internet, such as the ZDNet Software Library at www.hotfiles.com.

Getting Free Software Samples

Imagine this: You want to buy a new car, but you'd like to test drive it for a month before deciding whether to fork over the moolah. Or you'd like to use a new refrigerator for two weeks before deciding whether to turn over your cash. Sounds crazy, yes?

Well, when it comes to software on the Internet, it's not so crazy. In fact, you can get free, fully working, test-drive versions of most software to use for a month or more before you decide to buy. This kind of software is called demo software, or shareware, or try-before-you-buy software. And you'll find tens of thousands of programs such as this all over the Internet—everything from powerful programs from companies such as Microsoft and Symantec to games from big game companies such as Sierra Online to very useful utilities from companies you've probably never heard of. The software is available at a number of sites, such as the ZDNet Software Library at `www.hotfiles.com`. For information on how to use this kind of software, turn to Chapter 17, "Don't Be a Softie: Getting the Best Deal on Buying Software."

Should You Research Online and Buy Offline?

The odds are, you feel pretty comfortable about jumping onto the Internet and checking out the sites. No big deal; just fire up your browser and go. And as you go through this book, you'll also start to feel comfortable with researching products on the Internet as well. But you might not feel so comfortable about turning over $35,000 for the new Godzilla-like sports utility vehicle you're about to buy. In fact, researchers will tell you (if you ask them, that is) that more people use the Internet to research products and then buy through a store than use the Internet to actually buy online.

You'll find that the Internet is the world's best resource for helping you decide what you should buy. In addition to shopping sites, there are consumer sites, specialty magazines, discussion groups, and other places where you can get the precise advice you need before heading off on a shopping expedition. So, if you're an online shopping newbie and wary of buying online, my advice is to first use the Internet to research your purchase, and then buy the product in the real world.

Gradually, though, you'll want to start to use the Internet as a way to buy, not just research. If you've never bought anything online before and are worried about doing it, start small. Go to one of the big, reputable book sites, such as `www.amazon.com` or `www.barnesandnoble.com`. Browse and buy. When you see how easy it is, you'll find yourself more willing to branch out.

Some people might always be wary of buying big-ticket items, such as plane tickets or a car, on the Internet. If that's the case, you should still use the Internet to research your buying—you'll find yourself saving lots of time. I researched my last car buy on the Internet and, using the information I found, was able to save hundreds of dollars when I negotiated with the dealer. And, I always check online before buying plane tickets—that way, I not only find out what seats are available, but also know that I'm getting the best price. For example, recently, I was able to save my parents well over $1,000 by researching tickets for them online—we were able to find an deal online not available any other way—but they paid for the tickets the old-fashioned way. If you prefer to research online but buy offline, you should still use this book—except use the Internet for research instead of actual purchasing.

The Least You Need to Know

➤ Often the best way to find the products you need at a particular site is to use its search technology.

➤ The best way to buy online is to use your credit card—and be sure that you're first sent to a "secure area" before you buy.

➤ When creating a password to use with an online shopping account, be sure to keep away from common words or your initials. And always keep a copy of all your passwords in a safe place, away from your computer, should your hard drive crash.

➤ To get free samples of music, you need to install special plug-ins such as RealPlayer.

Chapter 2

Show Me the Money! Paying with Credit Cards and Electronic Wallets

In This Chapter

➤ Paying with your credit card

➤ Protecting your credit card online

➤ Paying with electronic wallets

➤ Ensuring your privacy online

➤ What are "cookies?"

So by now you're ready to go: You know the basics of how you'll buy, you know how to use virtual shopping carts, and you're pretty much revved up to do some buying. But, of course, one small detail is missing: How do you pay? What do you need to do when a site says to you, "Show me the money!"

The primary way you buy online is by using a credit card. You fill out a form, and as part of that form, you provide your credit card information. At some sites, you can order online and then send a check or a money order to do the actual payment. But many sites don't offer that service, and when you do use a check, you lose a big advantage of buying online—one-stop shopping.

Another way you might pay is with an electronic wallet, also called an eWallet. Using an electronic wallet makes it easier to pay online, because when you use one, you don't have to keep typing your information each time you buy something—that information is stored in your eWallet. Depending on your point of view, it's either a great convenience, or the quickest way to drop money fast on the Internet.

Playing Card Games: Paying with Your Credit Card Online

Just about all online purchases involve credit cards. It's the easiest way you can buy. But I can tell by that skeptical gleam in your eyes that you're worried about sending your credit card number out over the Internet. Won't wild-eyed hackers abscond with your number and use it to pay for all-night binges of Fritos, Jolt Cola, and calls to friends? Won't the site you send your credit card to simply take the money and run, financing a long-awaited European trip on your dime?

The answer to each of those questions is no, not if you play your (credit) cards right. It's very, very difficult for hackers to steal your credit card number if you do things right. In many ways, sending your credit card over the Internet is safer than the way you use it in real life. Think about how often you give out your credit card number to a stranger over the telephone when you're making hotel or car reservations or ordering something from a catalog. Do you know who is on the other end of the transaction, and are you sure that the reservation clerk or order taker is not copying down your credit card information for his or her own use? Worse yet, think of the last time you went out to a restaurant and paid with your credit card. Did the server vanish with your card for several minutes? What was he or she doing with it? Do you have any idea how many restaurant employees are out-of-work actors or standup comics? And would you trust an out-of-work actor with your credit card? If you would, I have two words for you: Mickey Rourke. Case closed.

On the Internet, your credit card number goes directly into an accounting and ordering system. No one handles or examines it. So in that way, your account information is safer than when you pay in person.

Techno Talk

What Is SSL?

No, it's not a new type of supersonic transport. SSL stands for Secure Sockets Layer. SSL is one of the most common technologies used to encrypt credit card numbers and other information sent over the Internet so that it's safe from prying eyes. If you're on a page that uses SSL, you might notice that the URL starts with https: instead of http:. Credit cards use a number of other encryption technologies as well, including Secure HTTP (S-HTTP).

When you send credit card information over the Internet, though, you'll want to make sure it's sent through what's called a "secure site." When you're at a secure site, any information you send is encrypted (often using Secure Sockets Layer, or SSL) so that no one will be able to understand it. *Encryption* means that all the information is scrambled into gobbledygook so that if any snoopers or hackers are able to see what you're sending, they'll see only gibberish, not your credit card number. Turn to Chapter 4, "How to Be a Cybersavvy Shopper," for more information about secure sites and how to know whether you're visiting one. Never order through a site that isn't secure—your card number could be stolen.

When you pay by credit card, you'll often be asked not only for your credit card number but also for some kind of identifying information, such as your mother's maiden name. That way, the site can always check to be sure you are who you say you are.

Paying with Electronic Wallets

Spend much time buying things online and it can get pretty boring, having to type the same credit card information, and other stuff such as your name, address, and phone number, over and over, each time you want to buy something. Pretty soon your little fingers are going to get awfully tired.

You Can Pay Online with a Debit Card

Most online sites will accept debit cards as well as credit cards, so if you prefer debit cards, feel free to pay with them. And debit cards generally offer the same consumer protections as do credit cards, and so are good for buying online.

A way to save time is to use electronic wallets, often called eWallets. The idea behind them is simple: Type information once, such as your name, address, and credit card number, and then whenever you visit a Web site and want to pay with your credit card, that information is automatically sent to the site.

Sounds simple, yes? Ah, but there's a catch. (If something is easy on the Internet, I've found there's *always* a catch.) An eWallet won't work on every site you visit. And some eWallets work on some sites, whereas other eWallets work on others. Still, eWallets can be timesavers. A popular eWallet can be found at—*surprise!*—www.ewallet.com. When you get there, you download a piece of software that you install on your PC—your eWallet. Install it and you're ready to start spending money. The following figure shows an eWallet.

Ready, set, spend: using an eWallet.

Whatever Happened to Digital Cash?

Until recently, many people believed that a big way we'd pay online is through the use of "digital cash"—money stored in a special place on our computers, and that could be used whenever we'd buy something online. Wrong! Two companies were pursuing the digital cash dream—and as I write this, one of them has abandoned the business altogether, and the other has gone belly-up, declaring bankruptcy. (Guess they were lacking the old-fashioned kind of cash—the kind that pays the bills.) So hang on to your credit card—it could be a long wait before we're paying with digital cash.

Another eWallet, called Microsoft Wallet, is built into some versions of Microsoft Internet Explorer. You don't have to download anything; it's already built in to the browser. Get there by choosing **Internet Options** from Internet Explorer's Tools menu, and then clicking on the **Content** tab. Then click on the **Wallet** button and fill out information. (Microsoft made it pretty hard to find their wallet. I'm not sure why—after all, they're only too happy to have you spend your hard-earned money.) The nearby picture shows how you can add a credit card to your Microsoft Wallet.

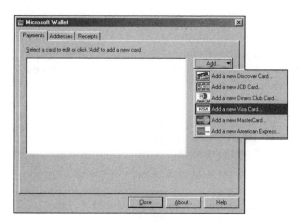

Stuff your wallet full of credit cards: Here's how to add a credit card to Microsoft Wallet.

Want to Be Alone? Privacy and Security Issues Online

One thing you should know when cruising the Net: On the Internet, you're never really alone. And nothing you do online is private. Everything that you do when you visit a site can be tracked—not just what you buy, but what products you look at, how long you spend on the site, what you read on the site, what site you visited before visiting the shopping site, and where you went next...no, probably not what toothpaste you used that morning, but based on your online activity, a market researcher can put together a fairly accurate profile of your shopping habits.

To go along with that, you should be aware of some security issues before heading off on your shopping expedition. Some of those issues were covered in Chapter 1, "Getting Started on Your Online Shopping Expedition," in the section about passwords. The rest of this chapter gives you the lowdown on what you need to know about privacy and security issues.

What You Can Do to Protect Your Privacy

The lifeblood of any shopping site is how well it knows the behavior of people who buy there—in other words, you. The more that merchants know about you, the better they can sell you things—for example, by targeting specific ads or special deals at you when you visit a site. One problem is that a site can cross the line of what's acceptable and start invading your privacy. For example, a shopping site could track your buying habits and then sell that information to direct marketing firms so that you'll be targeted by telemarketers and junk mailers (both standard mail and email). Shopping sites, more than any other kinds of sites on the Internet, can be tempted to profit from this information because they know so much about your buying habits.

You can take certain steps to protect your privacy online, though. Follow these six tips for ensuring your online privacy.

➤ **Ask about the privacy policy of shopping sites you visit and buy from.** Ask what information they gather, how that information will be used, and whether they share that information with anyone. Some sites will publicly post their policy; others will tell you if you ask. If a site won't reveal this information, realize that it could be sharing information about your shopping habits with other people and companies. If this situation concerns you, don't shop on that site.

➤ **Check for an "opt-out" policy on shopping sites.** Under an opt-out policy, the site would agree not to share information about you with any other companies if you opt out of this program. Send email or call the site to find out about any opt-out policies.

➤ **Provide minimum information when filling out forms.** When you fill out a form on a site to buy something or enter a contest, you'll be asked many questions. Sometimes those questions might cross over the line about what you want to be known about yourself, such as your annual income or age. You have to assume that the site will use any information you provide, so if you're uncomfortable with answering those questions, don't. Many sites put an asterisk next to the questions that must be answered, so answer only those.

Check Out *The Complete Idiot's Guide to Protecting Yourself Online*

Shameless pitch alert! If you're worried at all about protecting your privacy online and want to make sure that you're secure when you're on the Internet, get a hold of one of my latest books, *The Complete Idiot's Guide to Protecting Yourself Online*. It'll tell you everything you need to know about protecting your privacy and securing your safety online. Hey, exercise your e-shopping shopping skills and buy it online at a book site such as www.amazon.com or www.bn.com.

➤ **Read the fine print when filling out forms.** Often, buried at the bottom of the form, almost as an afterthought, you'll find an innocuous-sounding question or statement, something like, "Would you like to be informed about any special offers or information about products that might interest you?" Just say no! That's an invitation for the site to share information about you with direct marketers. Often the statement or question will already be checked (or unchecked), which means that you'll automatically be subject to junk mail and phone calls. If you don't want anyone else to get this information, be sure to read this fine print and to say you don't want to be contacted.

➤ **Never give out your Social Security number online.** There's no reason that you should ever have to give out your Social Security number online. If someone gets hold of your Social Security number, they could potentially "steal" your identity, pose as you, and even possibly get hold of your bank account. If a site asks for your Social Security number, buy somewhere else.

➤ **Check to see whether the site adheres to privacy rules from a privacy watchdog such as TRUSTe.** TRUSTe is a nonprofit group that serves as a watchdog on Internet privacy. The group allows sites that adhere to its policies to post an online seal (a "trustmark"). TRUSTe basically asks a site to tell you what information it gathers and how that information is used. And TRUSTe then polices the site to ensure it's following those standards. Head to www.truste.org for information about TRUSTe. You can see its Web site in the following figure.

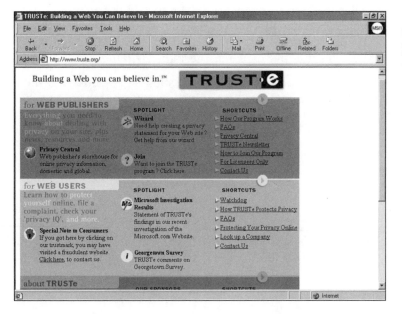

Visit the TRUSTe Web site to learn how to protect your privacy on the Internet.

Don't Lose Your Cookies Online

Online shopping sites have lots of ways to track your activity. Perhaps the most popular is through the use of "cookies." No, these cookies aren't Oreo or chocolate chip; instead, they're little bits of data that a Web site puts on your hard disk when you visit. (Why are they called cookies? Who knows? It's just one more example of the linguistic whims of the hackers and nerds among us.) Through constantly updating and checking that "cookie," the site can gather information about you—what pages you visit, how long you spend online, what you buy.

Before you start thinking conspiracy theory, don't be alarmed. These cookies usually aren't nefarious. In fact, they often make online shopping easier. They identify you to the shopping site so that you don't have to type in your username and password, credit card number, and similar information every time you buy something. And if used properly, cookies can help a shopping site tell you about the deals that you'd most be interested in because the site knows what you've bought and read online.

Still, you might not like the idea of a site putting a bit of information on your hard disk. Or you at least might like to know when a site is doing that. So go on a diet and control your cookie use. It's easy, and you can do it in both Microsoft Internet Explorer and Netscape Navigator.

In the PC version of Microsoft's Internet Explorer 4.0 and later, click **View** and then **Internet Options**. Now click the **Advanced** tab. Scroll down to the Cookies area. If you click on **Disable All Cookie Use**, your computer will automatically not allow any cookies to be put on your hard disk. Be aware that when you do that, though, you won't be able to use some shopping sites. If you instead click **Prompt Before Accepting Cookies**, you'll get a warning every time a site tries to put a cookie on your hard disk. You can then decide whether to accept it. Or you can just leave the default setting: **Always Accept Cookies**. For information on how to adjust cookie use in other versions of Microsoft Internet Explorer, check the Help file.

In the PC version of Netscape Navigator 4.0 and later, you should click **Edit** and then **Preferences**. Then click **Advanced**, and you'll be able to set options for your cookie use. For information on how to adjust cookies use in other versions of Netscape Navigator, check the Help file.

Be aware of one thing, though: If you turn off your cookies, you probably won't be able to use special shopping services such as virtual shopping carts, one-click shopping, and personalized buying.

The Least You Need to Know

➤ Never give credit card information to a site that isn't secure.

➤ Understand the privacy guidelines of sites before shopping at them.

➤ Check whether the site you buy from adheres to privacy guidelines from an organization such as TRUSTe.

So, Where Should I Shop Online?

In This Chapter

➤ Checking out metabuying sites

➤ Buying at department stores, online malls, and specialty–buying sites

➤ Buying through online services

When you're shopping in the real world, it's pretty easy to figure out where to buy things. You drive to your local mall or head downtown; you read ads in local newspapers and flyers; you watch TV; you get advice from friends. Let's face it: If you're looking to spend your money, there are too many places willing to accept your hard-earned cash.

But things aren't so simple on the Internet and in the online world. Thousands of shopping sites are already waiting for you, and new ones are popping up all the time. Although you find some hugely popular sites such as the booksellers Amazon.com (www.amazon.com) and Barnes & Noble (www.bn.com) taking out TV and print ads, many shopping sites don't have the kind of money needed to launch national ad campaigns, much less take out an ad in your local newspaper. And it's a whole lot easier driving downtown or to a mall to find stores than it is surfing at random on the Internet. On the Internet, if you just surf at random, you're as likely to find the ramblings of techies, geeks, oddballs, and malcontents as you are to find a good online store.

The first thing to keep in mind when looking for online shopping sites is that the Internet has many different kinds of sites—it's not a case of one size fits all. And, in fact, the kinds of sites you'll find online are often different from the kinds of stores you find out in the real world. Yes, you can shop at online versions of stores such as L.L. Bean at www.llbean.com, but the Internet also has all kinds of sites that have nothing to do with stores in the real world.

So what's a poor cybershopper to do? How can you go about finding places to spend your hard-earned money? It's not as hard as you think if you know where to look. In this chapter, I clue you in on all the different places you can shop on the Internet and show you how to find the right place fast. What are you waiting for? Let's go spend some money!

Everything Plus the Kitchen Sink: Browsing Through the "Metabuying" Sites

You want to buy a new watch online. Or a Matisse poster. Or a car. Or a computer, a pair of jeans, an airline ticket, three French hens, two turtledoves, and a partridge in a pear tree. Maybe you even want to buy the kitchen sink. Where's the best place to start?

Here's How to Find Your Favorite Stores on the Web

It's easy to find the online sites of your favorite stores on the Web—if they've set up shop there. In your browser, type in www, followed by a period, like this: www.. Next type in the name of the store with no spaces in the name, such as landsend, followed by a period. So you now have www.landsend.. Finally, type com at the end: www.landsend.com. It's there; try it.

If you're not exactly sure where to go and you're just getting started on a shopping expedition, head to one of the metabuying sites that are springing up all across the Internet. You don't actually buy something at these metabuying sites. Instead, they're lists, by category, of the many thousands of buying sites online. And they often offer more as well, such as coupons, cut-rate deals, and even ways to comparison shop online.

The best of these sites belong to the major search engines and indexes such as Yahoo! (www.yahoo.com) and Excite (www.excite.com). Search engines and indexes are sites that help you make sense of the Internet. They try to organize the general chaos so that you can easily find what you want. So if you're looking to find a site devoted to left-handed golfers from New Zealand, head to one of the indexes and do a search. Yahoo! and Excite, among others, have found that one of the most popular activities on the Internet is shopping, and so they've put together special shopping sites.

They all work in much the same way. For example, take a look at the Excite shopping area. It's easy to get there. First, point your browser to Excite at `www.excite.com`. Now click on **Shopping**. You'll see an index, as shown here, of just about every category of shopping you might ever do on the Internet, from auctions to clothes to music to sports.

Who's Excited? Online shoppers will be when they hit Excite's metashopping site.

The shopping directory on the right side takes up most of the screen. Here's where you'll spend most of your time. Click on the category that best describes what you're looking to buy, such as **Gourmet & Groceries** if you're shopping for a case of wine. (Save a bottle for me, please. I favor mellow Merlots.) Next you'll come to a page that does several things. It breaks out the main category (**Gourmet & Groceries** in this instance) into finer categories, such as **Alcohol**, **Candy**, **Coffee and Tea**, **Deli and Gourmet**, and **Health Food**. Click on any of them, and you'll get a listing of sites in that category. So when you click on **Alcohol**, for example, you'll get a list of dozens of sites that sell alcohol, including wine, on the Internet. Click on one, and you'll get sent to the shopping site. Now you can buy. (Again, remember to order a bottle for me. When you have it, send me an email and let me know at `preston@gralla.com`. Unfortunately, you can't yet deliver drinks over the Internet.)

You'll notice something else interesting on the **Gourmet & Groceries** page. In addition to having direct links to shopping sites by category, such as **Deli and Gourmet**, you'll also be able to search directly for wine or wine reviews right on the page. When you type in a search (such as for **Merlot**), it'll go to other sites on the Internet and find what you want and show you the results. This feature is called a shopping robot, a ShopBot, or a virtual shopping assistant. I cover ShopBots in more detail in Chapter 7, "Shopping Robots, Agents, Search Tools, and Virtual Shopping Assistants."

On the left side of any page on Excite's shopping area, you see special offers, deals, and other unique shopping tips.

You Better Shop Around

Let me issue a word of warning here: Just because Excite (or any other shopping index) highlights a particular online shopping site doesn't mean that it's the best site in its category. What it often means is that the particular site paid money to Excite to be listed there. (Are you shocked at such a concept? Don't be. Filthy lucre, after all, is what makes the world go around.) So although you might want to check out the highlighted sites, don't stop there—you might find better deals elsewhere.

Shopping metasites run by Yahoo!, Excite, and others do more than just offer an index to shopping sites. And they do more than give you special offers. Some of them offer "click rewards"—kind of like a frequent buying club. If you buy from certain merchants you find through their site, you get bonus money you can use to buy even more things from those merchants. Other sites offer consumer advice. Turn to Chapter 7 for more information about these shopping metasites.

Prosciutto, Futons, and Titanium Golf Clubs: Specialty-Buying Sites on the Internet

How easy is it for you to find one of the world's most comprehensive wine stores in your neighborhood? (If you do have one, remember that Merlot for me, please.) An electronics specialty shop? A store specializing in Generation X clothing? (Tank Grrrrl Tank and Full Metal Battle Skirt, anyone?) A massive office supply store? How about a futon shop or a florist or a gourmet shop where you can buy arincini (rice balls stuffed with onions, prosciutto, Parmesan cheese, and eggs) and broccoli di rape?

No, there's nowhere in the real world where you'll be able to buy all that in one small area—not on New York City's Fifth Avenue or Chicago's Magnificent Mile or anywhere else, for that matter. To get all that within easy reach (or to be more accurate, within easy click), you'll need to shop in cyberspace.

Sites Can Help Kids Buy Online and Manage Their Money

Kids and teens don't have credit cards, and so it's hard for them to buy online—they'll have to have their parents nearby. But several sites, including `www.doughnet.com` and `www.icanbuy.com`, allow parents to let their kids shop online. The sites let parents give kids a certain amount of money to spend, and also give parents tools for deciding where and what their kids can buy. And they have money management tools as well. Turn to Chapter 26, "More Than Child's Play: Buying Games and Toys," for more information.

One of the best reasons for shopping online is the incredible variety of specialty-buying sites you'll find. Whether you're looking for kosher foods, exotic roses, rare and out-of-print books, or any other specialty item, your best bet for buying is often online.

Your best bet for finding these specialty stores is to check in with one of the metashopping sites, covered earlier in this chapter. But there's always another technique as well: Type the name of the specialty product you're looking to buy. Want to buy wine? Try `www.wine.com`. How about a good cigar? Yes, no great surprise, it's at `www.cigar.com`. This technique won't always work, but many times it will.

For advice on how to buy and compare at specialty sites on the Internet, turn to the chapter in this book that covers the kind of product you want to buy. So for buying grooming products, turn to Chapter 25, "Where to Buy Clothing, Grooming, Beauty, and Jewelry Products," for example.

Online Department Stores

Another major place you'll shop on the Internet is at department stores—the online sites of places that are built of bricks and mortar (or maybe glass and concrete) in the real world. These department stores can be mail-order stores as well, such as Land's End.

You might wonder what the point is of visiting an online department store when you can simply drive over to your local mall or downtown and walk in. One reason, of course, is that you might not happen to have that particular department store within driving distance. Another is that online ordering can save you time—but still, those aren't the main reasons you'll hit the sites instead of the pavement.

Check Department Store Shopping Sites Before Visiting the Real Stores in Person

Just because you're planning to take a shopping trip to a department store is no reason not to check the store's online site. You'll find a number of reasons to visit the online sites of department stores before heading into your gas-guzzler and hitting the highway. Online stores clue you in to store specials and let you search to see whether the store carries a particular product. And some department stores even offer special deals online that you can't ever get in the real world. Whenever I check out the Sears site at www.sears.com, I find lists of store specials that otherwise I might not have known about.

The main reason to visit department stores on the Internet is for the extra services they offer. Yes, I know, it's hard to believe that I could actually use the words *department store* and *service* in the same sentence. After all, when was the last time you got anything other than a 100-yard stare and a look of disdain when you asked for sales help in a department store—if you could *find* any help, that is?

Online, though, it's a different matter. You'll be able to easily browse through everything the store has for sale. You can email questions about the merchandise—and actually get answers, instead of a shrug or look of incomprehension. You can get special deals at lower prices than in the real stores sometimes, and you can subscribe to email alerts that will clue you in on special deals not available in the bricks-and-mortar stores. And you'll get other special services that you can find only online. For example, the online version of the Land's End mail-order retailer has videos you can view online that help you know how best to measure yourself so that you order the clothes that will fit you best. And the smarter retailers even offer up-to-the-minute price alerts—they'll list their overstock that they need to sell fast. The longer the overstock stays unsold, the lower the price, so you can find yourself scooping up some pretty spectacular bargains.

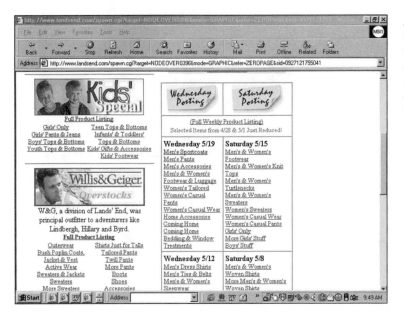

How low can you go? Closeout sales, such as this one at Land's End, are one reason you'll want to visit the online sites of department stores and mail-order retailers.

For more information about shopping at department stores online and to find the best ones on the Internet, turn to Chapter 15, "Mall Fever: Department Stores, Malls, Closeouts, and Bargain Hunting."

Online Malls: One-Stop Shopping Without the Mall Rats

Unless you're a teenage mall rat, or you really *do* love Food Court cuisine, malls might not be your favorite place to spend your free time. On the other hand, because of the variety of stores in them, they do make it easy to spend all your money in one place. Malls are among the few places in the world, after all, where under one roof you can buy a pair of jeans, a CD, a computer, a watch, underwear, Beanie Babies, baseball cards, the *Titanic* video, toothpaste, and the latest book to hit the best-seller list.

On the Internet, you'll also find malls—and those malls are much larger than their real-life equivalents. For example, the ShopNow.com site at www.shopnow.com has products from more than 25,000 stores. When you visit an online mall, you won't have to wear out your shoe leather getting from store to store, be forced to listen to the *Titanic* theme for the ten-thousandth time, or have to put up with the sight of nose-ringed mall rats wandering around aimlessly.

Be a Smart Shopper

One note here: Just because you find a site by typing the name of a specialty product doesn't mean that it's the best site out there. It just means that it exists. For example, a much better wine-buying site than `www.wine.com` is the Virtual Vineyards at `www.virtualvineyard.com`, and because the Internet has so many specialty shopping sites, be sure to check out more than one before buying. So if you're looking to buy from a specialty site online, the same rule holds true as in the real world: You better shop around.

As you might guess, you can pretty much buy almost anything in the world at these online malls—not just products and goods, but services as well, such as vacations, legal help, and mortgages. Hey, at `ShopNow.com` you can buy a used tractor for $18,900. Try buying *that* at your local mall.

You don't have to learn any great secrets to shop at these online malls. Most are well organized and list products and services by category. They also highlight specials and deals. Most let you search for a specific product by typing in the name or category of the product. Be sure to look closely for store specials—you often find big discounts and rebates. For more information about buying in online malls, check out Chapter 15.

Buying Through Online Services

In addition to Internet shopping, you can also enjoy cybershopping through online services, such as America Online, CompuServe, and the Microsoft Network. America Online, in particular, is morphing itself into a shopper's paradise and is by far the best online service for shopping. In fact, it's created an entire shopping "channel" with links to hundreds of online shopping sites. Some of these shopping sites are on the Internet, whereas others live only on America Online.

There's good reason for America Online's emphasis on shopping. In the long run, that's probably the only way it will make money. Because it charges a relatively low fee for its all-you-can-eat connection (in other words, you pay the same fee whether you're online for a minute or 1,000 hours in any month), it doesn't make much profit, if any, by providing you with your online and Internet connection. But it has many millions of subscribers and can make money by selling them things. So expect an even bigger emphasis on shopping in the future (and even more of those incredibly annoying ads that seem to pop up about every five seconds—no, America Online, I do *not* want to buy flowers right now or switch my long-distance phone company or buy an encyclopedia).

Oh, and That Sink I Mentioned Earlier...

And oh, by the way, if you are looking for a kitchen sink, Excite will give you plenty of places to buy one. Click on **Home & Garden** and then, from the page that comes up, click on **Kitchenware**. You'll find many places to buy that kitchen sink you've always wanted. Excite helped me find the CyberBath catalog at www.baths.com. You want sinks? They've got sinks—single bowl, double bowl, triple bowl, dual level, slimline, and Euro Dropin.

Because America Online has the best shopping area, I cover it in greater detail than the other online services. Check your online service for a shopping area, though, because they all have them to one degree or another.

Shopping on America Online

One good reason to shop on America Online is because it organizes shopping categories so nicely. From the main shopping area (KEYWORD SHOPPING), just click on what you're interested in buying, such as **Gifts & Gadgets** or **Auto & Travel**. From there, you'll be led to a directory type of page, such as the one you see here for gifts and gadgets. You'll find featured deals and stores, as well as a way to search directly for the specific product you want to buy.

There's a bonus to shopping on America Online. America Online offers a money-back guarantee if you buy at any of the merchants it lists in its shopping area. If you're not happy with your purchase and the merchant won't take it back, tell America Online. The service will try to get the merchant to allow you to return the product. If the merchant won't agree, America Online will refund your money.

Additionally, if you're the victim of credit card fraud at any of the merchants listed with America Online, report credit card fraud to your credit card company. Credit card companies will cover all but $50 of credit card fraud. America Online says it will pick up that $50, so you won't lose any money.

An online shopping paradise: the Gifts & Collectibles section of America Online.

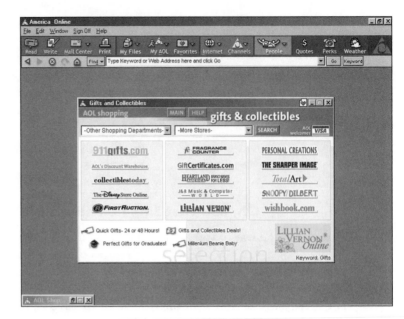

The Least You Need to Know

➤ Start your shopping expedition at one of the shopping areas run by Internet search engines such as www.yahoo.com, www.excite.com, or www.lycos.com.

➤ Even if you're heading out to a department store, check its online site first—there might be online-only specials and other good deals.

➤ To find a specialty-buying site on the Internet, start by typing the name of the goods you want to buy, surrounded by www. and .com. So to buy cigars, for example, try the www.cigar.com site.

➤ If you're on America Online and looking to shop, use the keyword SHOPPING.

Part 2

How to Be a Cybersavvy Online Consumer

You're a smart consumer—or at least you'd like to be a smart one. You check the labels of products before you buy. You know all about special sales, warranties, and return policies—so much so that salespeople quake when they see you coming. You are shopper. Hear you roar!

But how can you be consumer-savvy online? How can you get the scoop about warranties and return policies, and know you're buying the best product at the best price? How can you be sure that you never get burned—and woe to the person who tries? This part teaches you all that and more.

You learn how to check for hidden costs before buying, and how to be sure that you're buying through a secure, reputable site. You get the complete lowdown on online return and warranty policies. You see how you can get the inside skinny on shopping sites online—and you get a list of the best sites to check for when doing consumer research. You'll learn how to avoid Internet scams and con artists. And finally, you'll find out how you can get shopping robots and virtual shopping assistants to search the Internet for you, looking for the best bargains.

How to Be a Cybersavvy Shopper

In This Chapter

➤ Watching out for hidden costs when buying online

➤ Checking out return policies and warranties

➤ How to ensure you're buying through a secure site

The Internet can help you get some of the best shopping deals you'll find anywhere. And there's certainly nothing more convenient than shopping from your den, living room, or home office. That's the good news for Internet shoppers. The bad news is that on the Internet, you don't get to examine the merchandise (at least, until marketers come up with virtual scratch-sniff-smell-and-touch technology). And you have to be more careful on the Internet than you do in a physical store about whom you buy from—and on what terms you do the buying.

The Internet is also the best technology yet devised to make anyone a better shopper. With a few mouse clicks and a little Web surfing, you find the best merchandise at the best price and are able to ensure that you're buying from a reputable merchant.

In this chapter, I clue you in on all the ways you can become a cybersavvy shopper on the Internet. By the end of it, you'll know how to be sure that you're not going to be hit with any hidden costs when shopping online, and to be sure that you know your site's return policies. You'll also know how to be sure that you're getting the best deals at the best price.

Now You See It, Now You Don't: Beware of Hidden Costs When Shopping Online

Buy it now—40% off! Best deal ever: 45% off list price—only if you act now! Electronics blowout: 50% price cut now! The Internet is no different than any other marketplace; you'll be assaulted with outrageous promises, be offered impossible deals, and be subject to impossible-to-believe advertising. They all sound too good to be true, and with good reason: In general, the deals *are* too good to be true. The 40% discount deal that appears to be true on first blush might carry so many hidden costs that your supposed 40% discount vanishes faster than your bank account after a bout of binge shopping.

The truth is, shopping online can involve many hidden costs. You'll run across these costs not only when sites try to mislead you—hidden costs can be a normal part of almost any online transaction. Shipping costs, handling costs, restocking fees, and the like—they can add big bucks to any online transaction. Forewarned is forearmed, though: If you're aware of these costs, you can be sure only to shop at sites that minimize them. And there are ways to cut those hidden costs at any site.

Don't Get Burned: Watching Out for Shipping and Handling Costs

Any time you buy something on the Internet, you're going to have to pay shipping and handling costs. Get used to it: It's a way of life. Someone has to bear the costs of shipping the goods to you. Did you really think the merchant was going to eat the costs instead of you?

Be Sure Your Credit Card Is Charged Only When the Goods Ship

When you order from an online store, the goods you're buying might not always ship on the day you order them. Not all online stores have warehouses, and so it might take several days before the item is shipped. And in some cases—such as when you're buying a new, sought-after item—it can be weeks or even longer before the store can get its hands on the goods and send them to you. Therefore, be sure that your credit card is charged only when the goods actually ship to you—not on the day that you ordered the item. Otherwise, you might be carrying a credit card bill for months while you wait for the goods to be delivered.

(By the way, have you ever wondered what handling costs are? I have yet to figure it out. I, for one, don't like the idea of strangers getting their grimy fingerprints on my new pager by handling it. In fact, I'd consider paying extra if they *don't* handle my goods before shipping them.)

The costs for shipping and handling vary widely, according to the site you're shopping on, the goods you're buying, the method of delivery, and sometimes, considering how widely the costs vary, maybe the phase of the moon as well. At times, the costs of shipping are insignificant and don't eat into the discount you're getting by buying online. For example, when I was looking for a 3Com Palm V electronic organizer, I found one at the NECX computer and electronics site (www.necx.com) for $389.95, for a discount of over 13%—a savings of almost $60—off the $449 retail price I had seen for the little device advertised in local stores. The shipping and handling costs were $9.95, and so the final price of $399.90 would still save almost $50—a discount of 11%. Not a bad deal, especially considering I wouldn't have to fight the crowds and blink at the bad fluorescent lights at my local Staples chain store.

But shipping costs can also push the price of something you're going to buy well above whatever discount you're getting by buying online. Let's take an example. Say you were visiting the Barnes & Noble book-buying site at www.bn.com. You've decided that you absolutely, positively *must* have that scintillating, best-selling guide to the Internet, *How the Internet Works,* written by yours truly (pitch alert! pitch alert!). The list price is $29.99 (a deal at twice the price, believe me—pitch alert! pitch alert!). Barnes & Noble discounted it for 20% on the day I visited, so it would cost you a mere $23.99, a savings of $6. So far, so good. The book is so perfect, so true, so absolutely must-have (pitch alert! pitch alert!) that you need it the following morning. So you agree to have the book shipped to you via Barnes & Noble's option for United Parcel Service next-day-air service, which costs $8 per order, plus $2.95 per book, for a total shipping cost of $10.95. So for the pleasure of ordering the book over the Internet and then getting it delivered to you the following day, you'll pay a total of $34.94, $5 over the list price. (Hey, believe me, at that price it's still a steal—pitch alert! pitch alert!) You would have been better off heading to your local bookstore and buying the book.

Some sites let you choose the method of shipping, and here's where you can save big time. Let's go back to the Barnes & Noble example. Barnes & Noble gives you three options for shipping. The standard method, shipped via the U.S. Postal Service, delivers the book to you within three to six business days. That'll cost you $3 per order plus 95 cents per book. (So if you had bought *How the Internet Works, Fourth Edition* and had it delivered via this method, you'd pay a total of $27.94—a savings of $2 off the list price.) Or you can get it delivered via second-day service from Federal Express; your cost is $6 per order plus $1.95 per book. Or you can overnight it via Federal Express; this services goes for a whopping $8 plus $2.95 per book. The message here is pretty simple: Be sure to choose the lowest shipping price whenever possible.

Check Your Shipping Costs for Every Individual Product You Buy at Online Malls

Online malls, in some ways, are like bricks-and-mortar malls: They're a collection of different stores, all together under one roof, although in this instance, that roof is a virtual one. Each store in an online mall has its own shipping costs. In an online mall, though, sometimes it's hard to know when you're in one store or another because you can search them all simultaneously. So it's doubly important when you're in an online mall to check the shipping costs for every product you buy. Sure, you bought a shirt yesterday at an online mall that had a $3.95 shipping fee—but buy another shirt, and it might come from a different store and so might carry shipping and handling fees twice as high as the first.

There's another way to save on shipping costs. Whenever buying anything online, try to include several items in the same order, instead of having them shipped separately. Let's take the Barnes & Noble example. Say that in addition to wanting to buy *How the Internet Works, Fourth Edition*, you also want to buy another superb book by the same author (me!) about the use of Internet technology by private businesses, titled *How Intranets Work* (pitch alert! pitch alert!). If you ordered the books on different days and had them shipped separately, each via overnight express, you'd have to pay a whopping $21.90 in shipping costs. If, instead, you had them shipped (overnight, again) in the same order, you'd pay only $13.90, a savings of $8.

If you buy more than one item at an online store, there's a chance that one item will be ready for immediate delivery, whereas another might not be in stock and so might be delayed several days. Stores generally give you the option of deciding whether to ship the items individually or to wait until all the items are ready and then ship them together. You don't have to be an Einstein with numbers to see that you can save big time by telling the merchant to ship your items together. Sure, you'll have to wait a few days to get the goods, but you'll at least keep some of your hard-earned cash.

Most sites, not surprisingly, don't advertise their shipping costs up front. That's because their discounts and prices look better if you don't take their shipping costs into account. In rare exceptions, such as at the NECX site shown here, the shipping price is mentioned up front.

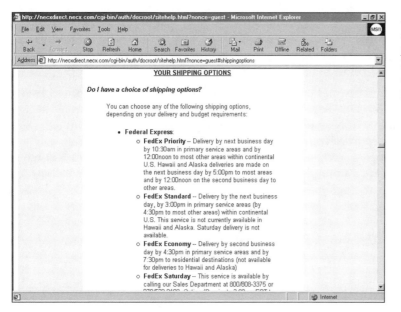

NECX is one of the few sites that states its shipping costs up front. On most other sites, you'll have to go searching to find the costs.

If a site doesn't mention shipping costs on the same page that has information about the goods you're buying, you'll have to go searching to find out shipping costs. If that's the case, I have two words for you: Good luck. Finding these costs before ordering isn't always easy. There's no standard place to look. If you're lucky (fat chance!), the site will have a link from the main page to a page with something such as Shipping Information or Ordering Information. If not, look for something such as Help Desk, Help, or even FAQs (Internet-speak for Frequently Asked Questions). Many sites also have a "site map" that makes it easy to find every page on the site. Check there if you can't find shipping information anywhere else—it always works for me. In general, though, you might have to nose around. In some cases, you won't be able to find out the shipping costs until you actually order an item. If that's the case and you're not happy with the shipping costs, just back out of buying by hitting the **Back** button on your browser until you're off the ordering page. No harm will be done. And you can always send email to the site before ordering to find out their shipping costs.

A Taxing Situation: Watching Out for State and County Taxes

You're buying over the Internet, rather than at a real store, so you probably figure that you'll save by not having to pay state or county taxes. After all, when you shop, you're not actually visiting a state and buying there, so you won't be hit with any sales taxes, right?

That sounds logical, but you hadn't counted on the long arm of the law, now, had you? As we all know, when it comes to taxes (and the Internet), nothing is simple, and so the answer is both yes and no. Usually, you'll pay no sales tax when you buy over the Internet. Sometimes, though, you will.

State laws require that companies collect sales taxes from anyone who buys and lives in a state in which a company has "established offices." Some county laws say the same thing. So if you live in New Jersey (You do? Which exit?) and buy from an Internet site that is based in New Jersey, you'll have to pay New Jersey sales tax. However, if you live in New York and buy from the same Internet site, you *won't* have to pay sales taxes. If there's a moral to be found here, I guess it's not to live in New Jersey.

Techno Talk

Use These Two Ways to Confirm Your Online Order

You should always have a written record of the purchases you make online, so that if something goes wrong, you have documents to use. But how do you get written records in a virtual shopping world? There are two ways. First, whenever you place an order, print out the confirmation page and keep it in a safe place. And second, always request that an email be sent to you with confirmation of your purchase. Any reputable site will do that for you as a matter of course.

So, for example, anyone who lives in California will have to pay sales tax when buying from the eToys site at www.etoys.com. And residents of New Jersey, New York, and Virginia will have to pay sales tax if they buy at the Barnes & Noble online site. That's because eToys has established offices in California, and Barnes & Noble has established offices in New York, New Jersey, and Virginia.

Now, you're probably thinking that Barnes & Noble has stores—and a lot of them—in every state in the country, so why don't people in every state have to pay taxes when buying on the Internet? I'm wondering the same thing. It has to do with the term "established offices." How do you determine what's an established office and what isn't—and why is the law so hard to understand? Don't ask me—why do you think God made lawyers? On the other hand, I've discovered that lawyers aren't so hot at figuring this out, either. I was once asked by an assistant attorney general in a state that will remain unnamed to be an "expert witness" in a case in which the state wanted to prove that an Internet business had an established office in the state and so had to pay sales taxes. I politely declined, on the general theory that the fewer taxes collected on Internet companies, the better.

Luckily, you don't have to be a lawyer to figure out whether you're going to have to pay sales tax when buying from a site. You'll find out from the site itself. As with other hidden charges, though, getting this information won't always be easy. Look for the Help, Ordering, FAQ, or similar area and nose around. Look for details about taxes. As with shipping charges, you might not find out that you'll have to pay taxes until you get to an ordering page. And as with shipping charges, you can always back out of the order by continually hitting the **Back** button on your browser until you're away from that page.

Many Happy Returns: Checking Out Return Policies and Warranties Before You Buy

You never buy anything expecting that you're going to have to return it, in the same way that you never fall in love expecting that you're going to break up some day. Unfortunately, though, breakups do happen—and not uncommonly, you have to return something you've bought online. Perhaps that orange dress shirt with the pointy collar didn't quite have the panache you had hoped for. Or perhaps the portable TV you bought was dead on delivery—the thing wouldn't even turn on, much less let you tune into your afternoon fix of *Gilligan's Island*. So you're going to have to return the goods.

What, you say you didn't check the return policy, and you won't be able to send that orange horror back? That's what you get for not being a cybersavvy shopper. Note this very important rule: Be sure that before you buy anything you first check out a site's return policies. There are a number of things you have to look out for: whether you can return the goods at all; what kind of warranty the site has; and who has to pay if you need to return what you've bought.

Return to Sender: Understanding Return Policies

All return policies are not created equal. One of the most important things you should get straight before buying is the kind of return policy a site has. Can you return the goods for any reason at all, or can you return an item only if it has a defect? How many days or weeks do you have in which to decide whether to return an item? Will you get a full refund or only a credit? What happens if you receive the wrong item—who pays the return shipping fees?

Don't Expect to Return Online Goods to Real-Life Stores

A lot of real-life retail stores, such as Barnes and Noble, the Gap, and many others, also let you buy online. So you might think that if you buy something from their online store, you can return it to their real-life store. Wrong! In general, if you buy something online, you'll have to return it via mail—you won't be able to return it to a retail store. Check before buying.

You'll rarely find this kind of information on the Web site itself—very few sites actually post their return policy. One shining exception is the eToys site, shown here, which makes its return policy clear. If the site you're thinking of buying from doesn't have a clear, posted return policy, send email or call the site to get the lowdown, and if you don't get answers to your satisfaction, don't buy there.

The eToys site is that rarity online—a site that actually posts its return policy in clear, concise language.

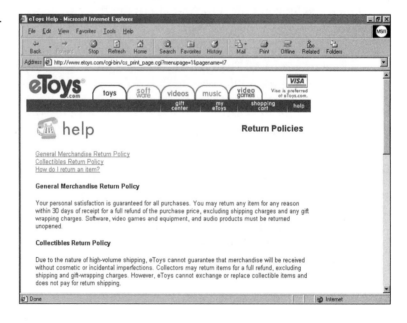

In general, most sites won't cover return-shipping fees unless the item was defective or the store shipped the wrong item. And not all sites will even pick up the shipping fees when they make a mistake or when they've shipped you some kind of damaged goods. Again, that's why you want to be sure to know return policies ahead of time.

If you're buying computer equipment via the Internet, you'll run into a whole host of complicated issues when it comes to returning a new computer—and if you're not careful, you could run up bills of well over $100 merely to return something. For more details about buying computer equipment over the Internet and ensuring you don't get burned in this way, turn to Chapter 16, "Drive a Hard Bargain on Hardware: Getting the Best Deal on Buying a Computer."

What You Need to Know About Warranties

Before you buy, check out the warranty or guarantee that the site offers for the goods you're buying. A warranty describes under what terms and conditions you can return goods and how the site has to replace defective products.

Yes, you guessed it—surprise, surprise, very few sites actually post warranties online. You know the routine by now. Nose around the site to find the warranty (again, good luck finding it). Then send email or call the site to find out its warranty. As usual, if you don't get an adequate answer, spend your money elsewhere.

Understand the Difference Between "Full" and "Limited" Warranties

All warranties are not created equal—and before buying, it's a good idea to know what kind of warranty you're getting, especially if it's for a big-ticket item. Full warranties, by federal law, guarantee that the warranty is offered free of charge and that return costs are covered if an item needs to be returned. They also guarantee, among other things, that the company will provide, according to your choice, a full refund or a replacement if the goods don't work. A limited warranty, on the other hand, is a much vaguer term. It means only that some kind of warranty is offered—and that it doesn't meet all the conditions for being a full warranty. Beware of limited warranties, unless you're given in writing exactly what the warranty covers.

When it comes to asking for a warranty, you have the law behind you. According to a little-known (and even less-used) Federal Trade Commission rule, a consumer product costing more than $15 must carry a warranty. And you have the right to demand and get that warranty in writing. Now, forcing the Federal Trade Commission to enforce the rule is another thing entirely. The odds are that the commission is not going to devote much of its lawyers' time to help you get a written warranty before you buy a $16.95 Slim Whitman album.

Some terms that merchants use entitle you to certain rights. According to the Federal Trade Commission, if a company uses a phrase such as *satisfaction guaranteed* or *money-back guarantee,* that merchant must be willing to give you a full refund for any reason at all—with no questions asked. Still, it's worth checking the site's warranty and return policies because it might or might not follow that rule. However, if you buy something at a site that uses words such as these and the merchant refuses to honor your request to return a product, send a threatening letter citing the Federal Trade Commission rule—and send a copy of the letter to the Federal Trade Commission. The odds are, the merchant will honor your request. Note that you might still have to cover return-shipping costs, though.

How to Know You're Buying Through a Secure Site

Probably the number one concern of anyone who buys anything on the Internet is security. How do you know that your credit card number won't be stolen by some money-hungry hacker intent on using it for buying tons of Jolt soda, nacho chips, first-class trips to Europe, and pimple cream? The answer is to buy things only on a secure site. Never, ever send your credit card number or other similar personal information over the Internet unless it's on a secure site.

Ah, but you're no doubt asking, how do you know what's a secure site and what isn't? Very clever of you to ask. Luckily, it's quite easy to know. At the point when you proceed to check out on a secure site, a window will pop up, alerting you that you're about to enter a secure site. Pictured here are the messages that Microsoft Internet Explorer displays when you're entering a secure site.

See the little check box in each of the windows? If you'd like, you can use that check box to tell your browser *not* to alert you each time you visit a secure site? Why would you not want to be alerted? Beats me—but that's the Internet for you. My advice is to be sure that the browser alerts you every time you're about to visit a secure site.

Note, by the way, that if you want to always be alerted when you visit a secure site, you ensure the box is checked in Netscape Navigator, but in Microsoft Internet Explorer, you ensure the box is *unchecked.* I guess that's just Netscape's and Microsoft's way of ensuring you're paying attention. Ain't the Internet grand?

Here's the message that pops up on Microsoft Internet Explorer when you're entering a secure site. Netscape Navigator displays a similar screen.

What Is SET?

No, it's not a portion of a tennis match. SET stands for Secured Electronic Transaction, and it's the electronic encryption and payment standard that a group of big companies, including Microsoft, Netscape, Visa, MasterCard, and others are pushing to become the standard for doing electronic commerce on the Internet. Some sites are already using it; soon every site might be using SET.

That little pop-up window is one clue that you're entering a secure site. But there's an even better way to know. That's to look for the little icon of a lock on the bottom bar of your browser. In Netscape Navigator, an unlocked lock means that the site is not secure. A locked lock means that the site is secure.

A locked lock such as this one means that the site is secure.

Microsoft Internet Explorer displays a similar lock icon if the site is secure, as shown here. If no lock appears at the bottom of the browser, the site is not secure.

The Least You Need to Know

➤ Get confirmation of all hidden costs such as shipping and handling fees, restocking fees, and state taxes before buying on a site.

➤ Check out return policies and warranties online before buying—and don't buy from a site that won't advise you of its policies.

➤ Be sure your credit card is charged only when the product is shipped to you.

➤ Get confirmation of all your orders via email and by printing out your order page.

➤ Buy only through sites that feature secure transactions—andy you can tell whether they're secure by looking for the locked lock at the bottom of your browser.

UM, IT LOOKED BIGGER ON-LINE.

How to Check Out a Site and Products Before Buying

In This Chapter

➤ Using the Better Business Bureau to check out a site

➤ Using the Internet to do consumer research on any product

➤ Best online consumer sites

You don't need a great deal of skill or very much money to put together a professional-looking Web site (although considering all the online dreck you come across when surfing, that might come as a surprise to you). It's not like a real-life bricks-and-mortar store where shoppers have clues as to whether it's on the up-and-up from how well the store is maintained, what the merchandise looks like, what kind of staff works there, and so on. Just because a Web site has a pretty front doesn't mean much—lurking behind that pretty face could be a merchant you'd be better off not trusting.

You can take a few steps, however, to check out a site before buying. If you do your homework, you can end up shopping only at stores that are honest and won't burn you.

First off, follow the advice from the previous chapter about finding out shipping policies, return policies, and warranties. Is any of that information posted? If it's not posted, when you send an email to the site, does someone respond quickly and with the specific information you've asked for? If you can't get this kind of information, then take a virtual hike—if a store treats you this poorly *before* you buy, imagine what happens if you have a problem *after* you buy.

How to Research the Shopping Site

What kind of information does the site post about itself? Does it include contact information, such as the address (or at least the city) of the site's main headquarters? Better yet, does it list the names of the company's officers (not many sites do so, by the way)? Is it a publicly traded company (if it is, it'll tell you so)? How about a contact telephone number—does it list any? The more of this kind of information a site is willing to post, the more likely it is that it's an honest one. If you can't find any of this kind of information about the site, be leery.

If there are message boards, check them out as well. Busy message boards usually mean a lot of active users, which can often be a sign that the site has return visitors and so is a trustworthy one. What kind of messages are being posted? Obviously, if you see a lot of unhappy campers there, it's not a place you want to be. Be careful, though, not to rely too heavily on what people say on message boards. The site itself can forge messages and weed out messages with complaints.

Have you heard of the site before—and is it associated with any kind of existing bricks-and-mortar stores? If the site has blanketed the airwaves or newspapers with advertising, there's a better chance that it's well funded and so will be around for a while than if you've never heard of it. And if the site is the online branch of a well-known retailer, once again, it's most probably a safe place to spend your money.

Doing all this is a good first step to figuring out whether the site can be trusted. But it's only a first step. You can do other things as well—particularly by doing some legwork (or is that keyboard-and-mousework?) and checking out whether there are consumer complaints against the site and how well regarded it is by other online shoppers. How do you do that? I'm glad you asked. Check out the following sections—they'll tell you everything you need to know.

Try the Better Business Bureau

The best place to go to check out a business is the Better Business Bureau. This local nonprofit corporation can give you the goods on any businesses that have less-than-savory reputations. And it will also let you know about businesses that have no outstanding complaints lodged against them.

You can get a free report from the Better Business Bureau about any company that it has a record of. The report will tell you how long the company has been in business, whether there have been complaints with the Better Business Bureau about the company, and how the complaints were resolved—if they were resolved at all. And if a government agency such as the Federal Trade Commission or a state Attorney General has taken actions against the company, the Better Business Bureau will let you know that as well. The reports usually cover the past three years and indicate whether the company is a member of the Better Business Bureau.

You Have Credit Card Rights Under the Fair Credit Billing Act

The Federal Fair Credit Billing Act covers credit card transactions over the Internet—and gives you legal rights if your credit card bill contains an error related to an Internet transaction or you're disputing a credit card bill because of an Internet transaction. If you've been billed incorrectly for some reason, such as for goods and services that you haven't received, an error in the amount charged, or unauthorized charges, the law covers you. Under it, you must write a letter to the company that made the incorrect charge, describing the error and including your name, address, and charge card number. When you send the notice, the company must, by law, send you a written acknowledgment of your claim within 30 days and must resolve the problem within 90 days.

The Bureau doesn't have reports on every business. If it doesn't have a report, it generally means that either the company is a new one or that no one has complained about it.

Better Business Bureaus are all local. So a Better Business Bureau in Burbank, California, for example, can't tell you about a business based in Secaucus, New Jersey (what exit was that again?). So before checking in with a Better Business Bureau, find out where the Web site's main offices are. If you can't find out, you've answered the question already—stay away.

There are two easy ways to find out where there's a Better Business Bureau near you. You can check the Yellow Pages or call directory assistance. Or if you'd rather not have to resort to such an old-fashioned, low-tech solution, go to the Better Business Bureau Web site at www.bbb.com. You'll be able to find contact information of a Better Business Bureau near where the company you're researching has offices. The following section gives more information about the Better Business Bureau Web site.

Try the BBBOnLine Site

The Better Business Bureau is no slouch; it recognizes that a whole lot of business is conducted over the Internet, and so it has put together a special program that can help you check out businesses that have online sites. The program is called BBB*OnLine,* and you can get information about it at the BBB*OnLine* site at www.bbbonline.com (stay tuned for more information about the Web site later in this chapter).

It works like this: A company agrees to participate in the program, and as part of that, agrees to abide by BBB*OnLine* standards. That means that the company agrees to resolve complaints quickly and fairly, have a satisfactory record with the Better Business Bureau, be in business at least a year, agree to correct or withdraw misleading Internet advertising, and provide contact information such as addresses, phone numbers, and company officials. And the company will also agree to binding arbitration with a consumer if there's been a complaint. All in all, not a bad set of guidelines.

But wait, as they say in late-night TV ads, there's more! Companies that participate can also place a BBB*OnLine* seal on their site. That seal shows not only that the company participates in the program but also, when clicked, gives a full rundown of information about the company including address, phone number, contact information, and how long the company has been in business. And best yet, if there have been any complaints against the company, you'll see that as well.

Here's part of the
*BBB*OnLine *report on a*
clothing store.

When I last checked, about 700 stores had signed up for the program. Not all of them, though, display the seal on their site, so you won't always know whether a particular company is part of the program. To find out, head to the www.bbbonline.com. From there, you can search for any company to see whether it is a member. And if it is, you can see the full BBB*OnLine* report on the company.

Try Those Wild and Crazy Accountants at CPA WebTrust

Here's another agency that can help you decide whether to trust a particular online merchant with your hard-earned cash. It's called CPA WebTrust, at www. cpawebtrust.com. Run by an association of certified public accountants (a bunch of wild and crazy guys and gals, no doubt—aren't all accountants?), the organization issues CPA Web Trust seals to companies that adhere to a set of online selling principles. These include posting warranty and return information, not using information gained about customers in a way that would invade the customers' privacy, and running a Web site that has secure transactions. If you see the seal on a site, you know it adheres to those principles.

Head to Usenet Newsgroups

Some of the best places to get the goods on an online merchant are in newsgroups and online discussion boards. A number of newsgroups provide this kind of information, but I've found that for information about which online sites to stay away from, misc.consumer is the best by far. In a single day, for example, three messages were posted warning people to stay away from buying at certain Web sites. Head there, read the messages, and post questions of your own. You'll most probably get answers—and honest ones.

Checking Out a Site's Privacy Policy Before Buying

When you buy at a site, you want to know more than whether they can be trusted with your money. You also want to know whether they can be trusted with private information about you as well. After all, when you buy at a site, they know a whole lot about you—your name, address, credit card information and similar private information. And they know your buying habits as well—and that kind of information is worth a lot of money to direct marketers and other companies.

Before buying at a site, you'd like to know that they won't share with the world and other companies the fact that you favor polyester leisure suits, Carpenter albums, and the collected films of Jerry Lewis. So you should check out a site's privacy policies before buying there.

To do that, head to the area of the site titled something such as "Privacy Policies," if there is one. Be prepared: It might be hard to find. Often the link to it might be in very small type at the bottom of a page. If you can't find a "Privacy Policies" area, look for something such as "FAQ" or "Help" or something similar. And you'll find that some sites don't post their policies. If they don't, email them to find out their policies. If they don't answer, buy elsewhere. There are a whole lot of places on the Internet that respect your privacy, so buy only at them.

What to Look For in a Site's Privacy Policies

Just because a site posts its privacy policy doesn't mean that the it's a good privacy policy. So here's what to look for:

➤ **Does it tell you what kind of information it tracks and collects?** Do they, for example, comprehensively track and analyze your buying habits, or just maintain a list of names?

➤ **What does the site do with your information?** Does it share information with other businesses? If so, what kind of businesses and what specific businesses—and what will those businesses do with the information?

➤ **Is information about you shared individually, or in the "aggregate?"** Some sites gather information about individuals primarily to put together demographic information about the site as a whole—not to track individuals. They then show that aggregate information to advertisers, to prove how valuable their Web site is. This isn't really an invasion of privacy, because your name and personal information will never be revealed. However, other sites release the personal information—and you should know whether they do.

➤ **Can you "opt out" of mailings?** Web sites ask for your email address not because they're curious, but because they want to send you email asking you to buy things. You want to be able to "opt out" of getting those mailings—in other words, you don't want to get them.

➤ **Is there contact information?** To whom can you complain if you think your privacy has been violated? There should be a person or email address to send your complaints to.

➤ **Does it carry a TRUSTe "trustmark" or similar seal?** TRUSTe, at www.etrust.com, is one of several companies that sets standards for protecting privacy on the Internet, and ensures that any companies that participate in its program adhere to these privacy rules. Check to see whether a company has the TRUSTe trustmark on its site. The Better Business Bureau Online at www.bbbonline.com, also has a similar seal that it allows sites to display if they adhere to privacy standards.

How to Research What You Buy Online

Ensuring you buy at a good site is only the first part of becoming a cybersavvy shopper. Ultimately, what's really important is *what* you're buying, not *where* you're buying it.

Know Your Rights About Shipping Times

You have the force of the law behind you when it comes to knowing when the goods you've ordered will be delivered to you. Internet shopping is covered by the Federal Trade Commission's Mail Order Rule. That rule says that companies must ship orders to you within the time they've promised—and if they haven't promised a time, then they must ship them within 30 days of when you've ordered them. If there's a delay, they have to notify you and ask whether you agree to the delay; if you don't agree, they must let you cancel the order.

One of the reasons to shop on the Internet is that it's the ultimate consumer resource. You can do comprehensive consumer research on any product you can imagine, whether it be a big-ticket item such as a car or a less-expensive product such as a bottle of perfume (that is, it's less expensive unless you buy a really, *really* big bottle of the stuff). Many great consumer sites can help you make your best buy. The best all-around consumer sites, listed here, are good places to start your research on any product. Later in the book, I mention other places to go for more specialized consumer advice. (For example, I'll list consumer sites about computers in—surprise!—the chapter about buying computers, Chapter 16, "Drive a Hard Bargain on Hardware: Getting the Best Deal on Buying a Computer."

The Best Consumer Sites in Cyberspace

You'll find a whole lot of consumer sites in cyberspace. Don't bother heading to all of them; here are the best of the best.

Consumer @ction

    http://www.consumer-action.org

This great site, run by the private, nonprofit consumer advocacy agency Consumer Action, is one of the premier online consumer sites. It posts reports and research on a wide variety of consumer issues, such as credit card shopping, long-distance phone rates, how to complain if you've bought a lemon of a car, and much more. And it also includes a comprehensive set of links to many other consumer sites on the Internet. If you head here, try out the Smart Shopper quiz to see how well you know your consumer rights. You'll probably be appalled at how little you know.

Consumer Information Center

http://www.pueblo.gsa.gov/

This site, created by the Federal Consumer Information Center, gives you access to hundreds of consumer booklets. Whether you want advice on getting the cheapest airfares or on the best interest rates from a bank, or on many other consumer issues, you'll find pamphlets here. Oh, one more thing: Just by going to this site, you'll save money. Normally, you'd have to pay for many of these pamphlets, but they're all available for free online.

Consumer Reports

http://www.consumerreports.org/

Here's the bible for consumers. Where else in the world can you find honest reviews of new cars, hotel rooms, house siding, and light bulbs? Nowhere else, of course. And you'll find reviews and advice on buying just about any other product ever created as well. For the visually minded, it comes with pictures as well—and who else other than *Consumer Reports* would display a graph comparing the concentration of gin-senoside, the supposedly active ingredient in ginseng, in the most popular ginseng capsules? By the way, there's one drawback to this site: Not all of the reviews and arti-cles are free—you have to pay for some of them. Nevertheless, the site is well worth a visit. The Web site is shown in the following figure.

One of the most trusted consumer magazines, Consumer Reports, *has a place online.*

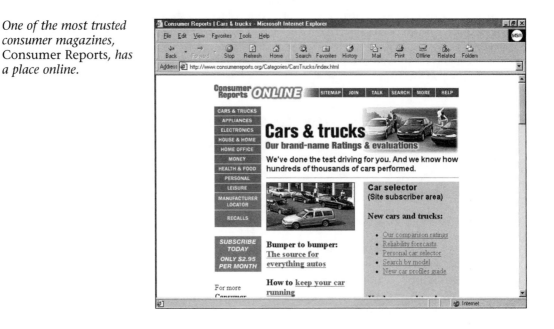

Consumer & Money Matters on America Online

KEYWORD CONSUMER

America Online has a whole lot of areas where you can do consumer research. Good luck finding them all because they're spread out all over kingdom come. If you are an America Online user, head here to find all of them in one place. From cars to personal finance to electronic gadgets, you'll find advice here. What's nice is that the site points to some Web sites as well, not just sites on America Online. But don't rely on this site completely; for some reason, it leaves out many of the best consumer research sites.

Consumer World

http://www.consumerworld.org/

The name pretty much sums up this site. Think of just about anything in the world a consumer might want to know about, and you'll find it here. Links to consumer agencies and consumer resources on the Web, links to the best consumer sites, bargains, discounts, news about shopping—it's all here.

GTE Superpages Consumer Guide

http://www.consumerguide.com

Here's a nice consumer guide to buying many different categories of products. Just click the kind of product you're looking for, and you'll get lists of the best products in that category (as rated by the site) as well as the best value for the money and other recommended products. There is also good general information on how to buy each different kind of product.

U.S. Consumer Gateway

http://www.consumer.gov

You pay a whole lot in federal taxes every year. Wouldn't it be nice to put that money to use for a change? Here's your chance. This gateway links you to the voluminous consumer information that the federal government has posted online. Want links to sites that warn of dangerous products and consumer recalls? They're here. How about a link to a site that focuses on consumer health issues? Or warnings about sleazy Internet businesses, vacation scams, dangerous drugs, advice on buying bicycles for your kids? Yes, there's all that here and more. This site is a must-visit for anyone who wants to find out what the feds have to say about any consumer issue or product.

Getting Advice from Others: Newsgroups, Discussion Areas, and Chat Areas

Thousands of newsgroups, discussion areas, and chats take place all over the Internet. Many of them have to do with consumer issues and buying things. If you're looking for information about a particular product, head to the newsgroup or discussion area that concerns that item. I'd suggest going to the Deja.com site at www.deja.com to find the right newsgroups. For discussions and chats, try Yahoo! at www.yahoo.com. And America Online has particularly busy chat and discussion groups, so if you're a member, check out those areas as well. For the shopping discussions, use the keyword SHOPPING BOARDS.

The Least You Need to Know

➤ Check to see whether a site lists its mailing address before doing business there.

➤ Look up a site with the Better Business Bureau to see whether any consumers have filed complaints.

➤ Ask questions about sites in Internet newsgroups devoted to shopping.

➤ Before buying a product, check consumer sites for product ratings.

CAN I HELP YOU?

Avoiding Online Scams and Con Artists

In This Chapter

➤ Top tips for avoiding online scammers

➤ What you should do if you've been burned

➤ How to make out consumer complaints

➤ Dealing with your credit card company

➤ Best sites online for filing consumer complaints

The Internet might be the ultimate shopper's paradise: All the goods in the world are a few mere mouse clicks away. Billions of dollars every year are sent through the wires, modems, and computers that make up the online world.

But the sad truth is that where there's money, there are also scams. In that way, the Internet is no different from anyplace else. There's a now-famous *New Yorker* cartoon in which a dog sits in front of a computer and tells another dog in the room, "On the Internet, nobody knows you're a dog." In the same way, con artists believe that on the Internet, nobody knows they're sleazy scammers. Con artists who in the past have used telemarketing and the mail to do their dastardly deeds have now turned their sights on the Internet.

Most Internet scams and cons are possible because it's so easy for anyone to pose as a legitimate business. Someone can spend a few bucks building a spiffy-looking Web site, and *voilà!* he or she is no longer El Slimo on parole from the Big House after conning poor old grannies out of their grandkids' milk money. Instead, a legit businessperson is taking your credit card number over the Internet.

But not to worry: You can ensure that you don't get conned online. And if, for some reason, you've been the victim of a scam or have a complaint against an online shopping site, you can do something about it. In this chapter, I offer you top tips for avoiding Internet scams and then clue you in on what to do if you have been burned. In most cases, you'll be able to get back any money you've spent—and you'll be able to file complaints against scammers online with a variety of private and public consumer groups and investigative agencies.

How to Recognize Online Scams

The truth is, it's not really that hard to detect online scams. Any undue hype and impossible-sounding promises such as these should raise a red flag: "Get a 500MHz computer for $300" or "Buy your dream house with no money down!" Sure, and you probably have a bridge you want to sell me as well.

It's not just hype you should be wary of. If you're contacted via email with a great-sounding offer or you come across a Web site that has no address or phone number on it, be wary as well. And any time a Web site seems just not right to you in some way, listen to your instincts—they're almost always right.

Fourteen Tips for Avoiding Online Scams and Con Artists

The Federal Trade Commission (www.ftc.gov) and a variety of consumer agencies, such as the National Fraud Information Center (www.fraud.org), keep a close watch on the kinds of scams that are common on the Internet. Based on what they've found, here are 14 tips for avoiding online scams and con artists:

➤ **Never buy from a site with no mailing address or phone number.**
It's easy to create a professional, slick-looking buying site on the Internet. Anyone with some Web-editing skills and a good eye can do it. But just because someone can create a great-looking Web site doesn't mean that he or she is on the up-and-up. That person can easily take your money and run. Buy only at a site that has a valid mailing address and phone number. When you get the address, check out the business with the Better Business Bureau and consumer agencies (refer to Chapter 5, "How to Check Out a Site and Products Before Buying") in the state where the company does business for more information. And if you still have doubts, listen to your instincts: Don't buy.

Watch Out for Unauthorized Credit Card Charges

A scam on the rise is unauthorized fees charged to your credit card for Internet services you never asked for. A warning sign is an unfamiliar business on your credit card, followed by an 800 number. Often, the charge will be for $19.95, the exact same fee that many Internet service providers (ISPs) charge. That fee is no accident—scamsters hope that you'll assume the charge is for your ISP, and so never notice it.

➤ **Don't hang up and redial in at the request of a merchant.** You might come across an online merchant who asks you to download a piece of software, log off your Internet service provider, and then log on to the Internet again using the software you just downloaded. The merchant might claim that redialing will make you eligible to win a prize or that you will be registered for some kind of free offer. Or the merchant might say that redialing with this software ensures a secure credit card transaction. Don't believe it. This common scam is potentially very expensive. When you dial in, you'll in fact be dialing a for-pay phone number, possibly somewhere in the wilds of Utter Nowhere, and you'll be charged a great deal of money every minute that you're online. People who have succumbed to this scam have been charged more than $100 for a single phone call. The most famous case of this kind had people dialing into Moldova and being charged a fortune without their knowledge.

➤ **Never respond to "spam."** No, I'm not talking about the much-maligned luncheon meat with a cultlike following. *Spam* refers to unsolicited email sent to your inbox, often touting too-good-to-believe offers such as investment schemes. Guess what? The reason those offers are too-good-to-believe is that they're not true. They're often scams. Spammers send out tens of thousands of emails in the hopes of roping in a few gullible, trusting souls. Don't be one. Never respond to spam—if you do, you could face worse consequences than mere indigestion.

What Is Spam?

Spam is junk email that is sent to many thousands of people, offering some kind of good or service for sale—and often it's a sleazy offer. Most people agree that the name comes from a famous Monty Python skit in which the most prominent—and ultimately only—food on the menu was the luncheon meat Spam.

➤ **Stay away from work-at-home offers.**   How would you like to work at home part-time and make $75,000 a year? Sure, so would I. Here's the bad news, though: It's not going to happen. These kinds of offers are common on the Internet. If you come across a work-at-home offer like this, jump as far away from it as you can. The odds are you'll be conned into buying a book, series of books, or expensive mailing materials and goods. And the only person making that $75K at home part-time will be the scammer, not you.

➤ **Don't buy "credit repair."**   The Internet is filled with con artists promising to repair bad credit records. They'll claim they have ways to get rid of your bad credit and start you off afresh. They'll, of course, charge you outrageous fees and ask for your credit card numbers. Not only will you be out the fees you pay to them, but they could well abscond with your credit card number and run up some pretty big bills in your name. So avoid them. And never, ever agree to create a second credit file for you with a second tax ID or Social Security number. It's illegal; you could be prosecuted if you're caught.

➤ **Be careful before signing up for any "free" trials.**   The hallmark of any "free" trial over the Internet is that you first have to submit your credit card number before the trial can commence. And you'll be told that you'll have a chance to back out of the trial before your card is billed. Be careful, though, because that free trial might only mask a con artist who's looking to get his or her hands on your credit card and who may continue to charge you every month, or worse. Agree to free trials only with large, well-known, reputable Web merchants.

➤ **Don't buy goods, stocks, or services solely on advice you come across on discussion boards, email, or chat areas.**   It's true that discussion boards, newsgroups, and chat areas are great places for getting consumer advice and shopping tips from others. But it's equally true that con artists have used them for a variety of nefarious purposes. It's easy for con artists to forge their names in these areas and log in multiple times, touting some great stock or service or goods that they, in fact, sell under a different name. Then, when you buy from them, they take the money and run. Con artists have used this approach to run up worthless stocks, and many people have been burned.

➤ **Stay away from online pyramid schemes.**   In a pyramid scheme (also called multilevel marketing, or MLM, schemes), you're promised a handsome profit if you pay an initial fee and then recruit others to join in the scheme. Along the way, you also often have to buy marketing materials or pay more fees. The problem is this: You never make any money; you only keep paying it. It's an online variation of one of the oldest scams in the book, known as a Ponzi scheme, and is one of the more common scams on the Internet. The Federal Trade Commission brought a case against a company called the Fortuna Alliance, which allegedly ran such a scheme, and then transferred all its loot to a bank in Antigua. Avoid these scams. Buying into this pyramid is like agreeing to buy the Brooklyn Bridge.

Double-Check Web Sites That Promise to Give to Charities

The idea is a great one: Buy at a Web store and a portion of the proceeds go to charity. Sometimes, however, that money might not end up where it's supposed to—and the site might keep the money or give less than you believe it will. So be careful, and check out a site that promises to do something like this. By the way, some great charity programs *have* worked in this way. For example, the toy site www.etoys.com and Visa credit card had a great program one holiday buying season in which someone who bought a toy at eToys could buy a second one at a steep discount—and the toy would be given to the worthy Toys for Tots program.

➤ **Don't agree to set up an offshore trust.**   One of the newer and more innovative scams to hit the Internet is one promising that you can legally avoid paying taxes if you let the con artist set up an "offshore trust" for you. You'll find many of these offers in a variety of newsgroups. They'll ask for access to all your assets and then say they'll set up the trust for you—and that you'll never have to pay taxes again. (And while you're at it, why don't you just turn over the keys to your car, house, and safe deposit box as well—that'll make it much easier for them to bilk you out of everything you own.) In the best of cases, the con artists just take your money and run—and you'll be out whatever fees you paid to them. In the worst of cases, they'll set up the trusts all right, but with themselves as beneficiaries—and they now own your assets. Follow this simple rule: On the Internet, don't trust trusts.

➤ **Be careful when buying directly from individuals online.** A good deal of person-to-person buying, trading, and swapping takes place online in newsgroups, classified ads, and swap meets. Be aware that you don't have the same legal rights when you buy from an individual as when buying from a business—and it'll be much harder to track down a person as well. That means you should be even more careful about paying for goods from an individual than from a business.

➤ **Watch out if you're asked for personal information, such as your Social Security number.** There's hardly ever any reason for you to supply this, and so it could tip you off that the person on the other end of the transaction isn't on the up and up.

➤ **Check your debit card before paying online.** Most debit cards carry the same protection as do credit cards—you'll be held responsible for only the first $50 of a charge if there's some kind of scam. To be safe, though, check with the issuer of the card to see whether your card carries this protection.

➤ **Be careful when buying at auction sites.** The most common scam reported to the Internet Fraud Watch group involves online auctions—and the most common scam there is when buyers don't get what they've been promised by sellers, or don't get anything at all. To protect yourself, check the insurance policy of the auction site, and pay using C.O.D. or an escrow service. An escrow service holds your money until you get what you've been promised—and only when everything is kosher do they pay the seller.

➤ **Don't call 809 numbers.** A common scam involves sending you spam mail, or making you another kind of online offer, and asking you to call a number that starts with an 809 or other unfamiliar area code. This code is used for numbers outside of the United States and is a favorite of scamsters who aren't subject to U.S. fraud laws. When you dial the number, you might be put on hold for a long period of time or talk to an operator who claims not to speak English. The entire time, the meter is running—and you might be charged $25 or more a minute. In a variation of this theme, a fraudulent email was sent to thousands of America Online customers, telling them they were now signed up for a pornographic Web site. (None of the people had, in fact, subscribed to the site.) For more billing information, they were told to call a number. When they called, they were put on hold, and were charged for every minute they spent on the phone.

Check out the U.S. Consumer Gateway for the latest news about Internet scams.

What to Do If You've Been Scammed

If you follow the previous advice on avoiding scams, the great odds are that you'll never be burned. Cyberspace remains a largely safe place to shop. However, there's a chance that no matter how careful you are, you might get burned. Perhaps you ordered a Palm III handheld organizer, and it was never delivered as promised. Or you were the victim of a stock scam. If you've been a victim, don't despair, because even if you've been a victim of a scam, you can still fight back. Follow my advice, and you might well be able to get your money directly back from the scammer. And if you can't, you could get your credit card company to cover most, if not all, of the costs of your scam. And you also have recourse to a wide variety of government and private agencies to help you get back your money—and even to prosecute the scam artist who targeted you.

Be Safe by Knowing the Latest Internet Scams

New scams crop up on the Internet almost every day. A number of Web sites report on the most current Internet scams. Check out the Web site of the Better Business Bureau at www.bbb.org and the Internet Fraud Watch run by the National Consumer's League at www.fraud.org. The federally funded U.S. Consumer Gateway at www.consumer.gov not only reports on scams but also lets you know what actions the Federal Trade Commission (FTC) has taken against Internet scamsters. The FTC site at www.ftc.gov also reports on actions it's taken against scamsters. And the Securities and Exchange Commission site at www.sec.gov reports on stock-related scams.

Dealing with the Company That Burned You

If you suspect you've been the victim of a scam, the first thing you'll want to do is deal directly with the company who did the con. Be sure to contact the company as soon as you suspect a problem; if you wait too long to complain, defending your position will be more difficult. Before you contact the company, be sure you have your ducks in a row—have all the information about your complaint ready. Here's what you should have:

➤ **All information about the sale itself**   Have ready the product name and price, its serial number, the date and time you bought it, and any other identifying information. If you were notified by the company via email about your purchase, have a copy of that as well. If you printed out your order from the Web site, have a copy of that.

➤ **A clear description of your complaint**   Write a paragraph describing why you think you've been wronged.

➤ **Canceled check or credit card bill**   If your check has already been cashed or your credit card has been billed, have that information ready.

With this information in hand, call the company and say you want to talk to someone about a consumer complaint. Then go over the complaint with them. Be sure to take notes, including the name of the person you spoke with, the date and time of the call, and what the discussion was about. Follow up the call with an email.

In most cases, this effort should resolve the problem. If it doesn't, however, you should make a formal complaint to the company. Do so in writing through the U.S. mail—*not* via email. There's no way to prove that your email was sent or received, so if the issue goes to a consumer agency, you'll still need the good old U.S. Postal Service to deliver your letter via snail mail.

It's Easy to Find the Mailing Address and Phone Number for Any Web Site

Many Web sites don't include information such as the company running the site, its address, and phone number. That's information you should have—especially if you're going to file a consumer complaint. Here's how to find the owner, address, and phone number for any site. Head to the site www.netsolutions.com and click **WHOIS Search**. From the page that appears, type in the name of the site, but leave out the www. So, for example, you'd type in ebay.com to find information about the www.ebay.com online auction site. You'll then get that site's mailing address, phone number, and sometimes names of people who run the site as well.

Writing a letter will preserve your rights under consumer laws. Include in the letter the information about the sale, detailed earlier in this chapter; a clear description of your complaint; and the number of your canceled check or information about when your credit card was charged. Include information about the person you spoke to at the company and what took place in your discussion. Also include all your contact information.

Here's where you play hardball. In the letter, give the company a specific amount of time in which to resolve your complaint—anywhere from 10 to 14 days. Say that you're also going to take legal action unless the company resolves the complaint to your satisfaction. Be sure the recipient knows that you're sending copies of your letter to your state consumer agency, consumer groups, and your state attorney general. (See the information later in this chapter on which groups to complain to.) When you've finished writing your letter, send it via certified or registered mail. That way, you'll be able to prove that the company received your letter.

If you do all this, odds are that you'll get the complaint resolved. If not, you'll at least have a written record of the complaint, which you can then send along to your credit card company and government and private consumer agencies.

Dealing with Your Credit Card Company

If you've paid with a credit card, the odds are that you'll be covered for all but $50 if you were the victim of a scam. Most credit card companies will investigate your complaint, and if it finds you're in the right, you'll have to pay only the first $50. (See, there's a reason you've paid thousands of dollars in late fees all those years.) And if you push hard enough, the credit card company might eat that $50 as well. Some credit card companies, notably those that advertise on the Internet, make it a point to promise you that you'll never be liable for a penny of Internet fraud if you use their card.

The Visa NextCard Guarantees You'll Never Pay if You're Scammed Online

The Visa NextCard is a credit card with a twist—it promises that you'll never have to pay a penny if you've been the victim of fraud while using the card buying online. So even the first $50 is automatically covered, unlike other credit cards through which you might be liable for that $50. For details, head to www.nextcard.com.

If you've been scammed, start by calling the credit card company and give the representative all the dirty details over the phone. Follow up with a letter. In the letter, explain your complaint in as much detail as you can, including information such as which site you're complaining about, its mailing address and phone number, the day and time of the purchase, the product you purchased (or thought you were purchasing), and any other pertinent information. Describe how you tried to resolve the complaint. Also include any letters or email that you've sent or received. The credit card company will investigate your claim, and if it decides in your favor, you're off the hook for all but $50, and maybe not even that. If it decides against you, though, don't give up. You can still do more, as I'll explain in the next section.

Complaining to Consumer Agencies

So, you've been scammed. Maybe you've gotten your money back. Maybe you haven't. No matter what, you owe it to yourself and others to go after the sleaze artists who wasted your time and money online. You can complain to a variety of government and private consumer agencies that can help you get back your money. They can go after the con artists and shut them down—and possibly even prosecute the perpetrators (the "perps" as crime shows would have it). There have been many Internet-related prosecutions for fraud and the like, so don't worry—you have a lot of people on your side.

Here are the best places online and in the "real world" to make complaints about getting burned on the Internet.

Complaining to Private Agencies

A great place to start is with the *Better Business Bureau*. Better Business Bureaus exist in every state in the country. In fact, some states have a half dozen or more bureaus.

As described in Chapter 5, businesses fund these agencies to promote good business practices. The agencies keep track of complaints filed against businesses. In addition, the bureaus try to resolve any complaints you have—they'll work directly with the businesses to try to get your money back. The agencies also keep your complaint on permanent file so that other people will be warned away. You'll need to complain to the Better Business Bureau where the company is located. To find a list of them in the entire country, head to the Better Business Bureau Web site at www.bbb.org.

The *National Fraud Information Center* is a good place to complain as well—especially because it has a major online presence. It will relay your complaint to the proper federal, state, and local law enforcement agencies. And your complaint will also go into the National Fraud Database maintained by the Federal Trade Commission and the National Association of Attorneys General. You can fill out a complaint form online. Head to www.fraud.org and fill out the form shown in this figure. If you prefer the telephone (how retro of you!), call (800) 876-7060.

You can also complain to the *Netcheck Commerce Bureau*, a private agency that specializes in tracking down online scams and frauds. Find it at www.netcheck.com and fill out a complaint form online. When you make out a complaint, the company you're complaining about has 20 days to respond to Netcheck. If the offending company doesn't resolve the problem to Netcheck's liking, Netcheck might then forward your complaint to the proper federal organization handling complaints.

You might not realize it, but just about any kind of business belongs to some kind of *trade association*, which, among other things, resolves consumer complaints. (Yes, Virginia, there is a National Soap and Detergent Association. And a National Turkey Federation. And a lot more where those came from.) To get a complete list of trade associations, head over to the Federal Consumer Information Center at www.pueblo.gsa.gov and click on the link to the "Consumer's Resource Handbook." It's a complete guide for consumers and includes a comprehensive listing of trade associations.

Don't get mad, get even! It's easy to fill out a complaint form online. Here's the one you'll find at the National Fraud Information Center.

Complaining to Government Agencies

You pay a lot of money in taxes to support government agencies. Put that money to good use for once: Take advantage of the government agencies that investigate consumer and online fraud. You can file many complaints online or do things the old-fashioned way and mail them in.

A good place to start is with your state's attorney general or with your state's Department of Consumer Affairs, if it has one. These are the two primary local consumer enforcement agencies. A good way to find out whether these agencies have online sites is to head to the ConsumerWorld site at www.consumerworld.org. You'll find a link to what's probably the most comprehensive list of government consumer agencies and attorneys general offices on the Internet. To be sure your complaint is heard, complain not just to the state agencies in your state but also in the state where the Web site does business.

The *Federal Trade Commission* is responsible for a variety of consumer laws involving the Internet. In fact, it's the primary federal agency that prosecutes Internet scams. Fill out a complaint online at its Web site at www.ftc.org. The information goes not just to the Federal Trade Commission, but to the National Association of Attorneys General as well.

If you've been the victim of an online scam involving stocks or securities, file a complaint with the *Securities and Exchange Commission*. Find it online at www.sec.gov. You can also directly email your complaint to enforcement@sec.gov.

Tell It to the Judge: Using Small Claims Court

You might be able to take the company that scammed you to small claims court. These are local courts in which you need no lawyer—you present your facts to the judge, and he or she can award you the amount of money you've been scammed. I've gone to small claims court and been awarded $250 worth of repair work from a used car dealer, so I can personally vouch that it works. Unfortunately, you have to go to small claims court in the locality where the Internet business operates, so you'll be able to take someone to small claims court only if he or she lives in your area. It's not going to be worth your while to fly to Tulsa from southern California to resolve a $225 rip-off—that is, unless you're in the mood for an Oklahoma vacation (where, after all, the corn is as high as an elephant's eye).

Online Tactics for Fighting Back

Where I live in Massachusetts, politics is a contact sport. There's a time-honored rule that prevails here: Don't get mad, get even. When it comes to online scamsters, play by the same rule. Use the Internet to get back at the sleazeballs who took your money—and possibly get your money back as well. Here are some online techniques to use if you've tried every other way to get satisfaction and can't.

Start by visiting the site where you made the purchase. Look around for any message areas, bulletin boards, or any other kind of public discussion areas. If you find one, publicly air your complaint. Odds are, it'll be taken down at some point, but that's no problem—keep logging in and complaining. The company will soon discover that it'll be much cheaper to settle with you than to risk a continual stream of public complaints.

You can also go to other places to stir up trouble for people who have ripped you off online. The most popular site on the Internet, Yahoo! at www.yahoo.com, has public message boards where people from all over the world participate. These boards are broken down by topic, such as Computer Hardware, and Auto & Truck Manufacturers. Go to the board that matches the kind of goods you tried to buy. Then sound off.

Next head to Internet newsgroups. These are public discussion areas in which millions of people all over the globe participate. Go to alt.consumers.experiences, alt.consumers, and misc.consumers. Let 'er rip: Tell the world about your experience. This tactic might not get your money back, but you'll at least warn away others.

As I detailed earlier in the chapter, many places online enable you to fill out complaint forms with private and government agencies, so make sure to do that as well.

The Least You Need to Know

➤ Buy only from online sites that also have real-life addresses and telephone numbers.

➤ Beware of any deals that sound too good to be true, such as work-at-home offers, "free" trials, and pyramid schemes.

➤ Be careful when buying from an individual online.

➤ Keep careful records of all your online purchases and use those records to write letters of complaints to the Web site that burned you, as well as to consumer agencies.

➤ Government agencies, such as the Federal Trade Commission (www.ftc.gov), and private agencies, such as the National Fraud Information Center (www.fraud.org), are good places to file online complaints against Internet scammers.

➤ Fight back against con artists by going online and airing your complaints in public discussion areas, newsgroups, and bulletin boards.

GO. SHOP.
FIND ME
SNEAKERS.

Shopping Robots, Agents, Search Tools, and Virtual Shopping Assistants

In This Chapter

➤ Understanding shopping search tools

➤ The best shopping search tools on the Internet

➤ How to get ShopBots to do your shopping for you

➤ Using the best ShopBots in cyberspace

"May I help you, Sir (or Madam)?" When was the last time you were in a store and heard those words spoken with civility? And when was the last time anyone in a store actually gave you any kind of real help? The great odds are that it's been a long, long time. Good luck going into a store and getting advice on which lawnmower offers the best value or which shirt is made of the longest-lasting material.

Amazingly enough, though, you can find many shopping assistants online. Mainly, they'll help you find the best deals—the lowest price on the new Pentium PC you've been craving, for example. They go out across the Internet, sweep all the shopping sites, and report to you on the lowest prices they find. These shopping assistants can help you save much time and much money—and they don't annoy you with sullen stares when you make a request or keep you squirming in line while they talk on the phone to friends about their newest tattoos and plans for body piercing.

Online shopping assistants go by many names, and you'll find many different kinds. They're often called shopping robots, ShopBots, shopping agents, shopping search tools, and shopping assistants. Some run as software on your own computer, whereas others are built into sites that you visit on the Internet. No matter what they're called, though, shopping assistants can help you find a product that you couldn't otherwise find, and many of them will find the best price online for it as well.

Someday (and probably fairly soon), you can expect to find a new kind of shopping agent—a 3D representation of a person (called an avatar) who interacts with you when you enter a shopping site, asks you questions, offers advice, and tells you where to find the daily specials. And you won't even have to listen to your agent describe his or her newest metal ring piercing an unspeakable part of his body.

What Are Shopping Search Tools?

The most popular kind of virtual shopping assistants today are sites that are essentially shopping search tools. With these kinds of online shopping assistants, you visit a site and describe the product or category of product you're looking for. Some shopping search tools will then find the product and give you a set of links that will let you visit sites where you can buy. Other shopping assistants actually comparison shop for you, reporting on the best deals they find. They'll give you a set of links to those best deals. Still other kinds of search tools are even more helpful—they'll offer side-by-side product comparisons to help you decide which product to buy in a particular category—for example, the Aiwa ADC-RF35 or the Blaupunkt CDC-RF6 car CD changers.

Techno Talk

What's an Avatar?

An avatar is a visual representation of someone on the Internet that can talk and interact with you when you enter a certain area. Avatars have been used in chat rooms for a while—when you're chatting, you don't merely see what the person types, you see a picture that represents the person as well. Avatar shopping assistants are being developed so that when you enter a shopping area, someone whom you can see as well as talk to on the Web might greet you.

These kinds of search tools are so helpful that I rarely buy online anymore without first checking in with at least one of them, and possibly more than one.

One thing to keep in mind about these kinds of search tools is that each one won't search every single shopping site on the Internet. Consequently, you might want to check a couple of shopping search sites to get the best deal. And also keep in mind that sometimes search tools have business arrangements with some stores—and part of those business arrangements might be not to search certain sites. Again, this is another reason to check more than one search tool before buying.

In addition to the general shopping search tools that I cover in this chapter, many specialized search tools cover only a particular product. For example, if you want to buy a book, the Acses site at `www.acses.com` searches through 25 online bookstores for the book you want and reports on the best price. I discuss specialized shopping search tools in the chapters that cover the corresponding products.

Okay, Already, So Where Can I Find the Best Shopping Search Tools?

Just as there are good and bad shopping sites, there are also good and bad shopping search tools. The bad ones might only search through a few sites, steer you only to certain sites, or simply not do their jobs right (kind of like clerks in most retail stores these days).

Still, many helpful shopping search sites are out there. The following sections describe the best general purpose search sites.

BottomDollar

```
http://www.bottomdollar.com
```

Here's a reasonably useful shopping search tool that will help you find the best prices on a wide variety of products. It's not nearly as comprehensive as some of the other shopping sites listed here, and searches through only about half a dozen places. Still, it's useful, to be sure you're getting the best deal possible.

CompareNet

```
http://www.comparenet.com
```

Here's the big mama of them all, the best site I've so far found for anyone who needs advice on which product to buy. You won't do any actual buying at this site, but let's face it, buying something is the easy part. The hard part is figuring out what you should buy. And that's where CompareNet excels.

As you might guess by its name, the main reason you'll go to CompareNet is to compare products to one another. First, find the category of product you're looking for (such as electronics) and then choose the specific kind of product you want (such as digital cameras). You'll then fill out a form describing what you're looking for in the product—in the example of a digital camera, factors such as price, number of images it can store, whether it has removable storage, and similar information. CompareNet then lists for you every product that meets what you're looking for. You can look at the product specs of any individual product. But that's not what you should do. Instead, click on **Add to CompareTool** for every product you're interested in. Then click on **Compare**, and you'll get a side-by-side comparison of those products—you'll see prices plus a comprehensive features list. Now you can compare the products, as you can see pictured here, and figure out which one to buy.

You can also easily look up a single product here or do a quick search to compare two products side by side. The site even has links to relevant newsgroups where you can talk to others about what product you should buy.

And you should be sure to visit the Buying Tips section here. It has great advice on what to look for when buying something—almost anything. Whether you're buying a sports-utility vehicle (feeling uncertain about our manhood, are we?) or any other kind of car, electronics equipment, home and garden goods, home office equipment, sports equipment, or a lot more, you'll find excellent advice here.

In fact, you should head to CompareNet before buying anything, whether you plan to buy it online or instead in a real-world store.

Techno Talk

Beware of "Sponsored Links" Inside Shopping Search Tools and Agents

Shopping search tools frequently make deals with certain online sites—and those deals could include putting links to those sites at the top of a search list. Consequently, when you go to a shopping search site and do a search for the best deal on a particular product, the first link displayed to you might not be the best deal—in essence, an online site could have paid to be put at the top of the list. Because of that, whenever you use a search site, be sure to browse through the entire list of results. You'd do well to check in with more than one search site.

Excite Product Finder

Go to http://www.excite.com and click on **Shopping**.

The popular Excite search engine has put together one of the better online shopping assistants on the Internet. Using it is a breeze—just click the category of product you're looking for (**Home Audio Equipment**, for example, or **Cigars**), and you'll go to a page that lets you search the Internet for the best deal possible. The nice feature here is that the page you're led to is customized for the product you're looking for. For example, in Home Audio Equipment, you choose the kind of equipment you're looking for from a list (speakers, subwoofers, and so on). You can then even further refine your search by typing a manufacturer and a product name or model number. Next, you get the list of products that match your search, along with their prices. Shown here is a listing of VCRs on the site. Click the product name for more information about the product, click the store name for more information about the [store] the **Buy** button to buy. That's all it takes.

What's the best digital camera for under $400? That's one of the many shopping questions that CompareNet helps you answer.

[...]'re given the option to either find the product [...]ion about the product. Finding reviews is an [...]ks to reviews, and other times you're sent [...]t getting any help. I'd use this site primarily for [...]ling reviews.

[...]ny favorite shopping search site. It's remarkably [...]about any product you can name, and searches [...]you a whole lot of money. A random example: [...]m V handheld computer for prices ranging [...]gs of $80.

Simon says find a hammock—using MySimon to find the best deal on the Internet for buying a hammock.

Product ReviewNet

http://www.productreviewnet.com

What's one of the best ways to comparison shop? To read magazine and newspaper reviews of products, of course. But good luck trying to find those reviews—you could spend the rest of your life tracking them down if you could even find them. This site comes up with a simple solution. Type in the name of the product or kind of product you're interested in, and you'll get links to reviews of it from magazines and publications all over the Web. You'll first get an abstract of the review. If a full review is available online somewhere, you can then click to that. The site also will do price comparisons for you. A very useful list of buying guides from different magazines and publication is also available.

Although the site is useful, you'll find yourself wading through outdated information here—some reviews of computer products, for example, are from 1996, which pretty much is the Paleolithic era when it comes to computer hardware these days. I'd suggest using this site only as a starting point.

Shopfind

http://www.shopfind.com

If you're into minimalism, this is the site for you. How minimal can you get? How about this: A search box and nothing else. That's the whole interface. But it works great: Type the word or words that describe what you're shopping for, and Shopfind finds all the products for you, along with price, information, and the site that sells it. Just click on a link, and you're sent there. It's the site for speed searchers.

Yahoo! Shopping

http://shopping.yahoo.com

The excellent Yahoo! Web directory has put together a—surprise!—excellent shopping search site. Start at the top and type in a word that describes the product you're looking for, and you'll get a whole lot of results—lots of sites are searched, and there's much to choose from. Better still: Go to the category of product you're interested in, and you get even better search tools. Definitely worth a visit on your shopping expedition.

Meet George Jetson and His Maid Rosie: Getting ShopBots to Do Your Shopping

Another way to nose out the best deal on the Internet is to use a ShopBot. Instead of visiting a Web site such as those outlined previously, you can download software to your computer and use that software to find the best deal. This way, you're not tied to any one particular site.

What's the Difference Between a Search Engine and an Index?

Many sites on the Internet, such as Excite, Lycos, AltaVista, and Yahoo!, are good jumping-off points for finding any information on the massive World Wide Web. Some of them are called search engines, whereas others are called indexes. Why is that? A search engine scans the entire Net and then puts everything it comes across in a humongous database that you can search. So it finds just about everything on the Net—and without human intervention. An index, on the other hand, is hand-selected by people and organizes Internet sites into categories so you can browse them by category—although you can search them as well. Yahoo! is an index, while AltaVista is a search engine. And Excite and Lycos combine functions of both indexes and search engines—they scan the whole Net, but also organize sites into easy-to-browse categories.

Some ShopBots are free; some are not. Why should you pay for one ShopBot if others are free? Beats me. I don't think most people will do it, even if the one you have to pay for is superior to the free one. I'd guess, though, that any ShopBot that charges money will eventually go out of business. With so many free search sites and ShopBots available on the Internet, you don't have much of a reason to pay for one. Still, if you fall in love with a particular ShopBot (kinky, kinky), you might want to pay for it.

ShopBots all work in a similar way. You run the software and then choose the category of product you're searching for. The ShopBot sends its various search agents scurrying across the Internet, searching shopping sites to do your bidding. The agents then report their results. Click any link to visit the site where the ShopBot found a deal for you and buy the product if you're interested. It's that simple.

In addition to the general-purpose ShopBots I'm covering in this chapter, specialized ShopBots look for particular products. In fact, some ShopBots work only on a single site! For example, some ShopBots watch auction sites, such as eBay, and check on your bidding, buying and selling for you. I cover the specialized ShopBots in the chapters that discuss the corresponding kind of product.

Macintosh users alert: You enjoy complaining about how the whole world is against you, don't you? Here's another reason to complain—as I write this, no shopping agents are available for the Mac; they're only for the PC. Must be a conspiracy! Call Steve Jobs, and man the ramparts!

Oh, one more thing you should realize when using ShopBots. They don't hit every site on the Internet—just a predetermined number of them. Because of that, you might want to use them as just one tool for researching the best deal online.

The Awards, Please! The Best ShopBots on the Internet

ShopBots are still a relatively new phenomenon, and there aren't nearly as many ShopBots as there are shopping search sites. Still, a number of ShopBots are already at work. Here are the best of the bunch.

By the way, don't look in your local computer or software store for these ShopBots—you won't find them there. You'll find them instead on the Internet. To get them, you download them to your computer and install them.

RoboShopper

This free program's name summons up images of an armor-plated RoboCop, committing mayhem against high-tech villains, in the name of justice and good fun. Well, this program will do shopping for you, but it won't go after the bad guys—for that, you'll have to buy the RoboCop movie. (And you can use this program to find the best deal on it.)

Figure In Shipping and Handling Charges When Using Shopping Assistants

Virtual shopping assistants of all sorts are great when it comes to finding you the best price on a product. But not all of them figure in shipping and handling costs when doing that price comparison. Shipping and handling costs vary widely from site to site, which means that what the shopping assistant tells you is the best price might not really be the best one. After you've obtained the information from the shopping assistant on the sites with the best prices, check out the sites themselves to see what their shipping and handling charges are. Only then will you know which site truly offers the best price.

You won't have any trouble using it—just pick the category of product you're searching for (golf equipment, computer products, electronics, and so on), type a word or word that describes the specific product, in some instances choose the manufacturer, and click on the **Shop** button. Your private shopping bot now goes out and searches online sites—and comes back and tells you what it finds. It reports its results as links right inside your Web browser. Click on any of the links to get details on the deal. You can see the results of one of its searches in the picture on this page. RoboShopper tends to work best on computer-related products.

You can also ask the program to instead research your buy by going out across the Internet and finding product reviews.

RoboShopper is a great place to start a shopping expedition, but the truth is, to some extent, it should be considered a work in progress. One problem it has is that it searches too few shopping sites. And the same problem bedevils its searching for reviews—it returns very few of them, and often they're old or don't even exist anymore. For example, I used it to try to find reviews of the newest IBM Aptiva computers. What did I find? Links to two-year-old reviews of a completely different product—and the links were so old, the reviews themselves had already been taken down. Methinks this robot might need a few minor adjustments.

The results of a RoboShopper search looking for computers for sale on the Internet.

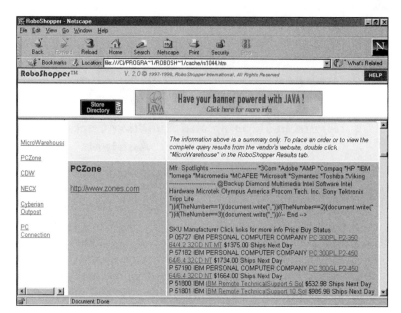

Still, despite some problems, the price is right because the program is free, and you can't go wrong with it. Get it at www.roboshopper.com or at download sites on the Internet such as www.hotfiles.com.

When you head to www.roboshopper.com site, you'll see that you can also search right on the Internet from the site, without having to download software—in essence, it's a shopping search site. But it's not a particularly good one, and you'd be better off with one of the better search sites mentioned earlier in the chapter.

Shopping Explorer

There's good news and bad news about this program. Let's start with the good news: It's the best ShopBot I've used. Now for the bad news: You'll have to pay for it if you want to use it for more than 30 searches. You can download and use the program for free, but after 30 tries, you're out of luck, and you'll have to pay. (The program will tell you how to pay for it.) Figure it'll put you back from $20 to $30. You should really have to pay only $20—the "list price" is $30, but every place I've seen it has a special on it for $20.

Like RoboShopper, you first choose a category of product. Then you type a word or words that describe the specific product you're searching for. Shopping Explorer then sends out its shopping agents to look across dozens of sites on the Internet to see what deals it can find. It then lists all the deals it finds. It gives a description of the product, the price, the name and location of the store, and tries to give information about whether the product is in stock, although that feature doesn't seem to work very well. And it even tells you what country the store is located in. Shopping

Explorer searches through shopping Web sites all over the world, from the United States to Great Britain to Singapore.

Double-click on an item on the list, and you get sent to a Web page with information about the product and where you can buy it.

The program is better than RoboShopper for a few reasons. Shopping Explorer searches far more shopping sites than RoboShopper does. It's much easier to compare products in this program. And the results were generally better—Shopping Explorer finds fewer products that have nothing to do with the product you're searching for.

Of course, on the other hand, it *does* cost $20. So what's a poor shopper to do? As the man says, you pays your money, and you takes your chances. You can download a copy of the program from the ZDNet Software Library at `www.hotfiles.com` or from `www.shoppingexplorer.com`.

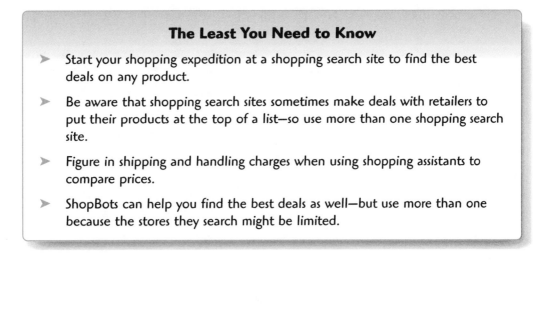

The Least You Need to Know

➤ Start your shopping expedition at a shopping search site to find the best deals on any product.

➤ Be aware that shopping search sites sometimes make deals with retailers to put their products at the top of a list—so use more than one shopping search site.

➤ Figure in shipping and handling charges when using shopping assistants to compare prices.

➤ ShopBots can help you find the best deals as well—but use more than one because the stores they search might be limited.

Part 3

In Search of Bargains Online

I can get it for you wholesale!

That was the mantra I grew up with. Buy a product at retail price! Perish the thought! No one in my family would ever think of doing it!

Going online means never having to pay retail price again. The Internet has become a bargain-shopper's paradise. You'll find an amazing number of ways to get online bargains. This part teaches you how to go about getting the best bargains, gives you inside tips for bargain-hunting, and leads you to the best bargain-hunting sites online.

You learn about the remarkable array of bargain-hunting sites, and learn how to get coupons, enter contests, and get all kinds of free stuff. You find out how to shop on classified ad sites, which offer great bargains. And finally, you become an instant pro and killer bidder at online auctions—those amazing sites, such as eBay, that offer anything you can imagine at great prices.

Chapter 8

Have I Got a Deal for You!

In This Chapter

➤ What are auctions and swap meets?

➤ How to buy and sell at auctions

➤ Buying at classified sites

➤ How to use and shop at Usenet newsgroups

What! You say you don't just want to merely shop in the Internet, but you want great deals, too? No problem. The Internet offers one of the best ways to get great deals. You'll be able to buy at online auctions, at classified ad sites, and in discussion areas called *newsgroups*. Here's how to do it.

Sold to the Highest Bidder: Auctions and Swap Meets

Among the most popular shopping sites on the Internet are online auctions. These sites are popular for a very simple reason: You'll find some of the best deals on Earth there. Participating in online auctions is probably the best way yet devised to get good stuff cheap. And you can make money as well because you can sell as well as buy.

Forget what you know about auctions in the real world; online auctions don't feature fast-talking auctioneers, and you can't accidentally buy a Ming vase for half a million in cold cash because you swatted a fly on your head and the auctioneer mistakenly thought you were making a bid. Unlike real-world auctions, the online versions don't focus only on antiques or collectibles. You can buy anything you can imagine, from toys to computers to collectibles to books, jewelry, and much more. Just how popular are these auctions? The numbers tell the tale. The last time I checked into just one of these sites, eBay at www.ebay.com, 2,170,430 items were for sale in 1,627 different categories—and every day there are over half a million new auctions. And that's just for a single site. Dozens of similar sites are all over the Internet—and more are coming online every day.

In some ways, online auctions are like their real-life counterparts. The basic idea is the same: You bid against other people in the hopes of buying something you want at the lowest price possible. If your bid isn't the highest, you don't get to buy—and so you don't have to pay anything. If your bid is the highest, then you get the goods.

One thing to keep in mind is that at many auctions, you're not actually buying the goods from the site you're visiting. Instead, you're buying from a private individual or a company. The auction site in essence serves as a broker—it's a place where buyers and sellers gather. The auction site provides the technology and the meeting place and does its best to draw a crowd. But when you do the actual buying, you might send your money to a person or company, not the site itself. Consequently, you're going to have to be really careful about whom you buy from—you want to be sure the seller is on the up-and-up. (Turn to Chapter 11, "Sold American! Buying Through Online Auctions," for more information about how to check out online sellers, as well as for more information about auctions in general.) Auction sites generally make money by charging a commission from the people doing the selling, not from those who do the buying.

How to Buy at Auctions

Each auction site is somewhat different. In general, though, here's how the process works and how you make your bids. Auction sites are divided into different categories of products, so you can browse through what's being auctioned to find something you're interested in buying (Princess Beanie Baby, anyone?). You can read descriptions of various items, and sometimes you can view a picture of the item as well.

There will be a starting price—essentially the minimum bid that will be accepted. (So, no, you won't be able to buy a Rolex watch for $25 or a nice laser printer for $35.) If the auction is already in progress, you'll be able to see the current high bid, and often, the history of the bidding as well. Also listed will be the increment that bids go up by—$1 or $5 or $10 or more, for example.

At Online Auctions, Beware of False Bidders

When buying online, don't get carried away by the fast and furious bidding. Pick a price you'll pay and stick to it. That fast-paced bidding you see might not be others really trying to outbid you. Instead, it might be the owner of the item or a friend artificially bidding up the price, in the hopes that you'll pay more than you normally would have. So don't get carried away in the heat of the moment.

To make a bid, you fill out a form, stating the maximum amount you are willing to pay for the item. You might, in fact, end up paying less. If you say your maximum bid is $75, for example, and other bidders drop out at $50, you'll pick up the item for $55 (assuming the bidding increment is $5). Each auction goes on for a set amount of time, and you can change your bid as the auction progresses. So if you absolutely have to have that set of "The Best of Elvis Playing Cards" or the "Evel Knievel Stunt Cycle in box, with figure" and the bidding is beyond your maximum bid, don't worry—you can always up the ante. By the way, if you're an Elvis fan, you'll find a whole lot more than just trading cards at eBay, as you can see pictured here. There are literally tens of thousands of pieces of Elvis memorabilia up for sale every day. And the "Evel Knievel Stunt Cycle in box, with figure" sold as well. As I said before, anything you can possibly imagine—and many things you no doubt have never imagined—is for sale at online auctions.

You want Elvis; eBay's got Elvis. Elvis playing cards are just one of the many of thousands of goodies you can buy at online auctions at sites such as the eBay site pictured here.

If you win an auction, you'll be notified, and then it's up to you and the seller to arrange for payment and delivery of the items. But before you send any money, don't forget to check out the seller's reputation (see Chapter 11).

Clean Out Your Attic and Make Money: How to Sell at Auctions

Got an old hand drill taking up room in your attic? How about an old Nikon camera instruction manual? Maybe some of your grandmother's costume jewelry is gathering dust. Or a pile of moldering *Life* magazines.

Don't throw them out! There's gold hidden up there. You'd be surprised how you can turn old junk into quick cash. To you, that camera manual might be a quick throwaway, but it's just the item that some shutterbug has been scouring the Internet for. Here are some sample starting prices at recent auctions: The Nikon instruction manual's bidding started at $15, as did an old hand drill. *Life* magazines were often starting at $10 and more. And some costume jewelry was starting at $300. No, you might not sell enough to pay for your kids' college education—but you'll find that cleaning out your garage and attic can bring in a pretty penny.

Selling an item is pretty simple and straightforward at most auctions. You fill out a form, describing the item, your starting price, and similar information. Many auction sites also let you include URLs to pictures of what you're selling. You'll pay the auction site a fee based on the selling price of the item. You can also choose to pay extra for advertising the item.

When the auction is finished, it's up to you and the highest bidder to arrange for payment and delivery. For more information and advice on selling at auctions, turn to Chapter 11.

Buying at Online Swap Meets

The terms *auction* and *swap meet* are often used interchangeably on the Internet. Many sites, such as eSwap at www.eswap.com, call themselves swap meets—but in fact, they work exactly like auctions. Six of one; half a dozen of another. Or as they say here in Massachusetts: same difference.

However, some online swap meets are not auctions—these sites are often classified ad sites. These swap meets are usually specialized classified ads and are usually held on special-interest sites, rather than on shopping sites. For example, motorcycle fanatics will be happy to learn about a buying site just for them: MotorCycleShopper.com at www.motorcycleshopper.com. One of its features is a motorcycle swap meet. Swap meets are more like classified ads than auctions. There's no bidding; instead, sellers advertise what they're selling and their asking price. If you're interested, you send them email and buy. And if you're interested in buying something that you don't see advertised, you can put up an ad, hoping that someone has that 1948 Indian Chief Roadmaster motorcycle you've been lusting for.

Ham radio swap meets, for some reason, are particularly popular on the Internet. I guess it's just plain easier to find 3-1000z tubes, ARC-5 transmitters, TenTec Omni Vs, and Ameritron AL-80B amplifiers online than anywhere in the real world.

The best way to find these kinds of swap meets is to head to special-interest sites, such as those for ham radio operators. Last time I checked, no ARC-5 transmitters were in sight at the general auctions.

Buying Through Classified Advertising

You're looking to buy a used bicycle at a good price—if you're like most people, the first place you turn is your local newspaper and go straight to the classified ad section. The problem with that approach is that it covers only your local area, and there's no way to do a quick search for a particular item. You can spend inordinate amounts of time staring at tiny print and ruining your eyes while your hands get smudged with ink from the cheap newsprint.

Surely, you've probably thought, there has to be a better way. Yes, there is. You can check out classified ads on the Internet.

You can also, of course, place classified ads on the Internet. Amazingly enough, a number of classified ad sites, such as Classifieds2000 at `www.classifieds2000.com`, shown here, let you place your ads for free.

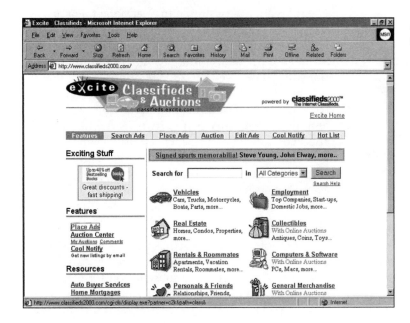

Place a free classified ad at Classifieds2000.

As with auctions, or any other kind of transaction when you're dealing with a stranger rather than a well-known company, be careful. For more information about how to buy or sell at classified ad sites and for more on the best sites online, head to Chapter 10, "Classified Information: Getting the Most Out of Classified Ads on the Internet."

Savings in Numbers: Online Buyers' Clubs

You've no doubt heard of buyers' clubs—places where you pay an annual fee and then, in return, get to buy products at cut-rate prices. Some of these buyers' clubs, such as the well-known Sam's Club, have online sites as well. Its URL? Right—it's at www.samsclub.com.

So far, buyers' clubs such as Sam's haven't really quite caught on to what the Internet is all about. You can join them online, but you can't buy that much online yet—aside from gazebos, tanning beds, hot dog wagons, and similar nonessential products. Not much use unless your business is selling wieners to well-tanned people lounging in gazebos. Still you can expect to find more buying clubs, including cyberspace-only buying clubs, at a Web site near you soon. You can join the NetMarket buying club on America Online with the keyword NETMARKET. You can also join it on the Web at www.netmarket.com. And the related buying club Shoppers Advantage is available at www.shoppersadvantage.com on the Web.

Before Joining a Buyers' Club, Check Signup Prices on America Online and the Web

Sometimes buying clubs have different sites on America Online and on the Web. And they'll often give better signup prices on one than the other. For example, it'll cost you $59.95 a year to join NetMarket on America Online, but $69.95 to join it on the Web.

The rules are pretty simple for NetMarket. For an annual fee ($59.95, last time I checked), you get a 10% to 50% discount on many products—some 250,000 of them, according to America Online. I'm not sure I'd believe that 250,000 number, but you get the point—a lot of products. You'll often get some other kind of bonus to join as well, such as a lengthened warranty period (two years when I last checked), as well as a free, cheap little gizmo that probably costs all of 75 cents, and that's giving NetMarket the benefit of the doubt, to produce. Many buyers' clubs, such as NetMarket, also sell goods to nonmembers, but nonmembers have to pay higher prices.

Whether joining clubs such as these is worthwhile depends on your buying habits. Here's my advice: Join only if you get a free subscription for three months or more (America Online has an offer like this). If you see in that time that you'll save money over an entire year, go ahead and join. If not, fuhgeddaboutit.

There's Savings in Numbers: Save Money at Bulk-Buying Sites

Here's some elementary economics: Usually when a whole lot of people want to buy the same thing, the price goes up. That's because they're all competing to buy the same product, and so they in essence are fighting one other to buy the same thing. Anyone with kids who's tried to buy Pokemon cards has seen this basic economic principle in action—cards that carry a retail price of $2.95 regularly go for $7.95 because so many people want to buy them, and there's a limited quantity of them.

But the Web, as we've seen, turns everything we know on its head. And so there are now ways for you to get a *lower* price on something if a lot of other people want to buy it at the same time. That's because the Web allows you all to band together and in essence get wholesale prices because together, you're all placing a humongous order instead of your diddly little one.

Several sites let you do this. The Mercata site at `www.mercata.com` has what it calls a "PowerBuys" section in which you set a maximum price you'll pay for items on sale. Other people are doing the same thing. As more people sign up, the price drops—and the lower the price goes, the less you'll pay. You'll never pay more than your maximum price, and you'll often pay less, as more people sign up. The nearby picture shows an example of some of the kinds of savings you'll get on the site.

The power of many: The more people who buy at the PowerBuys section of the Mercata site, the less you'll all pay.

A similar site is Accompany at www.accompany.com. One of the neater things about the Accompany site is that you'll be able to see graphs of the dropping prices, and see how many people need to sign up before the price drops more—that way, you can try to get other people to sign up to lower the price.

Buying Through Usenet Newsgroups

Answer this question quickly: What is a newsgroup? No, it's not that gas-bag John McLaughlin and his windbag friends who bloviate over the TV airwaves with their inflated, self-important talk about the news and doings down in Washington, D.C. Newsgroups, in fact, have nothing at all to do with the news. Go figure. But that's the Internet for you.

Internet newsgroups are, in fact, discussion groups. The full name is Usenet newsgroups. (Why the term *Usenet*? Don't ask—yet another one of those Internet odd turns of phrase that the hackers among us have devised, no doubt in order to confuse the great unwashed even more than they are already.) In newsgroups, people talk about their own special interests, which are just about anything in the world. Newsgroups are a cross between a public bulletin board, a town-meeting place, and, some people might say, a global lunatic asylum. Want to discuss the use of Esperanto as a universal language? There's a newsgroup for you (alt.talk.esperanto, among many others). Need a place to find out why your guinea pig is coughing up hairballs? Yup, you've got a place to go (alt.guinea.pig is your spot). How about talking with other fans of the fallen ice goddess Tanya Harding? Yes, you have a friend—in fact, many of them—at alt.fan.tanya-harding.

Thousands and thousands and thousands of newsgroups exist, each of them focused on a unique special interest. Anyone with an Internet connection can participate in them. They're of particular interest for Internet shoppers because many newsgroups are devoted to shopping, collecting, buying, and selling. That means you can buy and sell directly to other people on these newsgroups, and you can do consumer research on them as well. (For information on how to research buying anything on the Internet, turn to Chapter 4, "How to Be a Cybersavvy Shopper.")

On a newsgroup, you read what other people have written, and then you write a public response. Other people can see everything you write on the newsgroup, and you can see everything they write. When people post to a newsgroup, their email address is included. That means you can send them private notes via email if you want.

One thing to keep in mind when buying on a newsgroup: You don't have a clue who's on the other end of the transaction. Yes, it might well be that the person offering to sell you a used Magnavox TV for $75 is on the level. On the other hand, it might also be a scam artist trolling the Internet for gullible marks. So be very, very careful when buying through a newsgroup. I find that newsgroups are much better for doing shopping research than doing actual buying—although many great deals can be found as well. It's worth checking out newsgroups, though, because they also often have links to good shopping sites.

But how do you participate in newsgroups? And how do you find the ones that are best for you? Fear not, dear reader. Read on, and you shall see.

How to Use Newsgroups

To participate in newsgroups, you'll need what's called a *newsreader*. (BBC fans, take note: A newsreader in this context is not the person who reads the morning BBC news report to you in plummy, British tones.) A newsreader is a special piece of software that—well, not surprisingly—reads newsgroups. Microsoft Internet Explorer and Netscape Navigator both come with built-in newsgroup readers. So does Outlook, Microsoft's email package. And many other newsgroup readers are available for purchase or free trial. (See Chapter 17, "Don't Be a Softie: Getting the Best Deal on Buying Software," for information on how to try out software for free.)

If you use an online service, such as America Online, you'll probably have two choices on how to participate in newsgroups. You can use the service's built-in newsreader, or you can use a newsreader such as the ones that come with Microsoft Internet Explorer or Netscape Navigator.

Newsgroups live on special Internet servers called—surprise!—newsgroup servers. The Internet service provider (ISP) or online service that you use to connect to the Internet maintains these newsgroup servers. Check with your service for details on how to use your software to connect to the servers.

When you connect to a newsgroup server with your software, you'll be presented with a list—a very loooooooooong list—of newsgroups. There are many thousands of them. Many, *many* thousands of them. As usual with the Internet, at first things will be incredibly confusing to you. You'll see names such as `3dfx.game.upcoming` and `misc.fitness.weights`. And you won't have a clue on how to find newsgroups that might interest you.

It's actually not as hard as you might think. The first few letters of the newsgroup, before the first period (or *dot*, in Internet parlance) generally describe the broad category of newsgroup. So any newsgroup with `comp.` at the beginning is about computers. Any newsgroup that begins with `talk.` is for those who want to talk about a particular topic. The `alt.` newsgroups are particularly popular. Originally, `alt.` groups were devoted to "alternative" topics such as alternative culture, but these days `alt.` newsgroups cover pretty much everything. The same holds true for `misc.` (for miscellaneous) newsgroups. In fact, you'll probably use the `alt.` and `misc.` newsgroups in your shopping expedition more than you use any other newsgroups.

Try These Usenet Newsgroups

You could probably spend a good portion of your waking life wandering through newsgroups, looking for the best shopping-related ones. Save yourself some time and check these out. The `alt.marketplace` is always worth checking for general merchandise, as are the various related newsgroups, such as `alt.marketplace.books`, and one of my favorites, `alt.marketplace.funky-stuff.forsale` (Fu Manchu movie posters, Monkee memorabilia, Sky Ring pins, and more). Collectors should head to the `alt.collecting` group and its cousins (such as `alt.collecting.stamps`, among others). The `misc.forsale` groups also have many products for sale. And for general consumer advice, head to `misc.consumer` and related groups.

Another set of letters follow the first dot—for example, `alt.collecting`. This set of letters describes a broad category of newsgroups. So the `alt.collecting` newsgroups, not surprisingly, cover collecting. Sometimes those two sets of letters, separated by a dot, will be the entire newsgroup name, as `alt.collecting`. So if you want to talk about collecting in general, head to the `alt.collecting` newsgroup. But sometimes you'll find additional subcategories. Here are some examples: `alt.collecting.barbies`, `alt.collecting.beanie-babies`, and `alt.collecting.stamps`. (You can find a newsgroup for every interest. Want to talk about bizarre rabbits? No problem. Head over to `talk.bizarre.rabbits`.)

Does this all seem clear now? Well, at least a little clearer? Good. That must mean it's time to confuse you again. One problem you might run across is that not all newsgroup servers carry all newsgroups. So if you see one listed in this book and can't find it, your ISP or online service doesn't carry that specific newsgroup. Contact your ISP or online service and ask it to add the newsgroup you see listed here.

Haven't I Read You Somewhere Before? Reading Newsgroups at Deja.com

Another way to read newsgroups doesn't require special newsgroup software. Just go with your browser to the Deja.com site at `www.deja.com`. When you head there, you'll be able to read and respond to newsgroups from within your browser.

Deja.com also helps you find the newsgroups you're interested in. Instead of wending your way through all the listings for alt, misc, comp, and the like, you instead choose a topic. Deja.com then finds the newsgroups for you—no matter what their weird names. You can search by typing in a word or words that describe what you're looking for. Or you can go to one of the Deja.com *channels*, which are areas that group together similar newsgroups, such as Business & Investing and Arts & Entertainment.

The Least You Need to Know

➤ Watch out for false bidders trying to artificially inflate the bids at auction sites.

➤ You can make extra money by selling at auctions.

➤ A good way to find shopping newsgroups is to start at www.deja.com.

Chapter 9

Great Stuff Cheap! Coupons, Contests, and Free Stuff

In This Chapter

➤ How to get free samples and other goods, including free email accounts

➤ The best places to get coupons online

➤ Where to enter free contests and games

➤ How to get a free computer online

➤ How to get free Internet service

➤ Get paid to surf the Web

Get paid to surf the Web! Free email account for life! Win big prizes by playing free games! Get oodles of free stuff! Get amazing deals in classified ads! Get a free PC! Get free Internet access! Sounds like typical marketing bluster and hustle, doesn't it, like those old Crazy Eddie TV ads—"where the prices are *insane!*"

Well, get ready for a surprise—because that marketing bluster is true when it comes to the Internet. You *can* find sites where you'll get paid to surf the Internet; you *can* get free email accounts for life, you *can* get tons of free stuff online, you *can* win big time by entering free contests, and you *can* get great deals at many classified ad sites. And yes, with certain caveats, you can even get a free computer and free Internet access. The Internet is a bargain hunter's paradise if you just know where to look. In this chapter, I clue you in on the two Cs of shopping online for bargains: coupons and contests. And I show you how you can get all kinds of free stuff on the Internet just for the asking.

Yes, There Is a Free Lunch on the Internet

Let's cut to the chase. What are you really looking for when you shop? To get something for nothing, right? Well, you can do that on the Internet—a lot of free stuff is just waiting for you. Now, I'm not talking about a free BMW or a new VCR. But I am talking about things such as teddy bears, teas, soaps, perfume, CDs, and many kinds of samples. You can save yourself a pretty penny over the course of a year by getting all this free stuff. And you can even get free email accounts for life as well. There are even some free PCs lying around for the taking (now where did I put that computer?). And you'll be able in some cases to get free Internet access as well.

The best way to find free stuff is to go to free-stuff sites. They'll guide you to the many free offers you can get on the Internet. Be careful when visiting these sites, though; you need to be sure that what you're getting really is free and that it's something you want. Many free sites offer primarily catalogs—which, let's face it, is really just junk mail. And they also often offer "free trials," such as getting a month of a magazine for free while you decide whether to subscribe—an offer you can get from virtually every magazine on the planet without having to go onto the Internet. And some sites use bait-and-switch tactics—they'll offer you something for "free" only if you first sign up for a service or buy a product. Stay away from these kinds of sleazoids. The sites listed later in this chapter offer at least some truly free stuff, so you're safe heading to them.

When you get something for free on the Internet, you'll typically have to fill out a form or a questionnaire of some kind. See whether the site publishes information about how it uses that information, and if you care about your privacy, be careful about what kind of information you provide. The site could be sharing that information with marketers, and you'll be inundated with junk mail (*Preston Gralla, $10 million is waiting for you! Just call this 900 number for your free offer!*) And, of course, you can always use the tactic of—well, there's no way to put this politely—simply not telling the truth. You can give a fictitious name and address, put in a bogus occupation (crab census counter is one that I use regularly), and enter a phony salary (make it at least seven figures for the little jolt of *frisson* it will give you). That way, marketers won't target you.

A Free PC! Are You Serious? There Must Be Some Kind of Catch Here

Let's start off with the big-ticket items—free computers. In the topsy-turvy world of the new Internet economy, some companies will actually give you a PC for free, as in no cash, no dinero, free of charge—well, sort of. In some cases, you'll have to sign up for a fixed length of time at a certain price to get Internet access through a specific Internet service provider. And in other cases, you'll have to agree to have ads flashing on your computer at all times (kind of like Chinese water torture, done electronically).

Generally, these free PCs aren't exactly barn-burners. At a time when the fastest PC was running at 500Mhz, for example, the freebies poked along at 333Mhz or less. They don't have big hard disks or oodles of memory. And they won't play the fanciest action games very well.

But still, let's face it, free is free.

Getting a Completely Free PC

The granddaddy of the free PC offers comes from a company called, not surprisingly, Free-PC. You'll find it at `www.free-pc.com`, pictured here.

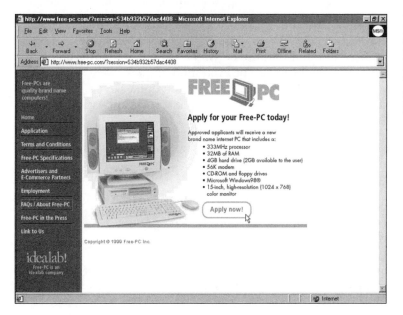

Yes, this computer can be yours for free. There's only one catch: You have to look at a whole lot of ads when using it. Oh, and there's not a whole lot of PCs available.

There are two catches with the Free-PC offer. The first is that whenever your computer is turned on, you'll see ads flashing by—and you can't turn them off. And if you don't use the computer at least 10 hours a month, you have to return it. Depending on your view of advertising (somewhere between being the spawn of the devil and the root of all evil, some people believe), this can be a very good deal.

Oh, yeah. Now for the second catch. It's really, really hard to get one of these free babies. And I mean *really* hard. How hard? When the offer first came out, one million people filled out a form requesting one. But there were only 10,000 free PCs available—so your chances of getting a free PC were one in 100. Not quite as long a shot as winning the lottery, but still, not a great bet.

Considering that all you'll waste is your time, it's a good idea to try to get one of these free computers. Go to `www.free-pc.com`, fill out a form, and hope for the best.

Getting a Free PC with a Catch

Most of the "free" PC offers are really come-ons for getting you to sign up with an Internet service provider for a certain amount of time. Don't get me wrong—these are still good deals. You'll get a computer in addition to Internet access. But, in general, you'll pay more for Internet access from these free PC companies than you will from other Internet service providers. You'll be locked in to using the Internet service provider for a certain amount of time. If you cancel your contract with the Internet service provider, you might have to pay a hefty fee of $500 or more. So read the fine print very carefully before signing up for a free PC. Also, be sure to check out the access numbers of the Internet service provider. If they don't have a local number for you to call, you might end up running huge telephone bills for long-distance service.

When deciding whether one of these free PC offers is right for you, figure out how much you'd normally pay for Internet access. Then see how much extra you'll pay for the free PC offer. Finally, keep in mind that the PC isn't a particularly powerful one—and if it's not particularly powerful today, it'll be even more underpowered in two or three years, the typical term of one of these offers. But if you don't have a need for a very powerful computer, or are looking to get a second PC, these can be good deals. Here's where to go.

Watch Out for Hidden Costs in "Free" PC Offers

When it comes to getting a free computer, There's free, and then there's free. Many "free" PC offers carry hidden costs. For example, you'll often be required to pay shipping costs, which can be $60 or more. And sometimes you'll be charged a "setup fee" of some kind that can be in the $40 range. So before you sign, be sure you know what you'll be paying for your "free" computer.

DirectWeb

`http://www.directweb.com`

One things makes this free PC offer different from the others: If you agree to pay more per month for Internet access, you get a more powerful computer. Be careful to do your math to be sure that the extra you pay is worth it for the kind of computer you'll be getting.

Gobi

```
http://www.gobi.com
```

Agree to pay for three years of Internet access and you get a free PC. It's pretty much the standard offer that you'll find at other sites.

InterSquid

```
http://www.intersquid.com
```

Sign up for 30 months of Internet access at $30 a month at this site, and you get a free PC thrown into the offer. You'll also be charged $60 in shipping, and $40 in setup fees in some cases.

How to Get Free Internet Access

How high is your tolerance for advertising? If it's pretty high, you can get free Internet access—you'll never have to pay a penny for getting online.

The deal works like this: You sign up for free Internet access. And then, whenever you're on the Internet, a toolbar of sorts will run on your computer—and ads will flow regularly through the toolbar. That's all there is to it.

Before signing up for one of these services, though, you'll want to be sure that it has an access number near your home and that's a local call. If it doesn't, you'll end up paying big-time for long-distance charges.

There are a number of these free services out there, many of them local. From my point of view, the best of the bunch is NetZero at www.netzero.com. It's a national service, available throughout the country. If you're going to try to get free Internet access, I'd say that's the way to go.

Mail for Free: Free Email Accounts

One of the best deals on the Internet these days is free email. Many of the most popular sites, such as Yahoo! and Excite, will give you free email accounts. To use these free accounts, you have to go to a particular part of a Web site for your mail. The following figure shows the free email boxes offered by ZDNet.

Offering free email accounts is all the rage these days. Every self-respecting major site seems to have them. The following is a very small list of sites that offer free email. They all pretty much work the same way and offer similar features:

AltaVista (altavista.digital.com)

BigFoot (www.bigfoot.com)

Excite (www.excite.com)

HotMail (www.hotmail.com)

Juno (www.juno.com)

Lycos (www.lycos.com)

MailCity (www.mailcity.com)

Yahoo! (www.yahoo.com)

ZDNet (www.zdnet.com)

Who said you can't get something for nothing? Here's an example of a free email account you can get, in this instance from the ZDNet (www.zdnet.com) site.

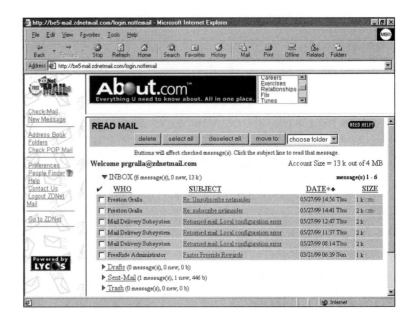

Free, Free, Free! The Best Sites for Getting Free Stuff on the Internet

If you're looking for more than catalogs and phony offers, check out the following free sites for the real McCoy.

The Daily Freebie

    http://www.gsmenter.com/dailyfreebie/index.htm

This free site has more links to more categories of freebies than any other site I've come across on the Internet. That's the good news. The bad news is that a good portion of the links either lead you to things such as catalogs or offers that aren't really free, or to sites that no longer offer free things. Still, just the volume of offers here is notable, and you'll find a lot of truly free stuff. You might want to take a few minutes to check it out.

Free Mania!

http://www.freemania.net

You just *know* this site will deliver the goods, based on the tacky flashing arrows that blink everywhere and its all-around tawdry look. But, hey, the *deals are insane!* (Sorry, I got carried away there.) Free Mania is one of my favorite free sites on the Internet because of the incredible variety of free stuff you can get here. Here's just a small sampling: Olympic pins, pantyhose, baseball caps, mouse pads, perfume, tea, coffee, T-shirts, teddy bears, cosmetics, health food, junk food, pecans, Excedrin, aloe vera gel—well, I think you get the point. Mucho free stuff.

Check This Out

Keep Your Mailbox Clean

Whenever you register to get something for free on the Internet, you'll be asked to supply your email address. As a result, junk email (also called "spam") from the free sites could flood your email box. To keep your regular email box clean of this kind of junk, first get a free email account from a site such as HotMail (www.hotmail.com). Now, whenever you register for something free, use that free email address as your contact information. All the junk email you get from the free offers will be sent to that account, and your regular account won't be compromised.

Internet Shopper Free Stuff

http://www.internetshopper.com/free/

Internet Shopper is a solid Web site, devoted to being an all-around consumer shopping resource. Its Free Stuff page always has about two dozen free offers, and they've been screened, so the offers are real. Another nice feature is that Internet Shopper gives editorial writeups of each free offer. Normally, sites like this just offer links. This site is a rarity: A free-stuff site that doesn't emulate tacky neon and eye-bending fonts.

Your Virtual Clipping Service: How to Get Free Coupons Online

As any thrifty shopper will tell you, one of the easiest ways to save money when shopping is to use coupons. And you can double your savings at some stores that double the face value of your coupon.

But you don't have to wait for the afternoon mail to bring you its fill of junk mail and perhaps a coupon or two. And you won't have to search through page after inky page of your local newspaper to get your coupons. You can get them on the Internet.

Coupon sites are generally straightforward. When you see a coupon you want, you click on it. You'll be able to print it—as long as you have either a laser or inkjet printer. Often, you'll click on a link that says something like **Clip**. When you've clipped all the coupons you're interested in, you can print them all at once. Other times, you'll get an email with the coupon attached—and again, you'll have to print it with an inkjet or laser printer. Sometimes, you'll get the coupon via regular mail. From that point on, the coupons work just like any other coupons: Take them to a store and cash them in.

Stay Away from Coupon Sites That Charge You Money

Strange but true: Some coupon sites charge a fee for their services. You might be charged an annual fee plus a certain amount of money per coupon. Two words of advice: Stay away! One ubiquitous coupon site, CentsOff at www.centsoff. com, charges $5.00 a year plus an additional $5.35 for every 50 coupons you clip.

You'll find national and regional coupon sites. The national sites offer free coupons at stores that you can find nationwide, and the regional ones cover only certain geographic areas. Some sites have areas for national and regional coupons.

By the way, be forewarned: Although many coupon sites exist on the Internet, most of them are not very good. Many sites have offers for things you'll never use, such as a lube job at a shop 200 miles from your home or a discount at a tribal craft boutique 1,500 miles away.

Clip, Clip, Clip: Best Coupon Sites on the Internet

Don't waste your valuable time at a site that specializes in coupons for goods you'll never buy in cities you'll never visit. Head to these coupon sites, instead, which for one reason or another are all worth visiting.

Alt.coupons Newsgroup

alt.coupons in your newsgroup reader

This newsgroup doesn't actually have coupons you can clip, but if you head here, you'll get the goods on all the coupon sites on the Internet. People here trade advice on coupon sites, and often, coupon sites post notices here when new coupons are available. People trade coupons here as well, so you might be able to get some good deals.

CoolSavings

```
http://www.coolsavings.com
```

Here's one of the best coupon sites on the Internet. Whereas many other coupon sites offer you piddling discounts on no-name products from no-name stores, CoolSavings specializes in big discounts from retailers and chains—Kmart, J.C. Penney, Alamo, and the like. You can get coupons for some serious savings here; on a recent visit, I found coupons for $50 off a trampoline, 15% off car rentals at Alamo, 20% off a day of shopping at J.C. Penney, and similar serious bargains. The only thing I don't like about this site is that to use its coupons, you have to download a coupon manager. No big deal, I know, but I like to keep things simple—and my hard disk clean. Check out the following figure for a sample of one day's worth of coupons.

You can save some serious moolah with coupons from the coolsavings.com site.

Coupon Directory

```
http://www.coupondirectory.com
```

This site is a combination coupon/free-stuff site. You'll find hundreds of offers for free coupons and free samples, organized by category. The coupons tend to be for good products from well-known brands, although you'll also come across some clinkers as well. Still, this site is great for bargain-hunting coupon seekers, as well as for anyone looking to get something for nothing.

ValuePage

http://www.valupage.com

Here's the best coupon site on the Internet if you're looking for supermarket coupons. It works differently from other coupon sites. You type in your zip code, and it displays a list of supermarkets near you that participate in the program. Click on any of the supermarkets, and you'll get a long list of products, along with discounts on them. The products tend to be national brands, such as Ragu, Beech-Nut, Gorton's, Mountain Dew, Gillette, Glad and—gasp—Ben and Jerry. (There goes my plan to lose five pounds this month.) Print out the list, take it to the supermarket, and present it at checkout. The register tallies up all the discounts, and that total is applied to your next purchase. It's that simple. You can save big-time here: ValuePage usually has about $40 worth of coupons per supermarket per week.

Coupon Sites Aren't the Only Places for Coupons

The Web site of the product you're interested often has coupons available. So before your next real-life shopping trip, visit a few Web sites of products you plan to buy to see whether they have any print-and-use coupons. The Beech-Nut site at www.beech-nut.com, for example, often has coupons.

Get Paid to Surf the Web

Here's a hard-to-believe deal: You can get paid to surf the Web. That's right. Several companies will in essence pay you when you visit certain Web sites, or buy from certain Web sites. They're "points" programs—think of them as frequent surfer clubs. When you visit sites or buy from sites, you get points. Then, when you accumulate a certain number of points, you can apply them toward free goods, such as CDs, videos, and movie tickets. So where to go? Head to the following places.

ClickRewards

http://www.clickrewards.com

Here's a great frequent buyer club. You earn rewards by buying at a lot of great sites such as Barnes & Noble online (www.bn.com), the Gap online (www.gap.com), and even for opening an account at the eTrade stock site (www.etrade.com). In addition to using your points to get goods, you can also exchange them for air miles in your frequent flyer club.

Head to eSmarts for the Best Information on Free Deals and Consumer Advice

The eSmarts site at www.esmarts.com is the best site I've seen anywhere for keeping track of Internet bargains. It reports on current special coupon deals and when they expire, has a page of links to free stuff, and also offers articles on topics such as where to find closeouts and bargains. Definitely a must-visit for Internet shoppers looking to save some money.

FreeRide

Here's a point plan with a twist—you'll get points not just for surfing the Web, but also when you buy things offline as well. (You mean, there's a shopping world apart from the Internet? Who knew!) HBO, Cinemax, and Kodak are a few of the offline merchants where you can get points.

MyPoints

http://www.mypoints.com

You earn points here two primary ways: By visiting Web sites and by receiving email. Then you can redeem the points for all kinds of goods, including from Blockbuster and Barnes & Noble. You can also get points by filling out forms and surveys.

Play Games and Contests for Free, Have Fun, Win Prizes

Is there some catch here? No, there isn't. You'll often come across places on the Internet where you play games or enter contests of all kinds, and if you're lucky, you get to win a prize.

Now, lest you think that these people are giving away prizes out of the goodness of their heart, think again. The purpose of these games and contests is to bring people to a site so that the site can sell them something or show them ads—and then those *ads* can sell them something. So for your own good, don't be distracted when you get to one of these sites—play the game or contest, take the money, and run.

A great site for this is the Riddler at www.riddler.com. You play a variety of games here, such as trivia games, and if you win you get "caps" that you can apply toward prizes.

Another site worth checking out is HuronOnline at www.huronline.com. Rather than having contests here, it points you to contest currently running all over the Internet. An even better site for finding Web contests is contestworld at www.contestworld.com. And ContestGuide at www.contestguide.com is worth a visit as well.

The Least You Need to Know

➤ When looking for free stuff on the Internet, be sure you visit sites that give you more than free catalogs.

➤ Stay away from coupon sites that charge money for their coupons—many coupon sites give away coupons for free.

➤ Look for coupons not just on coupon sites but also on sites of major manufacturers.

➤ If you're signing up to get a PC from an Internet service provider, be sure they have local numbers for you to call.

➤ Look for hidden costs such as shipping and handling when signing up for a free PC.

Classified Information: Getting the Most Out of Classified Ads on the Internet

> ## In This Chapter
>
> ➤ Different kinds of classified sites online
>
> ➤ How to shop at a classified site
>
> ➤ How to take out a classified ad
>
> ➤ How to ensure you don't get burned on a purchase
>
> ➤ Best classified sites online

In your home town, where do you think you can buy the most stuff at the best price—anything from bicycles to skis, a house, stamps, sporting equipment, and pretty much anything else? No, it's not the mall or Main Street; it's the classified ad section of your local newspaper or a free "shopper" newspaper that carries only classifieds. Classified ads are so popular, in fact, that they're often the most-read part of many daily newspapers.

The Internet is the same way. You'll find anything you can imagine in classified ads. Except that when it comes to classified ads, you'll be able to buy goods and find things not just in your home town, but in the whole world. And classified sites are fast becoming among the most popular sites on the Internet. It's no great surprise: Who doesn't like getting a great deal?

Classified ads are better on the Internet than they are in print in a number of ways. First is that you'll be able to buy things from all over the country—and, in fact, the entire world. Internet classifieds are also much easier to browse than print classifieds.

No more page turning; just type in words that describe what you want to buy, and you'll get your listing (yes, "remote-control helicopter" will find you that toy whirly-bird you've wanted since you were eight years old).

When you find something you want to buy, you'll either email or call the seller. Then it's up to the two of you to arrange for payment and delivery. It's that simple. Follow the instructions later in this chapter on how to buy and sell via classified ads.

Classifying Classified Sites: What Kinds of Sites Are Out There?

Classified sites aren't one size fits all. In addition to general classified sites, such as the Classifieds2000 site I mentioned in Chapter 8, "Have I Got a Deal for You!"you'll find sites that specialize in one particular kind of product, as well as help-wanted classified sites. And finally, you'll find newspaper and regional classified sites, where you can look for classified ads from people who live only in your area. Here's the rundown:

➤ **General classified sites**   These kinds of sites offer everything under the sun: apartments for rent, houses for sale, cars, bicycles, computers, clothing—pretty much anything you'll find in a print classified ad you'll find here.

➤ **Special-interest classified sites**   Have a special interest? Then there's a classified site just for you. Don't believe me? Okay, let's say you wake up one morning and decide that you absolutely *have* to own a Beech Bonanza 36 single-piston-engine airplane with retractable gear before the sun sets. No problem. Head over to the `www.tradeaplane.com` classified site and nose around. You'll find one. Just be sure you have a spare $345,000. I cover special-interest classified sites in the appropriate sections of the book.

Check for Internet Classifieds from Your Local Paper

Classified ads are big today, but they're going to get huge. In fact, many big newspapers are scared that the Internet will become the prime place for classified ads—which by far produce the most revenue for newspapers on a per-page basis than any other kind of ad. Many local newspapers already publish classifieds on the Internet, and a nationwide network of newspapers' classified ads will be coming sometime soon.

➤ **Help-wanted classified sites**   Help-wanted ads are the mainstay of newspaper classified ad sections. They've come to the Web big-time. Check out the Monster Board at www.monsterboard.com to see what I mean. How popular are these sites? Some companies have completely abandoned help-wanted advertising in newspapers in favor of these sites, especially when they're looking for technical staffers. Other good sites for job hunters are CareerMosaic at www.careermosaic.com, HeadHunder.Net at www.headhunter.net, Jobs.com at www.jobs.com, HotJobs at www.hotjobs.com, CareerPath at www.careerpath.com, and for technical people, jobEngine at www.jobengine.com.

➤ **Newspaper and regional classified sites**   The more forward-looking newspapers have realized that if you can't beat 'em, join 'em, and so they've launched their own online classified sections. Sometimes these sections are merely online versions of their print counterparts, whereas other times they're completely separate. And sometimes the newspaper posts only a selection of the ads available in its print edition. For a lot of things, you'll want to turn to these regional sites first. If you're looking to rent an apartment or buy a house, for example, regional sites, with their local listings, are better than national classified sites. And for things that are difficult to ship—such as a used car—you'll probably turn to regional sites as well. Pictured here is an example of a particularly good newspaper classified site, the *Boston Globe*'s.

For finding apartments and houses and for buying things that are difficult to ship, newspaper online classified sites such as the Boston Globe's *are often your best bet.*

115

Classified Intelligence: How to Shop at a Classified Site

As I mentioned earlier in the chapter, a big reason that the Internet can be better than print when you're buying through classified ads is that it's so much easier to find what you're looking for online.

Using classified ads is pretty simple. You head to a classified ad site (see "The Best General Classified Ad Sites on the Internet," later in this chapter) and then browse by the category of what you want to buy—or else search by typing a keyword, such as bicycle. If you want to buy from someone in your own area, you can often search by region or by telephone area code.

When you see something you're interested in, click it. You'll see a description of the item, the asking price, and contact information for the person selling the item. Sometimes you'll see a picture as well. Often, there will also be an email link. The following figure shows a typical classified ad; I found this one at the www.classifieds2000. com site.

A typical classified ad on the Classifieds2000 site.

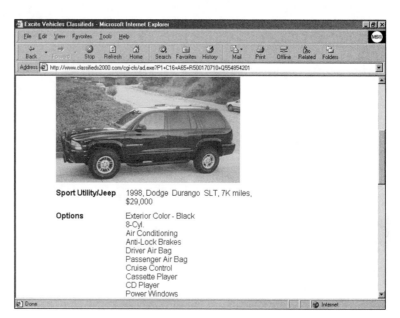

When you come to a classified site, you'll usually start with a list of categories of things you can buy—for example, vehicles, pets, computers, and software. Click the category you're interested in.

Sometimes, you'll see a follow-up list of subcategories of things to buy—for example, cars, vans, motorcycles, and many others if you've clicked on the vehicles category. (All this clicking is tiresome, I know, but hang on—it's worth the effort.)

So, now you would expect to be able to get a list of classified ads. Well, maybe yes, maybe no, depending on the site. At the better and larger sites, you'll have to go through yet another page. For example, the Classifieds2000 site asks whether you want to look at classifieds for the whole country or a single state. And you might have the option of getting really specific about what you want to buy. For example, people looking at the auto subcategory at the Classifieds2000 site can specify a model, a price range, and particular features, such as automatic transmission or air-conditioning.

Use a Hot List or Clipboard to Keep Track of Ads

Sites such as Classifieds2000 and ClassifiedWarehouse let you store all the ads you're interested in together in a separate place—called a Hot List, Clipboard, or similar name—so that you can refer to them later. It's a great feature that you should use often—that way, you'll never lose track of what you're thinking of buying.

Finally, after you do all that, you'll get to see a relatively straightforward listing of the items being sold. On many sites, you can get more details about an item by clicking on the listing; sometimes the additional information includes a picture.

Check out the classified ads. If one seems like a good deal to you, get in touch with the seller. All sites include a phone number, and some include an email address as well. My recommendation is to send an email before calling, especially if the call is a long-distance one. To start off, you save money. But it can also help you gauge how responsive the seller will be if problems develop with the sale. If you send an email and the seller doesn't get back to you fairly soon, that could mean it'll be even harder to get in touch after the sale. However, be sure to follow up any email with at least one phone call.

Oh, yes, and keep this in mind. You can certainly haggle over prices. Assume that the seller will take less than the asking price, so fine-tune your bargaining skills and get ready to save yourself some money.

How to Pay for Your Classified Purchases

Buying at a classified ad site is different from buying at other kinds of Web sites. When you buy at a classified site, you're buying from another person, not from an established business. That means that you'll pay that person directly.

Now, this situation is both good and bad. It's good because often you'll be getting a great price—there's no kind of markup involved. It's bad because you don't really know whom you're buying from—the seller could be your next-door neighbor, Jack the Ripper, Bill Gates, or Ginger Spice selling used Union Jack miniskirts.

Sort Ads by Area to See What's Being Sold near You

Sometimes you want to see what's being sold not just in your state, but in your city or near your city. At some classified sites, such as Classifieds2000, that's easy to do. After you see a listing of everything being sold in a particular subcategory in a particular state, click the **City** column. When you do, you'll see all the listings in alphabetical order by city. Now just scroll to your city or to cities near you to see what's for sale nearby.

Now, if you're buying from your next-door neighbor, you can be pretty sure she'll hand over the goods if you send her a check. I wouldn't trust Jack the Ripper, though. As for Bill Gates and Ginger Spice—well, you be the judge. The point is, though, that you'll want some way to be sure that after you send your money, you will receive the goods.

My advice is not to pay by check. If you do, it'll be only too easy for the seller to take the money and run. And whereas the law might be on your side, you'll find out that it's almost impossible to force someone to give you the goods after he or she cashes your check—especially if the seller is from another state.

One of the Best Ways to Take Advantage of Classified Sites Is to Use Their Email Alerts

These free email alerts let you know when something you want to buy goes on sale. The best classified sites, including Classifieds2000 and ClassifiedWarehouse, have this feature. Classifieds2000 calls it Cool Notify and ClassifiedWarehouse calls it AdHound. Despite the different names, though, the alert features work similarly.

Click the button on the site that leads you to the email alert feature—in the case of Classified2000 on the **Cool Notify** button and in the case of ClassifiedWarehouse, the **AdHound** button. When you get there, you'll fill out a form describing the kind of goods you're interested in buying and then have the alert created. In AdHound, for example, you choose the category you're interested in, such as Animals or Autos & Transportation. Then you click the button to create your AdHound. After you create the Cool Notify or AdHound alert, whenever a new classified ad comes in that matches your interests, you'll get an email alert.

An even better way to create a Cool Notify or AdHound is to first do a search for a specific product you want to buy. Then click the **Cool Notify** or **AdHound** button, and you'll be notified when another one of those specific products goes on sale.

To get around the problem, you should pay in one of two ways. The first is to arrange to pay cash on delivery (C.O.D.). That way, you won't have to pay for the item until you receive it. (And if it never arrives, you never have to pay.) C.O.D. costs a few dollars extra compared to regular shipping, but if it's the first time you're dealing with a seller, the extra cost is worth it. And you can always try to get the seller to pay for the extra C.O.D. charge or to at least split the charge with you.

The second way to pay is to use an escrow service. You pay this escrow service, instead of paying the seller. These services act as a good-faith go-between between a buyer and a seller. Escrow services cost more than C.O.D., so you'll want to use one only if you're buying a big-ticket item of $100 or more. The escrow service holds the money until you receive the goods. After you inspect the merchandise and are satisfied with your purchase, you tell the escrow service to pay the seller. Some classified sites, such as `www.classifieds2000.com`, have links to escrow services.

A number of escrow services handle this kind of transaction on the Internet: TradeSafe at www.tradesafe.com, I-Escrow at www.iescrow.com, and Trade-direct at www.trade-direct.com. They charge somewhat different fees, but generally the minimum is $5. A typical fee is 5% of the selling cost. You should haggle with the seller to get him or her to eat the cost or at least to split it with you.

How to Take Out a Classified Ad

It's been said that there are no problems, only opportunities. (Who said that? Me—I just did.) Where one person sees a chaotic mass of attic-clogging junk, a second person sees—well, a chaotic mass of attic-clogging junk. But that second person knows that there must be some way to metamorphose that attic-clogging junk into money, in the same way that the medieval alchemists were believed to have turned lead into gold.

When Buying Through a Classified Ad, Factor In Who Pays Shipping Costs

When you buy something through a classified ad in your local newspaper, shipping costs usually aren't involved—you drive to someone's house, slip them a check, and take the item home in your car. When you're shopping over the Internet, though, the goods will usually have to be shipped to you, so factor in those costs when you buy. Often, the buyer is responsible for shipping costs—but get that straight before completing a deal.

Yes, there is a way to do that. You can use the Internet to make some quick cash by selling stuff on classified ad sites. It's cheap, it's easy, it doesn't take a whole lot of time, and you just might end up with some spare change. And you can sell more than junk. You can also sell good-quality items, for example, your car (assuming that your car isn't junk).

Taking out an ad is usually pretty straightforward. You'll first have to register on the site by filling out information about yourself. Then you'll fill out a form describing what you're selling, including a picture if you have one, and setting a price. You'll usually include your email address and often your phone number and mailing address as well. Then sit back and wait for the offers to come in.

When you get a live one on the line, you're going to have to figure out how to get paid. It's the flip side of the buyers' dilemma: How can you be sure that the buyer's check is a good one? It's pretty simple: Don't send out the goods until the check clears. That way, you won't get burned. Or you can ship COD or use an escrow service. You'll have to bargain with the buyer to see who bears the costs. The fairest way is to split the costs straight down the middle.

The Best General Classified Ad Sites on the Internet

If you're looking for classified ads, here's where to start—the best of the best. Note that this list covers only general classified sites. For specialized classified sites, turn to the proper section of the book—for example, to Chapter 12, "Hot Wheels: How to Research and Buy New Cars Online," for classified car sites. And I don't cover newspaper and regional sites, either. For that, check out your local newspaper or city guide.

At Many Sites, You Won't Have to Pay a Cent to Take Out a Classified Ad If You're Not a Business

Here's a strange but true fact: The classified sites make their money by charging businesses to take out ads and by selling banner advertising space on their sites. That means you often won't have to pay a nickel.

America Online Classifieds

On America Online, KEYWORD CLASSIFIEDS

America Online users looking for a bargain will want to check out this area. It's a huge site, filled with thousands of classified ads. It's easy to browse as well. When you want to buy something, you send email to the seller's America Online email address. Note that America Online used to allow people to sell things directly on their message boards. That's no longer true—now you'll have to head to the classified area to buy and sell.

Classified Warehouse

    http://www.classifiedwarehouse.com

Former Speaker of the House Tip O'Neill once said aphoristically that all politics are local. This site applies that same aphorism to classified ads—all ads are local. The site covers the whole country, but when you're looking to buy or sell an apartment or a home or to find a job, you can restrict your search to a particular region. It's a great way to find local classifieds—and there are lots of them. My favorite part of the site is the AdHound feature. You tell it what you're looking for, such as a car or house or an antique wagon. Then, when a classified ad that matches your interests comes onto the site, AdHound notifies you via email.

Classifieds2000

http://www.classifieds2000.com

For my money, Classifieds2000 is the best classified site on the Internet. It has a huge selection of goods for sale (the site recently claimed 1.5 million items, but I have to admit, I didn't count). It has great features, such as a Cool Notify email alert that lets you know when the kind of product you're interested in is up for sale. It offers free listings for nonbusiness sellers. Its classifieds are listed on the major Internet sites Excite, and by various Internet service providers. There's also an auction section of the site. What can I say? It's the first and best place to go. Check out the picture on this page to see what the site looks like.

The best classified site on the Internet: Classifieds2000.

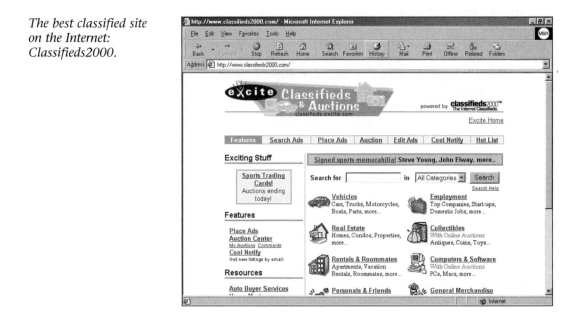

FreeClassifiedAds.com

http://www.freeclassifiedads.com

The name says it all: You don't have to pay to run ads here. If you're a buyer, there's a reasonable number of ads to peruse, so it's a good place to head. In addition to browsing, you can also search for exactly what you want by typing a keyword. It's a bit bare-bones but still worth a visit.

Lycos Classified Ads

```
http://www.lycos.com/classifieds/
```

Lycos, one of the major sites on the Internet, has a reasonably good classified section. There's not as much to buy here as at some of the other major sites, but still, it's worth checking out.

Recycler.com

```
http://www.recycler.com
```

Here's another top-notch classified site, run by the company that owns the Recycler classified newspapers in California, Texas, Arizona, Michigan, and other states. You'll find a sizable number of ads, and if you place an ad, it runs free for a week. This site also has bulletin boards where you can talk to other buyers and sellers although the boards aren't particularly active. One nice thing about this site is that you can search for classifieds in your local area if there are any.

Yahoo! Classified Ads

```
http://classifieds.yahoo.com/
```

I'd have to say that Yahoo! is a close runner-up to the Classifieds2000 site for the best classified section on the Internet. In addition to having a huge selection of stuff for sale and free ads, the site lets you browse by product and by region. So, for example, if you're looking for a rabbit in Boston, you can browse through all the classified ads from Boston—or you can go to the Rabbit area and ask to see all the ads for rabbits that live in Boston.

The Least You Need to Know

➤ Local newspapers run many of the best classified sites, so check to see whether your local paper has a site.

➤ For special products, head to specialized classified sites, instead of the large, general ones.

➤ Consider paying C.O.D. or using an "escrow service" when making a purchase from an online classified ad.

➤ Because some classified sites don't charge sellers any fees, consider taking out an online classified before paying for a printed classified the next time you want to sell something.

➤ Sign up for email alerts from classified sites so that you'll know whenever something you're interested in buying goes on sale.

Chapter 11

Sold American! Buying Through Online Auctions

In This Chapter

➤ Understanding how online auctions work

➤ Top tips for bidding at online auctions

➤ How to sell at online auctions

➤ Best auctions in cyberspace

"FivedollarsdoIhearfivedollars,IhavefivedollarsfromthemanintheStetsonhat,six!no,nomakethat sevenfromtheladyinthefeatheredboa!Eightdollars,doIhaveeight,yesIdofromthemanwiththe purpleascot,doIhearninedollars,no,idon't,goingoncetothemanwiththepurpleascot!goingtwice tothemaninthepurpleascot!!goingthreetimestothemaninthepurpleascot!!!soldAmerican!!!!"

Auctions summon up images of fast-talking smoothies rattling off bids and bargains in rat-a-tat style so fast you can't understand a word of what they're saying—and you're risking your bank account if you accidentally swat a fly away, lest the auction-eer mistakenly interpret your swat for a bid.

Online, though, things are different. Yes, it's true that the basic idea is the same—you bid against others, trying to buy something that you want, paying the lowest price possible. But the similarities end there. The auctioneer is absent, the pressure is decreased, and you can show up any time—auctions take place 24 hours a day, 7 days a week, at sites all over the Internet.

Why You Should Shop at an Auction

Auctions can get you the best deals that you'll find anywhere—whether it be in cyber-space or the real world. But a big part of the lure as well is that you never know what kind of bargain or buried treasure you will come across—so you'll want to visit auctions not only when there's something specific you need to buy, but when you're just interested in browsing as well.

Check Retail Prices Before You Buy at an Auction

It's easy to get carried away at an auction, assuming that you're getting the best deal possible—but are you? Before bidding on an item, be sure to find out its true retail price; otherwise, you might end up paying more than you would in a store.

Years ago, when I lived in a small hill town in western Massachusetts, my friends and I used to haunt small-time auctions held in farmers' barns on back country roads. You never knew what you'd find—an old daguerreotype of someone's forgotten ancestors, an ancient hand awl that no longer works, a bucket of bolts, a rusty old scythe, or a beautiful pearl-inlaid mandolin rescued from someone's attic. Sometimes we'd bid on a closed box of odds and ends, sight unseen, just to find out what was inside. Online auctions have that allure as well—where else in the world can you get deals on items as varied as an old shark-bone cane, a new 450 megahertz multimedia PC, a paua shell necklace, a Mickey Mantle sports card, and a new TV satellite dish?

Collectors, in particular, will be interested in online auctions, because some sites specialize in collectibles of all kinds. So will those looking to get good prices on new or used computer or electronic equipment because innumerable auctions online sell those kinds of items.

And auctions aren't just for buyers. If you're interested in making some money, and cleaning out your attic and garage along the way, you'll want to haunt auctions as well. You can make a pretty penny with very little effort selling off all kinds of things online. Don't look down your nose at those odd items collecting dust around your house. Just as realtors will tell you that every house, no matter how eccentric, has a buyer, any old junk has a buyer as well.

So How Does an Online Auction Work?

I'm glad you asked. Several kinds of auctions take place online, and they all work a bit differently. In all of them, though, you start off by visiting an auction site and browsing through the items that are up for bid. They'll be grouped by category. When you come across a particular item you're interested in, click it. You'll then be given details about the item, including a description and sometimes a picture of the item, the minimum bidding price, the bidding increment, the current bid, and other information, such as how long the auction on the item will last. The following picture shows the popular auction site eBay at www.ebay.com.

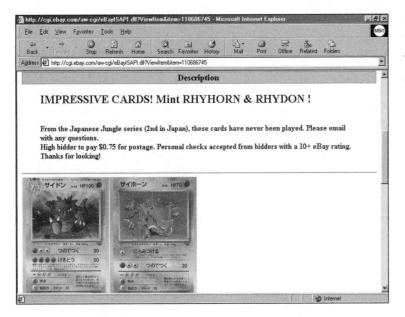

Catch Pokemon fever on eBay: Pokemon cards are just one of the millions of items up for auction every day at www.ebay.com.

If you're not interested in buying, don't do anything. Just keep on cruising the site. If you are interested in buying, you can now make a bid. To make a bid, you're going to have to register at the site. Registration is free. In some instances, you'll have to enter your credit card number and information if you're buying the item directly from the site itself. (Stay tuned—more on this topic later on in this chapter.) In other instances, you won't have to enter your credit card number, because you won't be buying the item from the site, but rather from a private person who put the item up for bid. (Again, more on this matter later.)

After you register for free at the site, it's time to make your bid. Look at the minimum bidding price and the bidding increment. Then look at the current high bidding price. Now decide how much you're willing to spend on the item. Go ahead now, bid. On some sites, that's all there is to it. Your bid is displayed on the site, and if someone wants to bid a higher price, he or she does so. You check back, and if you want to bid higher, you up the price. It goes back and forth that way for the length of the auction, until the highest bidder gets the item.

However, the most popular auction sites such as eBay handle things a bit differently— and they handle them in a way that's much better for you. In fact, they allow you to sometimes buy items for *less* than your bidding price. Yes, strange but true: There are times when you'll be able to buy something for less than you bid on it.

These specific online auctions work differently than their real-life counterparts. In a real-life auction, when you make a bid, it's public, and everyone can see it. In some online auctions, such as the ones run by eBay, your bid is private, and only you (and the auction software) know about it. So when you put in a bid, your actual bid might not show up—what'll show up is the increment above the current high bid. And if you end up getting the item, you might only have to pay that price, not your total bid. This kind of bidding is called proxy bidding—and it can end up saving you money.

Confused? I thought so. It took me a while to get it as well. The following example should help. Say you're bidding on a purple flyer advertising an *X-Files* pinball machine. ("Taking Pinball into the Next CENTURY!" And I'm not making this up, by the way; this item was up for bid at an auction site.) Let's say the minimum bid is $10, and the bidding increment is $1. The current high bid is $14. You really want this flyer (Why? Don't ask me; *you're* the one bidding.), and you're willing to pay $20 for it. So you bid $20. But the bid that will show up is $15, not $20, because no one except you has bid more than $14, and the bidding increment is $1. So you're shown as the highest bidder at $15. If no one makes another bid higher than $15, the flyer is yours, at the bargain price of $15, even though you were willing to pay $20 for it. Simple, no?

What's a Dutch Auction?

Sometimes someone has more than one of a particular item for sale. In that instance, the rules vary slightly from normal auction rules. On eBay, this kind of auction is called a Dutch auction. In a Dutch auction, the seller sets a minimum price for the items. Buyers then make their bids. When the auction ends, the highest bidders get the items—and they get it at the lowest bidding price of the highest bidders. So, for example, if five bird-shaped wind chimes are up at a Dutch auction and the five highest bidders bid $30, they each get the chimes for $30. If of the highest five bidders, four bid $35, and one bids $30, all five bidders get the chimes for $30 because the lowest high bid is $30. And if of the highest five bidders, one bids $40, three bid $25, and one bids $30, all five get the item for $25 because $25 is the lowest high bid.

Every auction lasts for a certain amount of time—usually several days and often up to a week. You'll want to check in regularly to see how the bidding is going. Suppose you made a bid of $20 yesterday. Today you check in, and you're still the high bidder—but now your high bid is listed at $18. Why is that? Because between yesterday and today, someone bid $17. And because you bid $20, your bid is automatically upped to the increment above $17, which is $18. (Hey, I might have been an English major, but I can add as well—at least single digits.) The next picture shows what you'll see when you check the bidding on an item at the eBay auction site.

Let the bidding begin! Twenty-three bidders are hot and heavy to get a deal on silver dollars on eBay.

So now you're on track to buy it at $18. There's a day left on the auction. It's nail-biting time. If no one bids again, the flyer is yours for the bargain-basement price of $18. Let's say, though, that someone outbids you in the interim, and you see there's a high bidding price of $21. You can change your bid now and try to outbid your rival—and the whole process continues until the auction ends and the high bidder gets the goods. Or you can just write off the *X-Files* flyer and hope to get another deal another day.

Let's say, though, that your dream came true, and you snagged that flyer for a mere $18. You'll be notified by email that you're the winning bidder. If the auction site is selling the item directly, you'll pay the site through your credit card. If, instead, you're buying the item from a private seller at the auction site, then you and the seller must arrange for payment and delivery. Information on the best ways to pay private parties for goods you've bought from them at an auction appears later in this chapter.

Various Kinds of Auction Sites

Two kinds of auctions sites do business online—sites in which you buy directly from the site itself, such as OnSale at www.onsale.com, and sites in which you buy from a private seller, such as eBay at www.ebay.com. Each type of site has its particular strengths and weaknesses:

➤ **Auctions in which you buy directly from the site**   These sites are good if you don't want to deal with a different private seller each time you buy. The transaction is done via credit card, which is safe and secure—and when you buy something via credit card, your credit card company offers you consumer protection in the case of fraud or damaged goods. When you deal with a private buyer, you don't get that protection (although, increasingly auction sites offer buyers' insurance when you deal with a private buyer, as you'll see later in this chapter).

The bad feature of these sites is that the variety of products is somewhat limited—often to hundreds or thousands of items instead of the hundreds of thousands or millions of items available at sites where you buy from private sellers. In addition, sites in which you buy directly from the site tend to focus on relatively high-ticket items such as computers and electronic equipment. Their products are often new rather than used, and so you often won't get as deep price cuts.

➤ **Auctions in which you buy from private sellers**   These sites offer an incredible variety of merchandise. On the monstrous eBay site, for example, on any given day more than half a million—that's right, you read correctly, half a million—different items are for sale. Because of the variety and because the goods tend to be used, you can usually get very good prices.

The downside is that you have to deal with private sellers—but if you follow the advice in this chapter, you shouldn't get burned. And sites increasingly offer "insurance" so that they'll cover your losses, in the unlikely event that you do get burned. And the ambience at these kinds of sites tends to be better—they tend to be just plain more fun because the sales are built by thousands of different people, not a single corporation.

At some auction sites, such as eBay, you'll find all kinds of goods for sale. Those are the kinds of auction sites I cover in this chapter. Other auction sites, such as the Cyberswap Auction House at www.cyberswap.com, specialize in a certain kind of product—Cyberswap, for instance, concentrates on computers and electronics. I cover specialized sites in the proper chapters.

You Can Buy Fine Art and Antiques at Online Auctions

You can buy a whole lot more than Pokemon cards, computers, collectibles and similar goods online—you can now buy fine art and antiques as well. Several sites specialize in these kinds of high-ticket items, including the well-known Christie's auction house at www.christies.com, the well-known Sotheby's auction house at www.sothebys.com, the antiques site iCollector at www.icollector.com, and the art site artnet.com.

By the way, you might come across sites that bill themselves as "swap meet"—or "trading sites." Those are pretty loose terms. Sometimes they're auction sites, whereas at other times they're classified ad sites. Just another reason why you can't tell a site by its name.

How to Become a Cutthroat Cyberbargainer: Top Tips for Bidding at Auctions

The whole point of an auction is to get the best deal at the best price. But if you go in blind, you might find that either you'll never be the top bidder or you'll overpay for an item. Follow these tips, though, and you'll be well on the way to becoming a cutthroat cyberbargainer:

➤ **Pick the highest price you'll pay and then stick to it.** One theory of bidding holds that you should immediately bid the highest amount you're willing to pay for an item and then just wait out the bidding, never upping your price. This kind of bidding works particularly well at a site such as eBay in which, as I explained earlier in the chapter, you can sometimes buy an item at a price lower than your bid. Some people call this strategy preemptive bidding, and it means that you'll know you'll never pay more than you want for an item—and you might well pay less. It's important, though, not to budge any higher after you pick your price; if you do, you can end up overpaying.

➤ **Become an auction "sniper."** Maybe you don't have the kind of personality that likes to sit around and wait to see what happens with your bid. And maybe you like living on the edge a little. (Wow, you drink caffeine after 5 p.m.? That's living on the edge, all right.) In that case, you'll be too antsy to become a preemptive bidder. Your best bet is to become an auction sniper. In sniping, you don't make a bid until the last few minutes—and in some instances, in the last few seconds—before the bidding closes on an item. And when you make a bid, you always make it for the smallest increment over the current bid. Sniping requires you to constantly watch the bidding in those last few minutes and to continually make bids at the speed of light (but, hey, with that caffeine in your system, that's no problem). You'll often be bidding against other snipers, so on a particularly good item, the bidding can get fast and furious. But if you're successful, you'll be able to get the best items at the lowest prices possible.

➤ **Use special auction software.** You can find a piece of software for pretty much every need you can imagine—and so you shouldn't be surprised to learn that a lot of software is available for people who buy and sell at auctions. Some is general software that keeps track of your bids and pertinent information at any site, but some is customized for a specific site. Look for software that enables you to follow bidding in real time and that allows you to make bids quickly and easily. And for the snipers of this world, you'll want supersniping capability built in. What is supersniping capability? Here's an example: You can tell some software programs to start sniping 10 seconds before the bidding ends and to send off bids 1 second apart. Where can you get auction software? Surprise—on the auction sites themselves. They're often auctioned off. One warning, though: Don't buy any of this software sight unseen. Some software vendors allow you to try out a program for free. That's the only kind of auction software you should consider buying.

Be Careful When Bidding at "Flash," or "Express," Auctions

Flash, or express, auctions are auctions that are done very quickly—often, they take an hour or less. In that way, they're similar to real-life auctions. These kinds of auctions get your adrenaline flowing because you're sitting there the whole time, in pitched battle against other bidders. When your adrenaline is flowing at one of these auctions, it's easy to get carried away—and especially because some of them allow you to chat online with other bidders, which means a bit of taunting can take place. In a hothouse atmosphere like this, macho posturing sometimes takes over, and you can find yourself bidding very high prices on an item just to prove you can win. But when the bidding is over, you might well find yourself paying well over top dollar for an item that isn't worth a plug nickel. So be sure before you bid at one of these to set a top price over which you won't go.

➤ **Use auction ShopBot sites.**   If you're looking for a specific item, how can you find out which Internet auction has the best deal? Forget trying to track all the auctions; with millions of items auctioned every day, that would be impossible. Instead, you can go to an auction ShopBot site that will let you search through all the auction sites and find the item you're looking for—complete with bidding prices. That's what the BidFind site at www.bidfind.com and Bidders Edge at www.biddersedge.com will do for you.

How to Pay at Auctions Without Getting Burned

So you've followed my tips for becoming a cutthroat auction bidder. You bought that *X-Files* flyer at a can't-beat price. Now it's time to pay for it. If you've bought it at a site that does the selling, no problem; the money gets charged against your credit card. But what do you do if you've bought it at a site such as eBay in which you buy from a private seller? How can you be sure the seller won't just take the money and run? Follow these tips and you should be just fine:

➤ **Research the seller.**   Before sending any money, you'll want to know how trustworthy the seller is. Some sites, notably eBay, allow you to get detailed information about how the seller has treated other buyers. At eBay, for example, you can see a profile detailing how other sellers have rated the buyer—you can see a tally of the total number of positive, neutral, and negative comments, and you can read the individual comments as well. If someone has several negative comments, stay away. (In fact, if someone gets four negative comments and eBay confirms that they're accurate, that person is kicked off the service and isn't allowed to sell anymore.)

The auction site will provide you with the email address of the seller. Send an email to that person to see how fast you get a response. If you don't get a response, or get a slow one, that's a bad sign. And certainly if you can't get an address and phone number, stay away.

If the site has a message board or chat area, head there and ask whether any other people have had dealings with the seller. If they have, they'll be happy to share their experiences with you—both good and bad.

➤ **Ask that shipping be done cash on delivery (C.O.D.).**   Here's a simple way to ensure that someone can't just cash your check and then not send you the goods—ask the seller to ship C.O.D. This way, you pay for the item only when you receive it. It costs a few dollars extra, compared to regular shipping, but if it's the first time you're dealing with a seller, it might be worth the cost. And you can always try to get the seller to pay for the extra C.O.D. charge or to at least split the charge with you.

➤ **Use an Internet "escrow" service.** If you are buying from a particular individual for the first time or you're spending serious money, more than $100 or so, you might want to use an Internet escrow service. These services in essence act as a good-faith go-between with the buyer and the seller. You make your payment to the escrow service, which holds your money until you are satisfied with the merchandise. Upon your instructions, the escrow service releases the money to the seller.

TradeSafe at www.tradesafe.com, I-Escrow at www.iescrow.com, and Trade-direct at www.trade-direct.com operate Internet escrow services. Fees vary. The minimum fee is $5, and a typical fee is 5% of the selling cost of the item. Again, haggle with the seller to get him or her to eat the cost or at least to split it with you.

➤ **Find out what kind of insurance the site offers.** Auction sites recognize that they'll be in trouble if people get ripped off when shopping there. So many auction sites now offer auction insurance—they'll cover all or part of your costs if you've been burned. Some cover the full amount, up to a maximum of $250 or so. Others have a $25 deductible—they won't cover the first $25, but will cover the rest up to a certain amount. Check your auction site to see what kind of insurance it offers.

Be Leery of Buying Collector Beanie Babies at Auction Sites

Beanie Babies—those furry little bean-bag-style stuffed animals so beloved by children—can be bought at many online auctions. As anyone knows who collects Beanie Babies (or has a child under 14), prices for some of these Beanie Babies can be astronomical, in the range of hundreds or thousands of dollars. Consequently, forgers have come into the market and created phony Beanies. Because you can't examine the Beanie when you bid online, there's no way to check whether it's a forgery. It's okay to pay normal prices for run-of-the-mill Beanies such as Chocolate the Moose (yes, that's his real name) because then it doesn't really matter whether you get a forgery or the real thing. But stay away from the high-priced Beanies when buying online.

Read the Fine Print on Auction Insurance

It's great that auction sites offer insurance—but be sure to read the fine print before bidding. Some sites have rules about what you need to do if you want to get them to offer you insurance—things such as only bidding on auctions in which the seller has been rated highly by auction bidders.

Become an Online Mogul: How to Make Money at Auctions

It's been said that there are no problems, only opportunities. (Who said that? Me—I just did.) Where one person sees a chaotic mass of attic-clogging junk, a second person sees—well, a chaotic mass of attic-clogging junk. But that second person knows that there must be some way to metamorphose that attic-clogging junk into money, in the same way that the medieval alchemists were believed to have turned lead into gold.

Yes, there is a way to do that. You can sell the stuff at an online auction. It's cheap, it's easy, it doesn't take a whole lot of time, and you just might get some spare change for doing it. That's what my kids are planning to do—they're going to put their Super Nintendo system up for bid. (No, they're not giving up video games—instead, they're going to apply the proceeds of their sale toward the purchase of a Nintendo 64.)

To sell at an auction site, you'll have to first register. You then fill out a form describing what you're selling. If you have a graphic of what you're selling, you can include that as well. You have to pay for your listing, and you have to pay a percentage of what you get for your item; you might also have to pay a low insertion fee whether or not you sell the item. The fee is usually based on your opening asking price. At eBay, for example, you pay 25 cents to list something with an opening value of under $10 and up to $2 for something with an opening value of $50 or more. If you sell an item, you pay 5% of the selling price for the amount up to $25; 2.5% percent for the amount from $25.01 to $1,000; and finally 1.25% for the remaining balance.

Use iShip.com for Easy Shipping

Often the most difficult part of selling an item on an auction site is dealing with shipping—you'll need to know things such as how much will you have to charge the buyer for shipping, where you'll get shipping materials, and how you'll ship the item. The iShip.com Web site makes it easy. You'll be able to see how much shipping on any item will cost, find out how long it'll take to get there, get help shipping the goods, and then even track the progress of what you've shipped.

When you find a buyer, check out the person in the same way that I suggested buyers should check out sellers. And ask buyers to send you a money order when paying. If someone pays by check, don't ship the item until the check clears.

Bid and Buy: The Best Auction Sites in Cyberspace

You'll find many dozens of auction sites on the Internet. Don't roll the dice when heading to a site; these are the best of the best.

Amazon.com auctions

```
http://www.amazon.com
```

Yes, it's true—the biggest online bookstore in the universe has started an auction site where you buy from other people. It's big, it's busy, and it offers free insurance. Check it out—well worth the visit.

Auction Universe

```
http://auctionuniverse.com
```

This well-put-together auction site is like eBay in that you buy from other people instead of from the site itself. A reasonable number of items are up for bid, and the site is easy to navigate and use.

Bid.Com

`http://www.bid.com`

This auction site specializes in closeout items, especially computers and electronics, although you'll find sports items and collectibles here as well. You buy from the site itself, and the products carry a warranty.

Bidder's Edge

`http://www.biddersedge.com`

Why look through just one auction site when you're looking to buy something when you search though many of them all at once? Bidder's Edge is an auction shopbot that lets you search through many auctions for what it is you want to buy. It searches through all the top auction sites, including eBay and Amazon.

Take into Account Shipping Charges When Figuring Out Your Buying Price

The price you pay at an auction might seem like a good deal—but when comparing auction prices to retail prices, don't ignore the cost of shipping. When you're buying a large item, shipping charges can add up—sometimes to $50 or more.

Have I Got a Bridge for You!

You knew it had to happen. Someone tried to sell the Brooklyn Bridge on eBay. Bidding started at 25 cents, and after a week had zoomed all the way to $5.50. Quite a steal, isn't it? Here's what the seller had to say about it: "The famous Brooklyn Bridge. You know what it looks like. It's kind of big, but I think I can fit it in a manila envelope, so shipping is $1. Should take a few days. Very nice keepsake (looks good on a bookshelf). Can earn you a good income (toll booths not included). Has some structural faults, but has at least another 10 years of life to it." Come on here! What kind of sucker do they think I am? After all, everyone knows there are no tolls on the Brooklyn Bridge. Sheesh!

eBay

http://www.ebay.com

As you've no doubt guessed by now, eBay is my favorite auction site in cyberspace. And I'm not alone—more than 2 million items are for sale in over 1,600 categories every day, so a lot of other people are heading here as well. What's for sale? Just about anything ever made it seems, as you can see from the following picture. You don't buy the goods directly from this site; instead, eBay acts an auction place where buyers and private sellers get together. The site is great not only for the variety of goods but also because it's so easy to use, you can easily check out buyers and sellers, and yes, it's just plain fun. eBay also has message boards where you can talk with other auction hounds.

From Pokemon cards to antique maps to computers, jewelry, and beyond—the eBay auction site.

First Auction

http://www.firstauction.com

Another one of the Web auctions in which you mainly buy directly from the site itself, First Auction specializes in computer products and electronics, although it has a decent selection of home products as well. Adrenaline junkies take note: Flash auctions are big on this site. They've also added a person-to-person auctions section, although it's not nearly as big as eBay's or Amazon's.

Check Warranties

One thing you might give up when buying at an auction is a warranty. For collectibles and similar items, this is no problem. But for something such as computers or electronic equipment, no warranty could spell big trouble. For those kinds of items, be sure that you'll get a warranty on your purchase.

OnSale

http://www.onsale.com

Here's one of the biggest auction sites in cyberspace. Unlike eBay, here you buy products directly from the site, so there aren't nearly as many items on sale—and the fun factor isn't quite so high. Still, OnSale is an excellent auction site, especially if you're looking for computer products, office products, and sports products. Much of the merchandise here is new and carries a warranty, unlike merchandise at many other auction sites online.

Yahoo! Auctions

http://auctions.yahoo.com

The world's most popular Internet site has an auction area, and while it's not as busy as eBay's, it's still a good place to go and get a deal. Lots of stuff for sale.

ZDNet Auctions

http://auctions.zdnet.com/

If you're looking to buy computers, hardware, software, and electronic gadgets at auctions, then this is the place to go. You can get great deals on powerful new computers, used computers, software, and electronics of all kinds. Definitely worth a visit for some great deals.

The Least You Need to Know

➤ At some auction sites, you buy directly from private individuals, whereas at others you buy from the site itself.

➤ For best bidding results, make your best bid at first and then don't budge.

➤ Use an auction ShopBot site to check multiple auctions at the same time for the item you want to buy.

➤ See what kind of insurance an auction site offers—and read the fine print before bidding.

➤ Before sending money to someone, check that person's (or the company he or she represents) background. For big-ticket items, use an Internet escrow company.

Part 4

How to Buy Anything in Cyberspace

Books. CDs. Cars. Houses. Perfume. Flowers. Toys and games. Gourmet food. Airline tickets. And yes, even clothes for your dog. That's just a small sampling of what you can buy online.

These days, you can buy anything online—absolutely anything. This section shows you how. For anything you want to buy, you get tips, advice, and insider hints on what you should know before buying anything from used cars to jewelry. You find out how to drive the best bargain. And then you get a list of the best sites to go to for shopping.

Just turn to the chapter that describes whatever you're looking to buy and read on. And then with the book open by your computer, head online and shop. There's a world of shopping out there—so get on with it!

Chapter 12

Hot Wheels: How to Research and Buy New Cars Online

In This Chapter

➤ Researching what car to buy

➤ Finding the true dealer cost of a new car

➤ Using information you find on the Web to bargain with car dealers

➤ Buying a car online

➤ Best car sites in cyberspace

If you take away only one piece of advice from this book, it's this: Use the Internet to help you buy your next new car. It will save you hundreds or even thousands of dollars—and you'll also be able to know that you're getting the best make and model possible. You don't have to actually buy your car over the Internet (although you can do that as well), but even just doing your homework online, and buying offline, can save you big bucks. Take it from someone who knows. I've researched my last two cars using the Internet and it saved me some serious money.

And let's face it, doing business with new car dealers is about as much fun as having your teeth pulled—except that you'll have to pay many, many thousands of dollars extra for the pleasure. The Internet helps make dealing with car dealers less painful in two ways: (1) You can buy cars directly online, and not have to deal with them at all; and (2) you don't need to wheel and deal if you decide to buy in person—armed with the information you got from the Internet, you can hold to a price.

You can use the Internet to

➤ Research what kind of make and model you should buy

➤ Find out the true dealer cost of the car

➤ Get information about hidden rebates and special offers

➤ Get bids from dealers who want to offer you the best price

➤ Research and take out car loans

So if you want to buy a new car, but don't want to get taken for a ride, read on and see how to use the Internet to get the best deal possible on a new set of wheels, whether or not you do the actual buying online.

Fast, Sleek, and Shiny: Using the Internet to Help Buy New Cars

Whether or not you plan to buy your new car over the Internet, be sure to do your prepurchase research online. Use the Internet to help decide which car to buy and to get the best deal possible from the dealer—or even to buy online. You'll get pleasure not only out of saving money, but also out of seeing car dealers gnash their teeth over the thought of how you were able to bargain them down to very little profit. There goes their trip to Cancun this year!

Step 1: Go Online to Research and Find Your Dream Machine

Your clunker has finally spit the last bit of black exhaust out of its tailpipe, and it's time to get a new dream machine. But what should you get? Should it be a superma-cho, ego-enhancing sports-utility vehicle? A trusty family station wagon? A hell-bent-for-leather sports car? Or just a plain old sedan? And which is the best model for your needs and pocketbook?

You'll find many sites to help you narrow down what you should buy. If you're not quite sure what you want, immediately head to the GTE Superpages Consumer Guide at www.consumerguide.com. Use the Interactive Car Finder—think of it as the *The Complete Idiot's Guide to Choosing a Car*. You select the kind of car (compact, sports-utility vehicle, and so on) the price range, fuel economy, and features such as air-conditioning, and voilà—you'll get a list of cars that match your pocketbook and the features you want. Browse the list, click on those you'd like to consider, and you'll get a quick comparison chart, shown in the following figure. Then click on each car and you'll get a complete rundown—and I do mean a *complete* rundown. You'll find out everything from legroom to workmanship to fuel economy, reliability, safety, steering and handling, braking, general pros and cons, value for the money—in short, the whole nine yards. And the site also gives out Best Buy awards to cars in each class.

What else could you ask for from a car site? Let me put it this way: If this site can't help you narrow your choices and come near a decision, then you're probably someone who spends two hours each morning deciding which socks to put on. (Choose the argyle.)

The best way to begin your car shopping expedition is to use the Interactive Car Finder at www.consumerguide.com.

Car aficionados who want to know what the insiders think about cars should head to the online site of *Car and Driver* magazine at www.caranddriver.com. Its Buyers' Guides are a good first step to help you decide. Choose the kind of car you're interested in (economy, sports-utility vehicle, and so on), the price range, and the manufacturer if you want, and you'll get a list of cars that match what you're looking for. You can then read the magazine's reviews of each car. When the magazine has given an award to a particular car, it notes that as well. If you want, you can browse by manufacturer only.

As you might guess, many, many more car sites online can help you decide which car to buy, and many also offer car reviews. I'd suggest that after you use the Consumer Guide and the *Car and Driver* site to narrow down your choices, you check in with as many sites as possible to get their takes on the cars of your dreams. One excellent site is Edmund's at www.edmunds.com. For a list of other worthwhile sites, check the section in this chapter "The Best New Car Sites in Cyberspace."

Step 2: Get Ready to Bargain—Find Out the True Dealer Invoice Price

Sure, the last time you bought a car, you probably thought you got a pretty good deal. The dealer might even have said something such as, "You got the best of me that time, Buddy." Guess what? The dealer was lying. (What a shock!) You got taken for a ride. The dealer got the best of you. And it's not because you're not smart enough to drive a good bargain. It's because the dealer knows exactly how much the car cost, and you don't have a clue. Sticker price, retail price, rebates, MSRP (what in the world does that stand for, anyway?—oh, yeah, Manufacturer Suggested Retail Price), the costs of all the "extras," (such as doors and an engine, it seems)—trying to put it all together makes your head start to spin. The whole pricing scheme for new cars is designed to confuse you. So what's a poor car buyer to do?

It's simple. Head to the Internet and find out exactly how much the dealer paid for the car (the dealer cost) to the dollar—including all the extras. When you're armed with that information, you can force the dealer to meet your price—or you can walk out the door and find a dealer who *will* meet it.

Find Out How Safe Your Car Is Before Buying

Sure, that cherry-red sports car looks great on the lot, but how well will it do in a crash? More to the point, how will you do in a crash? Find out how safe the car you're thinking of buying is at the National Highway Traffic Safety Administration (NHTSA) site at www.nhtsa.dot.gov. This government agency is charged with enforcing auto safety laws (and for creating the infamous crash car dummies), and it tests cars to see how safe they are in crashes. You can find the results of the tests, plus a good deal more information on buying a safe car, at the NHTSA Web site.

You can find the dealer invoice price at a number of sites on the Internet. But head to www.edmunds.com to get the best lowdown. It not only provides the most comprehensive information but also explains the ins and outs of car pricing, which is arcane enough to have confused a medieval philosopher. This site offers excellent how-to-buy articles as well.

When you get to Edmund's, find a review of the car you're thinking of buying by clicking on it. Then to get information about pricing, click on Vehicle Prices. The following figure gives you an idea of what you'll see at the Edmund's site.

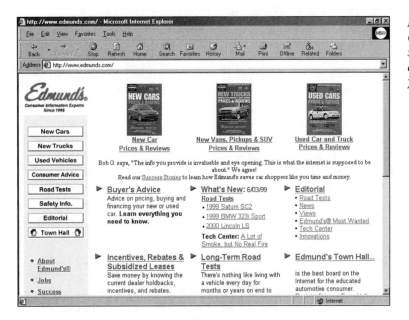

Head to www.edmunds.com *to get the inside skinny on what your dealer pays for the car you want to buy.*

You'll notice a few numbers there. The MSRP is the car's base price that the dealer will quote to you. Never, ever, ever pay that price for a car. If you do, the dealer and salesperson will be breaking out the champagne after you leave.

Find the Invoice price. That's the most important number on the page. It's the price that the dealer pays the manufacturer for the base model of the car, without any extras. That's the number you're going to use when you start to bargain. Do you notice something interesting about the MSRP price and the invoice price? I thought you did; you have sharp eyes. The MSRP (sticker) price is several thousand dollars higher than the invoice price. So if a dealer knocks off $1,000 from the sticker price, you might think you're getting a good deal, but you're not—the dealer is still making out like a bandit.

Next, check out the invoice prices of the options you want—things such as automatic transmission, a luggage rack, and a stereo. As you can see, each item has an MSRP as well as an invoice price, which means that the dealer is making money by marking up all your extras as well.

Now, add the invoice price of the car to the invoice prices of the extras you want. You now have the basic price that the dealer paid for the car—well, almost, anyway. You still need to know a few more things. But hang in there; we're almost done.

The dealer also has to pay a destination charge, which can be $500 or more. Edmund's reports that charge as well.

To figure out the true cost to the dealer of the car you're interested in buying, do this math:

Invoice Price + Invoice Price of Extras + Destination Charge = Dealer's Costs

Now here's a strange fact: Even if you pay only the dealer's invoice costs for a car, in most instances the dealer *still* makes a profit. That's because of a little-known program called the "Dealer Hold Back." The dealer hold back is a percentage of the MSRP of the vehicle, including all extras. When a dealer sells a vehicle, the manufacturer sends the dealer a check based on the hold back percentage and the MSRP of the vehicle. Domestic carmakers typically pay a 3% dealer hold back, and foreign makers often pay 2%. But the amount varies from manufacturer to manufacturer. Edmund's tells you the dealer hold back for the car you're buying.

Let's take an example. Say the MSRP of the car and extras you've bought is $25,000, and the dealer hold back is 3%. According to this formula, after you buy the car, the manufacturer sends the dealer a check for $750. Therefore, even if the dealer sells the car at invoice price, he or she is still making money. Note, though, that that money doesn't go to your salesperson—it goes straight to the dealer. So, no salesperson is going to agree to give you a car at invoice price.

Step 3: Psyching Out Your Dealer with Information You Got Online

So now you know the invoice cost of the car you want to buy, the destination charge, the dealer hold back, and any kinds of rebates and incentives available on the car you're interested in buying. What next? Let's say you want to buy a car from a dealer, not through the Web. (I cover buying through the Web in the next section.) First, print everything out directly from the Web so that you have a sheaf of papers you can refer to. When you walk in with the printouts, the dealer will realize you know your business and won't try to pull a fast one on you. (Well, the dealer might *try* to pull a fast one, but won't be able to succeed.)

148

Check for Rebates and Dealer Incentives Before Buying

Another way to save hundreds or even thousands of dollars when buying your next car is to find out what kinds of rebates and dealer incentives are available; on the www.edmunds.com site, just click on **Incentives and Rebates**. Car manufacturers regularly offer incentives to dealers to push vehicles that don't sell that well. The dealer won't tell you about these incentives—and in fact, the dealer might not even tell the salespeople about the incentives. But if you know about them, you'll know to knock off the price of the incentive when bargaining. These incentives are often short-lived, so be sure to check the Incentives and Rebates page before every visit to a car dealer.

Also, figure out on a sheet of paper how much you're willing to pay for the car. Base it on the invoice price of the car. You should hold the line at 3% over invoice cost if you can—and if the car isn't very popular or new models are about to come out, try to get it at 2% or less over invoice cost. If you're looking to buy a hot-selling car, you might not be able to drive such a hard bargain, but it's worth a try. For cars that aren't moving fast, you should be able to bargain down to your 2%–3% figure. Also, when figuring the price you should pay for a car, be sure to consider any rebates or incentives.

Let's take an imaginary example. Say you're buying a new car called the Gralla GoGetter. The base invoice price is $24,500. The destination charge is $500. You want extras, such as air-conditioning, power steering, power windows, AM/FM stereo, and an engine (just kidding) that have a total invoice price of $3,000. You've decided you'll pay 3% over dealer costs for the car. The GoGetter isn't selling that well, so the Gralla Auto Company (GAC for short) offers a dealer incentive of $3,000. (The MSRP for the car and extras, by the way, is $31,000.) Here are the formulas and math you'd do to come up with the number you should agree to pay:

Base Invoice Price:	$24,500
+ Extras Invoice Price:	$3,000
+ Destination Charge:	$500
Total Dealer Cost:	**$28,000**

Total Dealer Cost:	$28,000
? Percent over Cost You'll Pay:	.03
Dealer's Profit:	**$840**
Total Dealer Cost:	$28,000
+ Dealer's Profit:	$840
Your Price:	**$28,840**
Your Price:	$28,840
–Dealer Incentive:	$3,000
Your Bottom Line:	**$25,840**

So there you have it. When you go into a dealer, be prepared to hold to your price of $25,840. The salesperson will probably tell you that the MSRP is $31,000 and that you're asking for an outrageous deal. But tell the salesperson that you know the invoice number, the destination charges, and the dealer incentive; you can even display your printouts if he or she doesn't believe you. Hold to your price. If you can't get it, walk out the door.

Will this strategy work? Yes, it will. I know from experience. I've tried it; it's how I bought my last new car. The salesperson and the dealer frothed at the mouth. They lied. They tried the good-salesperson, bad-salesperson trick ("I'd really like to give you a better price, but my boss back there with the rubber stanchion won't let me!"). And finally, they gave in. That's the power of the Web for you.

Step 4: Buy It on the Web

Maybe you're tired of dealing with car dealers and salespeople. And maybe you want another way to try to get the lowest price possible on a car. In that case, try buying your next car over the Web. It's actually much easier to buy a car on the Web than to buy one at a dealer. And after you make an agreement to buy, you don't actually pay over the Web. Instead, you'll go to the dealer and finish the deal as you normally would.

Figure Out the Cost of Trading In Your Used Car

Sometimes when you buy a new car, you'll want to trade in your old car instead of keeping it or selling it privately. If you choose to do that, be sure to agree on a price for your used car before agreeing to a price on your new car. And when selling to a dealer, find out the book value of your used car (see the next chapter, for how to do that). Then don't accept anything less than 3% under the book value from the dealer.

A number of sites let you buy cars over the Web. The most popular are Auto-by-Tel at www.autobytel.com, AutoWeb at www.autoweb.com, and Microsoft CarPoint at www.carpoint.msn.com. They all work similarly and are amazingly simple to use.

The first step is to use the Web as outlined here to figure out the price you want to pay. Next, if you want to test drive the car, go to a dealer—but don't buy the car; just test drive it. Then, when you know the price and you're happy with the test drive, head to one of the buying sites. From there, you enter your zip code and provide details about the car you want to buy—make, model, extras, colors, and the like. The following screenshot shows the form you fill out at Microsoft CarPoint. You put in information about yourself, such as name, address, phone number, and email address. Within a day or so, a dealer will contact you by phone or email with a price on the car you're interested in buying.

Here's the good news about the bids you'll get: They're no-haggle bids and are final offers, so you avoid the usual kind of *mishegas* (that's Yiddish for craziness) that happens when you go to a showroom. If you don't like the bids, you don't buy. It's that simple. When you put in a request, you're under no obligation to buy, so you don't lose anything by using these buying sites—and you might find a great deal.

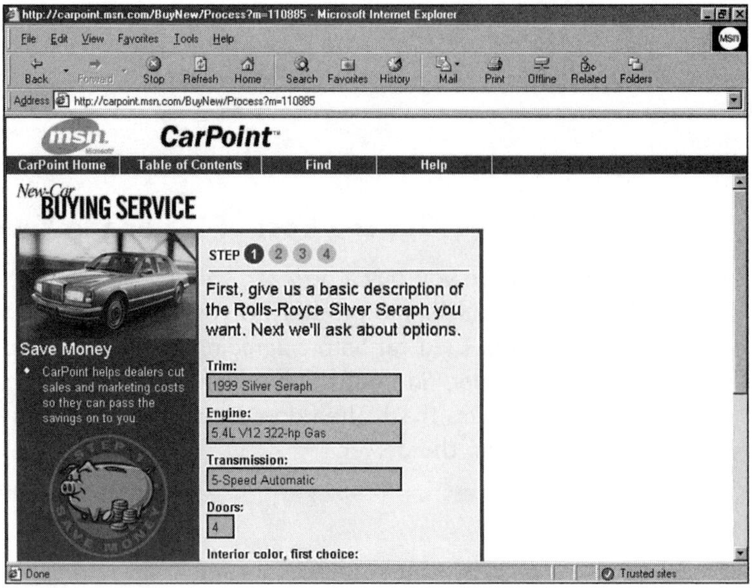

Here's the kind of form you fill out online when asking dealers to send you bids on a new car. Pictured here is the Microsoft CarPoint site asking for details about the new Rolls-Royce Silver Seraph I'm planning on buying...not in this lifetime!

Step 5: Get the Best Financing Deal on Your Car

If you're like most people, you don't have enough money socked away to pay cash for your new car. So you're going to have to finance your car. One option is to have the dealer finance it. Sometimes dealer financing can be the best deal, and sometimes not, so you'll probably want to shop around for the best financing deal before going to the dealer.

You can use the Web in one of two ways to get financing. You can do research to find out the best deals in your area for financing, or you can apply online for a car loan.

If you're looking to use the Web only for researching a car loan, you'll find that most of the Web buying sites have information about new-car loans. But I've found that the best site is a banking site: Bank Rate Monitor at www.bankrate.com. This site makes it a breeze to compare loans and offers useful tips and articles on car financing. Just fill in your state and area of the state you're in, and the site offers a side-by-side comparison of loan deals, as you can see pictured here. It's then up to you to contact the bank and get the loan. Note how much money this kind of comparison can save you—on the day I checked, the lowest rate in my area was 6.99%, and the highest, 9.50%, over a two-and-a-half point difference, which adds up to a lot of money.

Get Dealers to Match Your Lowest Price for a New Car

How's this for a switch: You decide how much you want to pay for a new car, and dealers scramble to meet your price. That's the idea behind Priceline.com at www.priceline.com. You head to the site, fill out a form describing the car you want and what you're willing to pay for it, and Priceline does the rest. It sends your price to car dealers in your area, and if any agree to meet your price, the car is yours. You pay Priceline only if you get the car at your price—and then the fee is a mere $25.

You can apply for a loan directly on the Web at CarFinance.com at www.carfinance.com. Applying is simple: Fill in the information about the loan you want and provide the necessary financial information about yourself—basically the same kind of information a bank asks for. There's no obligation to take out a loan when you apply, so you don't risk anything. If you're approved, you'll be notified and you can then decide whether to take the loan. You'll get a check in the mail, which you can take to the dealer to pay for a car.

Finding the best deal on a new car loan at www.bankrate.com.

153

The Best New Car Sites in Cyberspace

There are so many car sites in cyberspace that it seems you could spend your whole life visiting them all. Here are the best places to visit.

America Online Auto Center

KEYWORD CARS

If you're on America Online, you'll find that this area is helpful. It contains links to many useful auto sites within America Online and on the Internet. Because most of the information is available on the Internet, probably the best and most unique area here is the classified area, where you can look for used cars.

Auto-by-Tel

    http://www.autobytel.com

Auto-by-Tel is a must-visit site for anyone interested in buying a car through the Web. You can buy new and used cars here, and the selection is huge. Auto-by-Tel also offers reviews and specs. It's one-stop shopping: You can get insurance and financing from the site.

Autovantage

    http://www.autovantage.com

Here's another good site for those interested in buying a new or used car over the Web. You'll get reviews of new and used cars, and also get information about true dealer costs, so you'll know better what price you should pay for a car. All in all, it's a worthwhile site, especially if you want to see whether you can get a deal over the Web.

AutoWeb

    http://www.autoweb.com

If you're looking to buy your car over the Web, be sure to get a bid from here. Tell AutoWeb the car you want to buy and see what kind of bids you get from dealers. You can also get car financing, insurance, and other services from AutoWeb.

Car and Driver

    http://www.caranddriver.com

If you're a car aficionado, you'll want to visit this site. Its comprehensive reviews are written for people who love driving for its own sake, rather than from a purely consumer point of view. You'll find good buying guides and articles as well.

154

CarFinance.com

http://www.carfinance.com

Here's the place to find a car-financing deal on the Web. Select the state you're from, how much money you need, the car you want to buy, and similar information, and see what kind of loan you can get.

Carprice.com

http://www.carprice.com

Here's a site for getting the true invoice price of any car. Although not as good a site as Edmund's, reviewed shortly, Carprice does offer some excellent articles on topics such as negotiating the best deals and leasing tips.

cars.com

http://www.cars.com

Here's a solid, all-around site that offers good reviews, helpful pricing information, an area with classified ads where you can buy used cars, a loan calculator, and some useful general articles, such as understanding what a sticker price is. It's not good enough to make your first stop, but is worth a visit just to be sure you've covered all the bases.

carsdirect.com

http://www.carsdirect.com

This is a site with a twist—you buy your car directly through the site, instead of being directed to a dealer. And you see the price you'll pay upfront—when you select the make and model, you're told the price right then. Whereas there's some information here to help you decide which car to buy, it's not the most comprehensive. It's best to come to this site after you've decided the car you want to buy, and see whether it'll offer you a good deal. At press time, the areas the site served were limited to only a few cities, but it's expected to expand rapidly.

Car Talk

http://www.cartalk.com

Listeners to the best radio car show in the history of the universe—Car Talk, broadcast by National Public Radio to over 450 stations—will want to visit Tom and Ray Magliozzi (also Click and Clack, the Tappet brothers) on their Web site. You'll get here what you get on the radio—inspired lunacy mixed with superb car advice. These guys know their stuff, and I can speak from personal experience. They have an auto shop in my hometown, Cambridge, Massachusetts, and were able to fix a car problem that bedeviled many other mechanics—how to fix a car that often wouldn't start in rainy weather unless I hit the starter with a hammer. How they did it, I don't know, but they managed. In any event, stop here for entertainment and solid car advice.

Consumers Car Club

http://www.carclub.com

Useful reviews, the capability to buy cars directly over the Internet, helpful consumer information—that's what you'll get here. There are better overall sites, and better sites for consumer advice, but if you're looking to buy a car over the Web, put in your specs here and see what kind of dealer bids you get.

Edmund's

http://www.edmunds.com

When you want to find how much you should pay for a new car, Edmund's is *the* place to go. You'll get the most comprehensive pricing information, as well as good advice on how to use that information to get the best bargain. Edmund's also has good reviews and specs of cars, a discussion area, information about used cars, and much more. Anyone buying a car should visit here.

When Buying on the Web, Ask for Bids from Many Sites

When you use one of the auto-buying sites on the Web, you're under no obligation to buy a car when you ask for a bid. The different buying sites often send your requests to different dealers, so if you want to get bids from as many dealers as possible, go to as many auto-buying sites as you can and ask for bids.

GTE Superpages Consumer Guide

http://www.consumerguide.com

If you're trying to decide what car to buy or you want to compare several makes and models, here's the spot for you. For both new and used cars, you should head here first. The Superpages interactive car finder helps you narrow down your choices. And its reports on new and used cars are the most comprehensive and helpful you'll find online. You'll also find excellent articles on subjects such as how to negotiate your best deal.

Intellichoice

http://www.intellichoice.com

Intellichoice is a good site if you're looking for solid car reviews, good pricing information, and a nice touch that you won't find anywhere else. This site estimates the cost of ownership of a particular car over several years, taking into account not just what you'll pay for it but also the cost of gas, maintenance, insurance, and similar factors.

Microsoft CarPoint

http://www.carpoint.com

CarPoint is one of the better all-around car sites on the Internet, whether you're just researching a car or want to buy a car via the Web. CarPoint has information on new and used cars, useful buying guides, and good consumer articles offering tips on things such as test-driving cars and whether to buy a new or used car. If you want to buy a car on the Web, CarPoint is one of the must-visit sites.

Yahoo! Autos

http://www.autos.yahoo.com

The most popular index of the Web offers a solid, if unspectacular, car area. You'll find no-nonsense links to articles, and buying and pricing information. Probably the best part of the site, though, is the classified ad area where you can search for used cars.

The Least You Need to Know

➤ Before buying a new car, find out the true dealer cost at www.edmunds.com.

➤ Be sure to look for any rebates or special offers before bargaining with a dealer.

➤ Try to pay no more than about 3% over the true dealer cost of a car.

➤ If you're buying your car over the Web, get bids from as many sites as possible.

Chapter 13

Avoiding Clunkers and Lemons: Using the Internet to Help Buy a Used Car

In This Chapter

➤ How to do consumer research to find the best car for your budget

➤ Finding the book value of a used car

➤ Buying a used car over the Web

➤ Best used-car sites online

➤ How to sell a used car over the Internet

One of the best ways to save money on your next set of wheels is to buy a used car. But how can you be sure that you don't buy a lemon and that you pay the absolute minimum price? Unless you've been lucky enough to be able to afford to buy a new car every time you need new wheels, you've had to deal regularly with used-car salespeople—one of the few life forms lower on the evolutionary scale than garden slugs, and just about as appealing.

So what's a used-car buyer to do? Easy, head online. You can use the Internet and online services to get the best possible car at the lowest possible price. You use the Internet to buy a used car in much the same way as you do to buy a new car. (Refer to Chapter 12, "Hot Wheels: How to Research and Buy New Cars Online," for information on how to use the Internet to research and buy new cars.) You can use the Internet to research what you should buy and then to find out what you should pay for it. You can find out which used cars hold up best (and which don't), which hold on to their value the longest, which have the best service and repair records, and which are the best for your budget. You'll also be able to find out the "Blue Book" value for a used car—the generally accepted going rate for any used car. That way you won't overpay for that 5-year-old sports car you've been eyeing. You can also use the Internet to find the car itself and then either buy the car online or contact the seller and buy the car offline. (Check the information in the previous chapter on researching a new car; you can go to the same sites for information on older models.)

Finally, you can use the Internet to sell your car.

Getting the Best Deal on a Used Car

So if you're looking to buy or sell a used car, what are you waiting for? Get cracking! Follow these steps to get the best car at the best price or to sell your car easily for the most possible money.

Step 1: Go Online to Find the Best Car for Your Budget

You've checked your bank account—and no, you don't have the money to buy that new Alfa-Romero you've been salivating over, but still, you have enough money to buy something better than a 10-year-old Yugo that has about the same horsepower as your lawnmower. But what should you buy?

Start your used-car search by using the Internet to find the best car for you. If you already know the make and model of a car you're interested in, you can get more information about it online. Alternatively, if you don't have a clue about what make and model number to choose, but you have a budget in mind and know what kind of features you want in a car, you'll find that the Internet will help there as well.

Most of the sites covered in Chapter 12 that have information about new cars also offer information about used cars. Once again, your first stop should be the GTE Superpages Consumer Guide at www.consumerguide.com. From there, click on **Used Cars**. You can use the used-car guide both to research a specific model and to help you narrow down your choices.

If you already know the year, make, and model of the car you're interested in buying—because, for example, you've seen it advertised in a classified ad or have seen it on a dealer's lot—click on **Used Car Reports**. You'll then get the best reports on used cars in cyberspace. You'll get the rundown on the difference between several model years, a full review of the car, and what you should expect to pay for the used car, depending on its condition. But best for used-car buyers is the Recall/Repair record. Here's where you'll get what you *really* need to know about a used car: How reliable is the make and model, what kind of repairs can you expect, and, if applicable, the car's recall history. You'll get a full report on "trouble spots," what kind of parts break down, wear out, and are likely to need repairs. You'll also get the rundown on replacement costs and repair costs.

Get Advice on How Much Repairs Should Cost

Need a brake job or have to replace your radiator? That's the kind of thing you might run into after you buy a used car. It would be nice to know how much money you should expect to pay, even before you go to your local mechanic. The Web can help you out. The AutoJob portion of the `www.autodigest.com` site tells you how many hours common repair jobs should take. Find out how much your mechanic charges per hour, add in the cost of parts—and you then will be able to know ahead of time how much you should pay.

If you're at the beginning of your search and don't yet have a year, make, and model number, click on the **Interactive Car Finder**. You fill in information such as the price range you're willing to pay, how old a car you're willing to buy, and other factors that are important to you, such as performance or economy. You then get a list of cars that match your description. You can do side-by-side comparisons of them. And then when you narrow it down, you can get the full rundown of the used car, as described earlier.

Another excellent site is AutoConnect at `www.autoconnect.com`, a site that specializes in used cars. You answer an incredible number of questions about what you're looking for in a used car—everything from price to performance, safety, and much more—and you'll get a list of years, makes, and model numbers. Shown here are some of the questions you'll answer. You'll also get a basic report about each car. After you've narrowed your choices down at this site, I suggest heading to the GTE Superpages Consumer Guide to get more information, such as recall and repair records.

Worth a visit is the area of the site that lets you compare cars on just about any feature you can name—everything from price to fuel economy to headroom, performance, safety record, and technical specifications such as horsepower, type of engine, and whether the car is front-wheel, rear-wheel, or four-wheel drive. AutoConnect is a great place to visit when you've narrowed down your choices to two, three, or four makes and models and want to see how they stack up against one another.

*At AutoConnect at
www.autoconnect.com,
you'll get step-by-step
advice on choosing the
best used car for your
needs.*

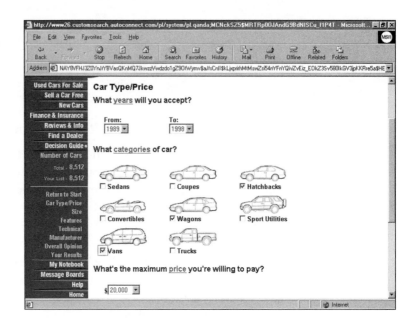

Get Inside Advice on the Best Late-Model Used Cars

Let's say you can't afford a new car, but you do have the cash for a late-model used one. Which one should you buy? The used-car buying section of the GTE Superpages Consumer Guide has the insider tips you need to get the best deal. From the used-car section of the site, click on **How Do I Shop for a Used Car?** and then click on **Best Late Model Buy**. You'll get recommendations on the best late-model cars to buy.

The site also has a useful area where you can calculate the cost of a car loan. And AutoConnect lets you locate used-car dealers near you. Finally, if you're interested in selling your car, you can use the site to sell your car as well. See the section "There's Gold in Them Thar Wheels: Selling Your Used Car over the Internet," later in the chapter, for more information on how to use the Internet to help sell your used car.

Step 2: Play It by the Book—Find Out the Book Value of the Used Car

Figuring out the value of a used car is simple. Many Internet sites will provide it for you. But the best one, by far, is Kelley Blue Book at www.kbb.com, shown here. At most sites, you can describe the year, make, and model of the used car you're interested in. Now, you might think that should be all you need to determine the price of a used car. That's what I thought. But nooooo, this site isn't content with that level of detail. Instead, you provide much more information. For example, you also supply the car's mileage and check off the car's extras, such as air-conditioning, automatic transmission, and more than a dozen other extras, because those factors alter the price of the car. More amazing, still: You also enter your zip code. That's because the same used car can sell for different prices in different parts of the country. For example, a used 1993 Lexus SC-400 Sport Coupe 2D sells for $2,450 more in California than it sells for in Massachusetts, according to Kelley the last time that I checked the site. That's those car-crazy Californians for you, I guess.

Use this price as a guideline when looking at a car and be prepared to make adjustments up or down, depending on the condition of the car and on how desperately you want to buy it.

If you're buying a new car and want to see what kind of trade-in you should expect to get for your used car, then click on **What's My Car Worth?**. You'll find the price you can expect the dealer to pay for it.

What's a used car really worth? Figure that out at the Kelley Blue Book site at www.kbb.com.

The Kelley Blue Book site isn't the only site on the Internet that tells you the price of used cars. Another is the Edmund's site at www.edmunds.com. Edmund's isn't as accurate as the Kelly Blue Book, though, because Edmund's doesn't take into account things such as the area of the country where you'll be buying the car. It does, however, tell you how much to adjust the price up or down based on the car's mileage. So be sure when trying to get an accurate price to go to the mileage adjustment section.

Although the Kelley Blue Book might be more accurate, you'll still want to go Edmund's to see the price Edmund's gives for the car you're considering buying. That way, you'll have a range of prices to consider. And better still, print out the lower of the two prices and take it to the dealer or individual from whom you're buying the car. You can say that this price is the one you want to pay. This tactic might or might not work—but it certainly can't hurt to try.

Read a Comprehensive Guide on the Edmund's Site to Buying and Selling a Used Car

Edmund's has a great guide for anyone interested in buying or selling a used car. It covers everything from pricing a car to evaluating a car to negotiating with a dealer. You'll find it at the Edmund's site at www.edmunds.com. Click the **Buyers Advice** section in the used-car area and then click the **Comprehensive Guide to Buying and Selling a Used Car** link.

The Edmund's site is useful for more than just finding the price of a used car. It also offers plenty of advice about used cars, full reviews, and ratings of any car you're considering. Edmund's rates every car on a scale of 1 to 10 for features such as safety, reliability, performance, comfort, and value. And it gives an overall rating for the car as well.

You can also get links to buy used cars from the site. When you're pricing a car in which you're interested, you can type in your zip code and you'll get a list of cars available. You'll actually be sent over to the Auto-by-Tel site (reviewed later in this chapter) when you type in the zip code.

Step 3: Use the Web to Find a Used Car

The Internet is chock full of sites that offer classified ads where you can buy used cars. Turn to Chapter 10, "Classified Information: Getting the Most Out of Classified

Ads on the Internet," for a list of classified sites, as well as advice on how to buy at them. Classified ads are a good bet for finding cars when you're looking to buy from an individual rather than a dealer. But looking in classified ads is a hit-and-miss affair. Although you can look in general classified-ad sections online, your better bet in the long run might be to go to car sites, which usually have a much wider selection of used cars than do most classified sites.

AutoConnect at `www.autoconnect.com` is a good place to start. Type your zip code, describe the kind of car you're looking for (such as by make and model, price, and year), and you'll get a list of matching cars, information about the cars, and contact information for sellers. Amazingly, AutoConnect also tells you how far away the seller is. Microsoft CarPoint at `www.carpoint.com` offers used-car classifieds with similar searching features. At both sites, when you see a car you're interested in, you can contact the seller the traditional way—by telephone or visiting—or you send them email.

Figure Out Your Monthly Used-Car Payments

When buying a used car, what matters to you as much as the selling price of the car is how much the loan will cost you—in other words, how much money you're going to pay every month for your car loan (if you don't pay in cash) and the total price you'll pay for the car when you take into account the interest on the loan. How can you find that out? Head over to the Bank Rate Monitor site at `www.bankrate.com`. In addition to calculating the cost of the loan (based on different interest rates), this site tells you the current average car-loan interest rate and enables you to compare different loan deals. It's also a good place to shop for a loan—you'll be able to take out a loan straight from the site, an especially good idea because this site also reports on the lowest loan rates in your state.

Auto-by-Tel at `www.autobytel.com` and AutoWeb at `www.autoweb.com` let you do more than just find used cars—you also use the sites to contact the owners. In both instances, when you're interested in a used car, you fill out a form, which is sent to the owner via email, saying you're interested in looking at the car. You can even schedule a specific day and time. Auto-by-Tel also offers a 72-hour money-back guarantee—if you buy a used car that you find on the site and then decide you don't want it, you can return the car for a full refund within 72 hours.

Best Sites for Buying Used Cars Online

A lot of places online list used cars. Here are the best sites to check out. In addition, many sites that specialize in classified ads have a used-car section. For a list of the best classified sites, turn to Chapter 10.

Auto-by-Tel

http://www.autobytel.com

This popular car-buying site is good for buying used cars as well as new ones. Auto-by-Tel not only has an extremely large selection of cars for sale but also provides reviews, specifications, and links to other car sites, such as Edmund's and Kelley Blue Book for used-car pricing. You can also get insurance and financing on this site. And you buy directly from the site itself. The following figure shows what the site displays when you search for a car near your home.

Buy a car close to home: Auto-by-Tel lists models of used cars for sale within a certain distance of your home.

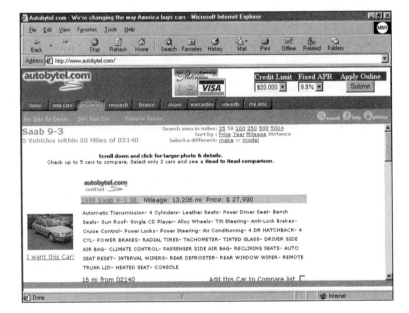

Use the `rec.autos.marketplace` Newsgroup to Buy or Sell a Used Car

Web sites aren't the only places on the Internet where you can buy or sell a used car. You can also use Internet newsgroups—public discussion bulletin boards—to buy and sell used cars as well. The best one is `rec.autos.marketplace`, which has hundreds of messages from people looking to buy and sell cars. It's all free—you don't pay anything to post a message or to respond to someone. For information on how to get to and use newsgroups, turn to Chapter 8, "Have I Got a Deal for You!"

AutoConnect

http://www.autoconnect.com

AutoConnect is a great place to find a used car. It's easy to search for precisely the car you want. Each used car you look at has a link to the Kelley Blue Book valuation so that you can check the car's book value. AutoConnect also includes links to recalls and safety ratings information.

Autovantage

http://www.autovantage.com

In addition to offering used cars for sale, Autovantage provides reviews of used cars. Its advice isn't nearly as comprehensive as other sites, so don't rely on the reviews here. If you find a used car you like in Autovantage's classified listing, you must contact the dealer and make the arrangements offline.

AutoWeb

http://www.autoweb.com

Here's one of the sites where you can actually buy a car over the Web. The process can't be any simpler: Tell the site the car you want to buy, and you then get bids from dealers. The site also has links to much useful information for used-car buyers, such as to the Kelley Blue Book value, to a loan calculator, and to information about recalls. You can also get car financing, insurance, and other services here.

CarPoint

```
http://www.carpoint.com
```

CarPoint focuses more on new cars than used ones, so for buying used cars, it isn't as comprehensive a site as AutoConnect is. But CarPoint has a good classified area where you can search for a used car to buy. A helpful feature is that you can limit your search to used cars for sale within your area code. You don't actually buy the car at the site. Rather, it points you to a dealer who has the car; you then buy it in the traditional way.

cars.com

```
http://www.cars.com
```

Here's a site with a very good classified area for buying used cars. In addition, you'll find reviews, pricing information, a loan calculator, and useful articles.

Yahoo! Autos

```
http://www.autos.yahoo.com
```

Here's a classified site where you can search for used cars. Some articles and related information are also available, notably used car prices from Edmunds.com. But the truth is, you'd be better off going directly to Edmunds for the information. The reason to come here is to search the used-car classifieds.

Best Sites for Getting Information About Used Cars

Most of the sites I covered in the previous chapter that sell or provide information about new cars do the same for used cars. Here are the best of the sites that provide information about used cars. Also check out the used-car buying sites, reviewed earlier in this chapter, because many of them also offer information about buying used cars.

Edmund's

```
http://www.edmunds.com
```

This site isn't as good as Kelley's Blue Book for getting the most accurate used-car prices, but Edmund's is worth checking so that you have two prices when going to buy a car. Edmund's also offers excellent car reviews, links to sites selling used cars, and a superb guide for advice on how to buy used cars.

GTE Superpages Consumer Guide

```
http://www.consumerguide.com
```

If you are trying to decide what car to buy or you want to compare several makes and models, here's the spot for you. For both new and used cars, you should head to GTE

Superpages first. The interactive car finder helps you narrow down your choices, and the reports on new and used cars are the most comprehensive and helpful anywhere online. You'll also find excellent articles on subjects such as how to negotiate the best deal.

Kelley Blue Book

```
http://www.kbb.com
```

Here's the bible for finding how much a used car is worth. Don't even try to find a better site for this type of information. Kelley also offers pricing information for new cars, although in this area the Kelley site is not as comprehensive as Edmund's, covered in the previous chapter.

There's Gold in Them Thar Wheels: Selling Your Used Car over the Internet

You can use the Internet to sell a used car as well. (Nice to know that on occasion it can be used to help you *make* money, not just spend it, isn't it?) Here's how.

Get a Free "Lemon Check" to Be Sure Your Used Car Isn't a Lemon

The AutoWeb site at www.autoweb.com has a free lemon-check area to help you avoid buying a lemon. Go to the lemon-check area of the site and then type in the vehicle ID number (sometimes referred to as a VIN) found on the dashboard of the car or in its title documents. The site checks a database to see whether that VIN is a known "lemon"—a car that has had a problem so severe that it was bought back by the manufacturer, and then later resold.

The first thing you'll need to do is determine a price for your car. If you've gotten this far in the chapter, you already know where to turn—to the Kelley Blue Book site at www.kbb.com and the Edmund's site at www.edmunds.com. Be sure to go to both of them and to use as your guide the *higher* of the two prices. In fact, you'll probably want to state a listing price that is a bit over that price to start, to give yourself a little wiggle room when bargaining. Figure on adding about $200 to $300 to your absolute rock-bottom price. Of course, if the person looking for a used car has a copy of this book, no doubt he or she will offer the lower of the two prices. Hey, don't blame me. I just offer the advice.

After you set a price, it's time to figure out where to sell. You have two choices here: You can either head to a classified site, or you can go to a site that specializes in selling used cars, which I covered earlier in this chapter. Check out Chapter 10 for information on how to sell at classified sites and on the best sites for placing a classified ad.

Although some car-selling sites accept cars only from dealers, many sites, including AutoConnect at www.autoconnect.com, Auto-by-Tel at www.autobytel.com, AutoWeb at www.autoweb.com, and Autovantage at www.autovantage.com, welcome private sellers. However, you have to register at the site to sell your car there. Some sites let you advertise your car for free, whereas others charge for the privilege. AutoWeb, for example, charges $19.95.

When you get a live one on the hook and you're ready to sell, it's time to get the money and turn over the car. All the services and classified sites leave the details of the transaction to the seller and buyer.

The Least You Need to Know

➤ Use the Internet to find the repair record of a used–car model before buying.

➤ Find the book value of a used car at Kelley's Blue Book at www.kbb.com before buying.

➤ If you're buying a used car on the Web, check multiple sites for the best selection.

➤ Use the GTE Superpages Consumer Guide at www.consumerguide.com for advice on the best used cars to buy.

➤ Use a loan calculator on a Web site to figure out the real cost of buying your car.

Chapter 14

That's Entertainment: Buying Books, Tapes, Movies, and CDs

In This Chapter

➤ Buying books on the Internet

➤ Buying CDs and tapes on the Internet

➤ Buying movies on the Internet

Books. Movies. CDs. So much entertainment, so little time. Shopping on the Internet is a great way to pay a low price for your favorite titles—and the best way to find little-known or out-of-the-way books, records, or videos that aren't available at the local mall or downtown store. Here's how to find the best deals in cyberspace.

As the Bookworm Turns: Finding and Buying Books on the Internet

Buying books over the Web practically single-handedly launched the Internet shopping phenomenon. One day, it seems, no one bothered to buy anything online; the next day the bookseller Amazon.com came online, and the Internet hasn't been the same since—the gold rush was on.

If you buy nothing else over the Internet, you should consider buying books there. It's easy, the books are cheap, and you won't get paper cuts. I love browsing through bookstores, and I live in Cambridge, Massachusetts, which may well be home to more bookstores per capita than anywhere in the world—and yet even *I* regularly buy books over the Internet. I still shop at my local bookstores, but they don't carry everything—and online bookstores do. When I'm looking for an obscure book, I immediately turn to the Web. I've bought new hard-to-find books, and I've had companies do searches for me to find out-of-print books. And if you live in an area that doesn't have as many bookstores as Cambridge has, you'll probably use the Internet to order quite a few of your books.

You can use the Internet to find and buy new books, used books, remaindered books, and rare and antiquarian books. Here's how.

Get 'em While They're Hot: Buying New Books on the Internet

Book-buying sites are the easiest places to shop on the Internet. Surf over to one, check out the featured books, or search and browse. Then with a few clicks, you can send a book on its way to you. You'll find conveniences such as shopping carts and one-click shopping. (For more information about these kinds of services, turn to Chapter 1, "Getting Started on Your Online Shopping Expedition.") You'll also find lists of featured books and special offers.

Make Extra Money

If you have a personal Web site, here's the easiest way yet devised to make some extra cash: Put links from your site to sites such as Barnes and Noble and Amazon.com. Those sites will pay you for every book someone buys from a link on your site. The percentage you get varies from 5% to 15%. Just head to the book sites to sign up. You won't find a simpler way to earn moolah.

You'll get discounts of up to 40% on new books at book-buying sites, which certainly is a big reason for buying. But you also have to pay for shipping and handling, which eats into your discount. If you're buying multiple books, though, you can cut down on shipping costs. However, if your entire order isn't in stock and you ask the seller to ship the books as they become available, you'll have to pay full shipping costs for each book, which can add up to big bucks for big books. Instead, tell the site to hold off on shipping your order until all the books are in stock. That way, you'll save big-time.

The two most popular sites for buying new books are Amazon at www.amazon.com and Barnes and Noble at www.bn.com. Their prices, offerings, and shipping rates are nearly identical. One of the main benefits that online bookstores such as these have over traditional bookstores is the sheer volume of titles they carry. Last time I checked, Amazon boasted that it had three million titles.

If you already know what book you plan to buy, it doesn't make a whit of difference whether you buy the book at Amazon, Barnes and Noble, or any of the other dozens of book-buying sites. After you've decided what book to buy, all you really care about is getting the best price. So if you know the book, shop around for the best price.

To turn a phrase, a book is a book is a book is a book (or is that a book by any other name would smell as sweet?). The book you buy at Amazon is the same as the one you buy at Barnes and Noble. And prices on the main sites are all pretty similar. So why should it matter which store you buy from?

What sets these sites apart from one another is the kind of extra services they offer—services such as reader reviews and ratings, recommendations for other books to read, discussion areas, and the like. Here's where Amazon shines. Its reader reviews and ratings are exceptionally helpful. And when you read the reviews, you'll also find links to similar books, or books by the same author. The site will also recommend books to you, based on books that you've already bought there, as shown in the following figure. And you can also sign up to receive email alerts about books and subjects you're interested in. Although other book sites offer similar recommendation services, Amazon's the best at it. Check out the section "Best Book-Buying Sites in Cyberspace" later in this chapter for a list of other Internet booksellers.

Amazon.com offers the best book recommendations online. Here's a section of the site that recommends books based on books you've already bought.

Using Book-Buying Bargain Agents

With so many bookstores on the Net, doing comparison shopping can be tough—you could wear out your mouse trying to find the best deal on new books. Make it easy on yourself: Use a book-buying agent to find the best price on the Internet. You tell the agent the book you want to buy, and it then goes out and checks many book-buying sites simultaneously, reporting back to you on the deals it finds. You then choose the best deal.

The best of the bunch is Acses at www.acses.com. It searches through 25 bookstores for your book, and when it reports back, includes the *total* price you'll pay, taking into account shipping and handling charges. It also shows shipping time. Just click on a link to jump directly to a page from which you can buy the book. Check out the section "Best Book-Buying Sites in Cyberspace" later in this chapter for a list of other book-buying agents.

Oldies but Goodies: Buying Out-of-Print, Used, and Rare Books Online

What's a Shopping Agent?

Shopping agents are sites or software that head out to the Internet, check multiple sites, and then find the best deal for you. Various kinds of agents scour the Internet, including some that specifically search for the best book prices.

The Web is great for buying new books. But where it really shines is in finding out-of-print, rare, and used books. Let's face it; most good bookstores have a decent selection of new books. But where do you go when you need to find an out-of-print title?

Many sites cater to helping you find these rare, old gems. For a full list, see "Best Book-Buying Sites in Cyberspace" later in this chapter.

Two kinds of sites can help you find used, rare, and out-of-print books on the Internet. In one, you do an online search for the book, much as you would at an online bookstore such as www.amazon.com or www.bn.com. The site then does a search and finds the books you're looking for. The best of these sites is Bibliofind at www.bibliofind.com. It searches many bookstores that specialize in used, rare, and out-of-print books and then shows you every copy of the book in every store—including the price, condition of the book, and shipping costs. How good is Bibliofind? I searched for books by a little-known (even in his time), long-forgotten novelist from earlier in this century, named Hervey White. I immediately found several original editions of his books through the site. By way of contrast, years ago, before the advent of the Internet, I spent months scouring the used and antiquarian bookstores of Boston and Cambridge before I found a single book of his—and in less than three minutes at Bibliofind, I found several of them. Just one more example of how the Internet has changed the world for the better.

Use Amazon to Find Out-of-Print Books

The Amazon.com site offers a simple method for finding out-of-print books. Head to the site and type the name of the book (or author) you're looking for. If Amazon has a record of the book and it's out-of-print, the company will do a free search for you. To initiate a free search, just proceed to check out as if you're buying a book. Then tell Amazon to search for the book. Within one or two weeks, if Amazon can find the book at a used-book dealer, you'll get an email telling you the price of the book. If you're interested, order it. If you're not, don't bother, and you won't have spent a penny.

In the other kind of site for hard-to-find books, you send email to the site describing the book you want. The site then does a search for you, and if it finds a book, lets you know the cost. Because there are enough of these sites around, I suggest you not pay an up-front finder's fee. Do business only with sites that do book searches for free.

Finding Remainder Books on the Internet

If you're a book fan, no doubt you've seen books being sold at amazing discounts—sometimes up to 90% off the list price. Often you'll find a small red or black mark at the bottom of the book. These books are "remainder" books, which is a polite way of saying that the publisher printed too many copies, and is looking for a dirt-cheap way to dump them.

You can easily find these bargain books on the Web. The best place I've found for remainders is Book Express at www.bookexpress.com. It has thousands and thousands of remainder books, available at top discounts. Sometimes you'll find remainders at other online stores as well. They're usually in the section called Bargain Books.

Best Book-Buying Sites in Cyberspace

The Internet is home to hundreds, if not thousands, of book-buying sites. You'll find online sites of book chains, individual bookstores, as well as book sites that exist only on the Internet. Here are the best, divided into three sections: those that specialize in new books; those that specialize in out-of-print, rare, used, and remainders; and book-buying agent sites.

Top Sites for Buying New Books

Looking for the latest new hardcover bestseller, a new paperback thriller, or any other new book? Here's where to go.

Amazon

`http://www.amazon.com`

Here's the site that started it all and is still, for my money (and I've spent a good amount of money there), the best book-buying site you'll find. It offers a huge selection, great advice, good discounts, and more help and features than any other book site you'll find. It's also cleanly designed and has expanded into selling CDs, drugstore items, and gifts as well. It even has an auction site. And if you're interested in buying books from other countries, Amazon has a site for buying books from the United Kingdom (`www.amazon.co.uk`) and Germany (`www.amazon.de`). Amazon is always my first stop when I'm out to buy books.

Harry Potter Fans Can Buy the U.K. Versions First

If you have a kid under the age of 13 in your house, you may well know of the Harry Potter series—the superb, award-winning children's books about the witch-in-training, young Harry Potter. The books are published in the United Kingdom before they are in the U.S., so Harry Potter fans often have to wait months before the newest book comes out. Ah, but not if they shop on the Internet. You can buy books all over the world on the Internet, from sites such as Amazon's U.K. site at `www.amazon.co.uk`. So you can buy the Harry Potter books before they hit the U.S. shores. That's what I do every time a new Harry Potter book comes out—and the truth is, I read them and enjoy them just as much as my son Gabe does.

Barnes and Noble

`http://www.bn.com`

The 800-pound gorilla of the bricks-and-mortar book-buying world has a Web site that rivals Amazon's. With a huge selection of books and a slew of features including chats and author interviews, it's trying to catch up to the kind of service that Amazon offers. Barnes and Noble is not quite there yet, but I always check in to see whether its deals are better than Amazon's. As often as not, they are.

Books.com

http://www.books.com

Here's another solid book site with good discounts. Last time I checked in, the site had several book excerpts you could read online as well as a number of author interviews. And Books.com has daily news reports about books and bookselling.

Borders.com

http://www.borders.com

Yet another book behemoth has entered cyberspace. Its site is not nearly as well-designed or as easy to use as Amazon's or Barnes and Noble's. Still, the prices are competitive, and the remainder section is worth a visit.

City Lights

http://www.citylights.com

Among the heroes of my adolescent youth were the beat writers of a generation before mine: Allen Ginsberg, Jack Kerouac, and Lawrence Ferlinghetti, among others. They all were published by the City Lights publisher in San Francisco and spent time at the City Lights bookstore there. When I graduated from college, I headed across the country on my own hejira to the City Lights Mecca. I still get to San Francisco regularly, but don't get to visit the City Lights bookstore as much as I'd like. So I occasionally visit it on the Web. True to its roots, the City Lights site features the works of the great beat writers as well as many other unique books. You'll also find excellent historical material about the beats and the bookstore itself. So pop on some cool shades, put Miles Davis' *Kind of Blue* on the stereo, and head to this site. You'll swear you can see people in black berets strolling across your screen.

FatBrain

http://www.fatbrain.com

If you're looking for computer books, FatBrain is a great place to go. It has just about any computer book you can imagine, offers good discounts, and even offers email alerts about books. For the techie crowd, FatBrain is a must-visit.

WordsWorth

http://www.wordsworth.com

Cambridge, Massachusetts, where I live, might well be the book capital of the United States. And when I go out to a bookstore (which is quite often), I usually go to WordsWorth, an independently owned bookstore right in the center of Harvard Square. WordsWorth also has an online site, and it offers its usual good discounts online.

177

Top Book-Buying Bargain Agents

So many bookstores, so little time. Instead of heading all over the Internet yourself, use book-buying agents to find the best deals. Here's a list of the best agents.

Acses

http://www.acses.com

Acses is the best book-buying bargain agent on the Internet. It searches the most sites, its search engine is the simplest to use, and unlike other agents, it shows you the *true* price you'll pay for your books, including shipping costs, and shipping times. Acses searches for both out-of-print and in-print books. And it also searches for the best deals on videos and music, so you can save money on those as well.

Best BookBuys

http://www.bestbookbuys.com

Here's an easy-to-use bargain agent that searches a number of bookstores and shows you all the prices. One good thing about the site is that it also searches some non-bookstore sites that sell books. Sometimes these sites have the lowest price on the books you want. Best BookBuys also has giveaways (a Palm IIIx personal digital assistant when I last checked) and finds special deals on books.

BookFinder

http://www.bookfinder.com

BookFinder is one of the better book-buying agents on the Internet. You can use it to find only new books, only used or out-of-print books, or both at the same time. BookFinder doesn't search as many sites as other agents, however.

Top Used, Bargain, and Out-of-Print Book Sites

There's a world of books beyond what's just come out this week—or what's still in print. You can use the Internet to find used and out-of-print books, as well as bargains. Here's where to go.

AbeBooks

http://www.abebooks.com

AbeBooks is a great site for out-of-print and hard-to-find books. It searches many booksellers simultaneously and gives you the choice of which one to contact and buy from. It searches international bookstores as well, and you can choose individual countries for a search. Collectors can search for first or signed editions, or for books with their original dust jackets intact.

Bibliofind

http://www.bibliofind.com

You want to find an old, used, or rare book? Most likely, you'll find it here. The site claims to have records of six million such books offered by 2,000 booksellers around the world. I've looked here for a lot of oddball and out-of-print books. I've found every one—and usually, more than one copy from more than one store so that you can price shop as well. Bibliofind is the best place to find used and out-of-print books on the Internet.

BookExpress

http://www.bookexpress.com

Bargain hunters, head here. It's the best site I've found for remainder books—dirt-cheap closeouts and books that publishers are looking to unload. You can get up to 90% off the list price in some cases. Just be prepared to spend some time looking.

Play, Maestro! Buying CDs and Tapes Online

Whether your tastes run to rock, pop, classical, jazz, blues, folk, the tasteless and bizarre (yes, Yanni fans, that means *you!*), or any other kind of music, you can buy it online. Not only can you get deep discounts online, but you can also listen to music clips before you buy. Even if you don't buy music online, you should check out CD sites before heading to your local music store. Online, you can listen to music clips and decide whether you really want that new CD from Weird Al Yancovic. You can listen to most of the clips you'll find online with software called RealPlayer. Head to www.realnetworks.com to get the software you need.

Techno Talk

What's "Streaming Audio"?

At most music sites, when you want to listen to a music clip, it'll be in a format called RealAudio, which is a streaming-audio format. Streaming means that you can start listening to the music clip before the whole thing downloads to your computer. Otherwise, you would have to wait several minutes before you could start listening to the music. Some other music formats, such as MPEG, aren't streaming, and so although the quality might be higher, you can be in for a real wait before you can listen to the music.

CD sites have attempted to gussy themselves up with bells and whistles as the book sites have. In general, they haven't succeeded. For example, CDNow offers a music adviser that recommends CDs to you, based on musicians that you like. I found it to be useless. I told it I like Miles Davis, and it recommended nine records—eight of them were by, you guessed it, Miles Davis! As my daughter would say: Well, *duh*!

You'll find two kinds of CD sites online: those that sell new CDs and CD-buying clubs. Before I go into detail about this, here's a brief primer on how you can sample music before buying.

Easy Listening Guide: How to Get Free Music Samples Before You Buy

One of the best reasons to shop over the Internet is that you can often try out the goods before deciding whether to buy them. When it comes to CDs, you can frequently listen to sizable portions of every single song on the CD, over the Internet.

So how can this be? Won't you soil the merchandise? What about the you-touch-it, you-buy-it ethos that prevails in so many retail stores? And how can you get free samples like this over the wires that make up the Internet?

You can get these free samples because they're all just a bunch of bits and bytes that are sent from a computer somewhere on the Internet to your own computer. You'll be able to listen right on your computer—you won't actually pop a CD into your CD player.

Here's everything that a cybersavvy shopper needs to know to take advantage of these free samples.

Listening to music samples is pretty simple, but you do need special software. The most popular software programs for this application are RealPlayer or RealSystem G2 (RealSystem G2 is the newer one, and so the one you should get). Pretty much any audio site that lets you listen to or view free samples will let you use RealPlayer or RealSystem. Head to the RealNetworks site at `www.realnetworks.com` and download a copy. Then just follow the instructions for installing it. It's free; you won't have to pay a penny for the software unless you want a version with some extra bells and whistles. Take my advice, though: You don't need the bells, and you certainly don't need the whistles. Stay with the free versions.

You can also listen to music with the Windows Media Player, which comes with many versions of Windows. You can also download it for free from the Microsoft site at `www.microsoft.com`. And there is a lot of other music formats that require special music players, such as one called Liquid Audio. For all of them, you'll need special software—and it's almost always available for free.

When you have that software installed and you're browsing a music site, you'll just have to click on the music you want to listen to. Then, voilà! In a few seconds, you'll be listening. After you check out the samples, you can decide whether to buy. As a bonus, you can use this software to watch the latest music videos at the MTV site (www.mtv.com).

Get Ready for MP3 Madness

The latest music craze to hit the Internet is a special music format called MP3. Files in that format are of a very high quality—in fact, they're almost as good as CD quality. Better yet, the files aren't that big, and so don't take a very long time to download. To listen to MP3 files, you'll need a special MP3 player. There's a lot of them out there. My favorite is called WinAmp. You can get it at the ZDNet Software Library at www.hotfiles.com, along with many other MP3 players.

There's one problem with MP3 files—they're very controversial. Many MP3 files you'll find on the Internet are *pirated*—pirated files have been recorded illegally, and are illegal to distribute because they violate the recording artist's and recording company's copyrights. Because of this, record companies and many recording artists don't like MP3 files.

You Can Listen to MP3 Files on a Walkman-Like Device

Here's one more reason that MP3 files are popular: You can download them to your computer, and then transfer them to a small, Walkman-like device, and listen to them wherever and whenever you want. With these devices, you can mix-and-match your favorite songs. The first one out there was called the Rio, but there are others as well.

There are, however, sites where you can download legal MP3 files, and you can even buy individual songs in that format, or entire albums in that format. Two of the best sites for doing this are www.mp3.com and www.goodnoise.com.

Buying New CDs and Tapes Online

Buying a new CD or tape online couldn't be easier: Find the album you want, maybe listen to a few tracks, and then buy it. Case closed. You'll, of course, have to pay shipping costs—and sales tax if applicable. You'll find online sites of big retailers such as Tower Records, at www.towerrecords.com as well as Internet-only sites such as CDNow at www.cdnow.com.

What's a Plug-In?

No, it's not a new electrical gadget for your wall outlet. When you're shopping on the Internet, you might come across a site that requires you to have special software to look at something or do something—to play a game, perhaps, or to see a video or listen to music. That special software is called a plug-in because it plugs in to your Web browser. (These geeky programmers certainly do have a clever way with words, don't they?) RealPlayer and RealSystem G2 are two examples of plug-ins. But there is a lot more of them as well. Here are a few you might want. The QuickTime plug-in (www.apple.com) enables you to view videos, and the Shockwave plug-in enables you to view special animations and play games (www.macromedia.com). For the latest list of up-to-date plug-ins, go to one of the popular download sites on the Internet, such as the ZDNet Software Library at www.hotfiles.com.

Obviously, the CD you buy is the same at any site, so you'll do well to shop around before placing an order. For reasons not at all clear to me, the prices of CDs seem to vary much more from site to site than do the prices of books. For example, when I shopped around for Lucinda Williams's album *Car Wheels on a Gravel Road* shortly after it was released, I found a difference of about $4 between the CD sites—a low of $11.88 on the CDNow site at www.cdnow.com versus $15.79 at Tunes.com at www.tunes.com. That's a whopping difference of 25%. Other sites I checked ranged somewhere between the two. Unfortunately, you can't count on using a bargain-shopping agent for CDs. The few that exist don't check enough sites to be worthwhile. You'd do best to do your own comparison shopping. Also, when checking for CD prices, be sure to check in at online malls and department stores such as Wal-Mart at www.wal-mart.com. Sometimes the prices at these general-shopping sites are better than the prices at the dedicated music sites.

Save Money and Buy Used CDs over the Internet

Bargain hunter, if you really want to make your music dollar go the furthest, then you'll want to buy used CDs instead of new ones. There's a great site to get used CDs over the Internet: CD Bargains at www.cdbargains.com. It has a large selection of used CDs, which you can get at bargain-basement prices—some as low as $5 and $6, and most for under $9.

Check out the section later in this chapter, the "Best CD Sites in Cyberspace."

CD Club-Hopping on the Internet

If you're a heavy-duty music fan, and most of your disposable income seems to go toward buying music, then you should consider joining a CD club. The best-known club with an online site is Columbia House. Believe me, you've seen Columbia House. It seems to run ads in every magazine in existence.

The pitch at all CD clubs is generally the same. You get to choose a dozen or so CDs for free or practically free. Then you agree to buy a certain number of CDs within the next year or two at club prices. If you buy a lot of CDs—and if your musical tastes run toward fairly common and not-too-offbeat artists— then these sites can save you big money. But if your musical tastes are a bit off the beaten track, the clubs probably won't carry what you like. The two CD clubs on the Internet worth checking out are Columbia House at www.columbiahouse.com and BMG Music Service at www.bmgmusicservice.com.

How to Figure Out Which CD Club Is Best for You

The CD clubs on the Internet offer CDs at different prices. Deciding which one to join can be tough, but the CD Club Web Server at www.cd-clubs.com can help. Type an artist or a title, and this site shows you what's available at each club—and the price. You'll know ahead of time where you can get the best deal.

Best CD Sites in Cyberspace

It's time to buy that Miles Davis classic or the latest from the Big Bad Voodoo Daddies. Where to go? Check out these best CD-buying sites for your next music fix.

Amazon

```
http://www.amazon.com
```

Yes, the giant online bookseller sells CDs as well. And no, it's not just an after-thought. I've found some of the best deals online here. Amazon is good site for comparison shopping but has yet to show any real music savvy when it comes to making recommendations.

CDNow

```
http://www.cdnow.com
```

Good site, good selection, good vibes. CDNow is a nice-looking site with good prices—and as far as I'm concerned, any site that highlights blues legend Charlie Patton from the 1920s and 1930s has something going for it.

CDUniverse

```
http://www.cduniverse.com
```

You'll find a good selection of CDs at CDUniverse, and often it features good prices, so you'll want to make it one of your stopping points. Where this site falls down is in making recommendations to you—it simply doesn't do it. Know what you want before you get here, because it's bad for browsing.

CDWorld

```
http://www.cdworld.com
```

CDWorld is really an all-around entertainment site, not just a CD site. It sells movies, software, video games, and even posters. Because it's so large, it doesn't offer much in the way of help or advice. And how seriously can you take a site whose fourth most popular album at one time was *Ally McBeal: TV Soundtrack*. Still, I've found some extremely good prices here, so you'll want to stop in when comparison shopping.

Create Your Own Personalized, Custom CD from the Internet

Ever wished that you could have a CD filled with only your favorite cuts—and from different artists? The Music Maker site at www.musicmaker.com can make that wish come true. Just choose your songs and artists, and Music Maker will cut the CD for you and ship it to your mailbox. Cost is $9.95 per CD for five songs. For each additional song, you pay $1 more. The only problem with the site is that its selection is somewhat limited. But if you like blues, folk, and other music that doesn't get a lot of airplay, you'll find a lot to like.

MusicSpot

http://www.musicspot.com

Here's a music site with a twist. In addition to being able to buy the normal kinds of CDs, you can also make your own CD by buying songs individually, and putting them together on a CD. You can put only some songs on CD—but I found a lot of old favorites here to build my own CD, including James Brown, Chet Baker, and the Yardbirds with Eric Clapton.

Tower Records

http://www.towerrecords.com

The retail music monster also has an online site, and it's worth a visit on your online shopping expeditions just to check out the prices. Tower is heavy on pop and rock and tends to highlight the usual suspects. Still, it has a large selection and is worth the trip.

Tunes

http://tunes.com

When I'm in the mood to browse and look for CDs and listen to samples, I head to Tunes. Its highlighting and suggestions are the best I've found online, especially if you're looking for more than the usual music industry hype. Shown here are its suggestions for blues records. With most CDs, you can listen to clips. Bookmark this site.

You have to suffer if you want to sing the blues, but if you're only looking for great advice on blues records, or records of any other genre, head over to Tunes at www.tunes.com.

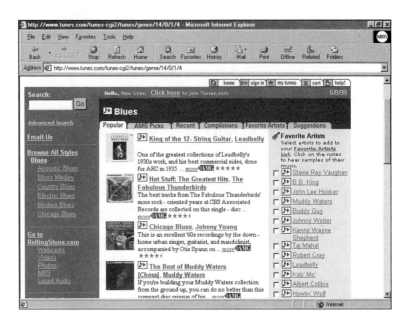

Lights, Camera, Action: Buying Movies Online

Whether your taste in movies runs to the *Terminator* series, *Grand Illusion* by Jean Renoir, or anything in between, you'll be able to buy whatever you want online. Figure that you'll get at least a 15% discount off retail price and often more on new releases. However, shipping charges, which frequently run about $3 for the first movie of an order and $1 for each additional title, are sure to cut into that discount.

You can reduce your losses somewhat by buying several tapes at a time.

Video prices are all over the map online, so it pays to do comparison shopping before you go. Be sure to check out not only the video-specific sites such as Reel at www.reel.com, but also the big department stores and online malls, which sometimes have the best prices. The video-specific sites are usually easier to use and offer more recommendations.

Most Movie Sites Also Sell DVDs

Have a DVD player and want to buy some movies? Fear not. Most sites that sell videos sell movies in DVD format as well.

At some sites, you'll be able to buy used videos as well, sometimes at extremely low prices, such as $5 per video. Be sure, before you buy, that the site offers a money-back guarantee—otherwise, you could be stuck with a low-quality video.

As with CDs, you'll find video clubs online—most notably Columbia House at www.columbiahouse.com. Here's the deal: You get seven or so videos almost free (you still have to pay for shipping), and then have to buy a certain number of videos over the next several years. If you buy a fair number of videos and your tastes don't run to the unusual and the eccentric, then video clubs are a good deal.

Avoid Renting Movies over the Internet

You can now rent movies over the Internet—you pay a fee, the videos are shipped to you, and when you're done watching, you ship them back. But you'll pay a steep premium to rent over the Internet. Figure on it costing from $3 to $5 per movie, plus round-trip shipping, which often costs about $6 for a single movie and $10 for four movies. That means you can pay up to $9 to rent one movie! You'd be better off heading to your local video store.

Best Movie-Buying Sites in Cyberspace

So you know you want to buy a movie online—but where to go? Check out these best buying sites. I've also listed the best movie-review sites as well, for advice on what to buy.

Columbia House

http://www.columbiahouse.com

If you buy lots of movies and your tastes don't run off the beaten track, consider joining this movie club. Get a load of movies for just the cost of shipping when you join and then buy a certain number at club prices over the next several years. You can save big-time—but the selections might be too limited for you. (I couldn't find *Eraserhead* or *Broadway Danny Rose* at Columbia House, for example. It didn't get my business!)

Goodmovies.com

http://www.goodmovies.com

Here's a nice site for buying movies that offers reviews not only of movies you can buy, but new releases playing only in theaters as well. Good site, well worth the visit.

Reel

http://www.reel.com

Here's the first place to stop if you're movie shopping. Good prices, excellent recommendations, and good search tools combine to make Reel a top site. You can also buy used movies here, as well as rent movies.

Film.com

    http://www.film.com

No, you won't be able to buy movies here—but if you're looking for a great site for movie reviews and recommendations, it's the place to go. Reviews, news, and movie trailers you can watch on your computer—it's an all-around great site for movie fans.

Internet Movie Database

    http://www.imdb.com

Check This Out

Use the Acses ShopBot to Find Deals on Videos

The Acses ShopBot doesn't just find bargains on books—it also will find the best deal on videos as well. Go to www.acses.com and do comparison shopping to find the best deal on a video you want to buy.

You won't be able to buy movies here, either. But movie buffs will want to head to this site to find every piece of information about every movie ever made. Believe me, it's true. Oh, you don't believe me? Okay, what was the title of Humphrey Bogart's first full-length movie, what famous director directed it, and when was it made? Now try this one: Name the director of one of the worst movies of all time, *Santa Claus Defeats the Martians*—and for which two of the best-loved TV series of all times did he direct episodes? You'll find all that and more here. (Answers to the questions: Humprey Bogart's first full-length movie was *Up the River,* directed by John Ford in 1930. The director of *Santa Claus Defeats the Martians* was Nicholas Webster, who also directed episodes of *Bonanza* and *The Waltons.*)

The Least You Need to Know

➤ Use book-buying bargain agents to find the best bargain at the dozens of book-buying sites on the Internet.

➤ You can get great prices on books at remainder and used-book sites.

➤ Prices for CDs vary greatly from site to site, so be sure to check multiple sites before buying.

➤ Don't bother using bargain-shopping agents for CDs and movies—these agents don't check all the best sites and therefore don't give you the best deals.

➤ Avoid renting movies over the Internet—you'll spend too much on shipping costs.

Chapter 15

Mall Fever: Department Stores, Malls, Closeouts, and Bargain Hunting

In This Chapter

➤ The best ways to shop at online malls

➤ The best department stores on the Internet

➤ How to hunt down closeouts, liquidators, and bargains online

You don't need to listen to piped-in Muzak, eat bad food at a food court, or walk past the sullen stares of angst-ridden adolescents if you want to shop at a mall or a department store. You can instead head to the Internet. You'll find online malls that are many times the size of any mall you've ever driven to, and you'll be able to browse the aisles in comfort. And you'll find great closeouts and bargains online—in many cases better than the ones you'll find in real life. So fire up your browser and read on to find out how and where to shop at malls and department stores and to find out about closeouts and other bargain-hunting excitement online.

I'll Skip the Food Court: Shopping at Online Malls

Online malls aren't all that different from their real-life counterparts. You can buy anything from light bulbs to CDs to computers and clothing in one place. You can generally find discounts and a big selection. Of course, you also have to pay shipping fees, so check those fees before buying to see what kind of discount you're actually getting.

At online malls, you'll find much more than just products—you can find services as well, such as getting insurance, booking travel, or even, perish the thought, finding a lawyer. And many malls even have classified ad areas. Almost anything you can buy or might need is available at an online mall. (I've yet, though, to find any yak meat—and believe me, I've tried.)

Generally, malls list products and services by categories, such as Electronics or Fashion. Most let you search for a specific product or kind of product by typing in a word that describes what you're looking for. Malls highlight deals, specials, and anything they're trying to push on you that day. The iMALL at www.imall.com, shown here, is fairly typical.

From cigars to soccer to software: shopping at the iMALL online mall.

Different Types of Online Malls

Although online malls all look somewhat the same, two different kinds prevail—and before you place an order you should know what kind of site you're buying from.

Check Shipping and Return Policies

Even if you buy at a mall in which you buy through the mall itself, the shipping and return policies might vary, according to what product you buy. For example, the shipping charges on a computer may be many times the charges on a bottle of perfume—and they'll often have different return policies as well.

One kind of mall is much like a traditional mall in the real world. It's a collection of different stores, all under one roof for convenience—although in this instance, the roof is a virtual one. When you buy something from this kind of online mall, you are buying from the individual store located in the mall—just like at your local mall.

So, you think, who cares whether you buy from the mall itself or an individual store? Well, you should care. Each individual store at the mall might have different policies about shipping costs and times, returns, warranties, and the like. There's nothing wrong with shopping at a mall where you buy from individual stores—you should just be sure you know whom you're buying from and what their policies are before buying.

At the other kind of mall, you buy everything through the mall itself, not from individual stores. It's easier to buy at these kinds of malls because you won't have to set up separate accounts every time you buy a different type of goods. And the site will have common warranty and return policies.

So how do you know which kind of mall you're in? If you have to fill out a different form each time you place an order for a different kind of product, you're in a traditional mall. If you don't have to fill out a new form, you're probably buying everything through the mall itself, but not necessarily. The only way to really know is to dig down and check out the Help or About or similar area of the site.

If you've gotten this far in the book or have spent any time on the Internet, you know that nothing is simple when it comes to the Internet and that the world is always more complicated than it seems. It's true with malls as well. Some malls, in fact, combine features of both kinds of malls—most of what you buy might be through the mall itself, but there could be "sponsored links" or highlights to goods or sites that are separate stores. Again, the best advice is always to check before you buy.

Check the Sales Tax

State laws require that you pay sales tax on an item if you buy it over the Internet from a site that has a business presence in your state. Oftentimes, when you buy through a mall, you'll be buying from different stores. That means that even though you bought a book and paid no sales tax, you still might have to pay sales tax on a pair of sneakers from a different store.

Best Online Malls in Cyberspace

These days, it seems there are as many malls on the Internet as there are in the real world. Here's the best of the best.

AOL Shopping Channel

On America Online, KEYWORD SHOPPING

The AOL Shopping Channel is a cross between a mall, a directory, and a site that lists bargains on individual products and points out bargain-hunting sites. It's the central place on America Online to go shopping and is organized by category, so finding what you want is easy. Sometimes you'll buy directly from AOL, sometimes through another store on the site, sometimes on the Internet—it's all over the place. But for America Online users, the Shopping Channel is a good place to start shopping.

Buy.com

        http://www.buy.com

You won't be able to buy everything at this site—at last look, they sold only computer and electronics products, software, books, video games, and videos. But the deals they offer are often spectacular—the site regularly has the lowest prices on the Internet for many products.

iMALL

        http://www.imall.com

Big site, big specials, big discounts. When comparing prices, be sure to stop here; it's one of the better malls in cyberspace, with one of the biggest selection of goods. iMALL is a mall of separate stores, so be sure to check shipping and handling when you buy.

192

iQVC

http://www.iqvc.com

Here's the online shopping mall of the QVC Shopping Channel cable network. What you see on the mall is a lot like what you see on the air, which means just about anything. There's a Last Clicks area where you can get closeouts and even a place to click to see what they're hawking on TV. Women who care about style, fashion, and makeup can check out My Style Adviser for recommendations based on your hair, eye, and skin color; the kind of makeup you like to wear; and the kind of fashions you like.

Deals can be had at www.iqvc.com, *the online outpost of the QVC Shopping Channel*

NetMarket

http://www.netmarket.com

Here's a mall that offers great discounts, but also goes beyond them—it also has an auction; a flea market where you can get closeout goods, coupons and discounts; and a "haggle zone" where you get to haggle and bargain over prices.

Check This Out

What? You Can Go to a Mall of Malls?

Here's a twist: A mall site that doesn't sell anything itself, but instead is a way to find other online malls. Malls.com at www.malls.com lets you find malls that have stores that sell products you're interested in.

ShopNow.com

```
http://www.shopnow.com
```

You think you've been in a big mall in the real world? Fuhgedabout it! You haven't seen big until you've been here. ShopNow.com claims to house more than 25,000 stores under one big virtual tent. In addition to the huge selection, the site does a great job of organizing what could otherwise be an impossible mall to make your way through. And it offers daily specials on everything under the sun, as you can see in the following figure.

Shopping.com

```
http://www.shopping.com
```

One of the premier malls on the Internet, Shopping.com not only offers a huge selection of goods (looking for orthopedic bedding for pets—yup, it's here), but excellent prices as well. In fact, I've found that its CD and book prices are often the best on the Internet. The site is also well organized and fast. And it has some of the best searching capabilities on a shopping site that I've ever seen—you can search by product, price, and manufacturer.

Spree.com

```
http://www.spree.com
```

Here's a mall with a twist: Every time you buy something, you earn points, and when you accumulate enough points, you get a check in the mail. And if you get people to come to the site and sign up at your request, you get even more points—and more cash. Even if this site didn't offer that extra cash for shopping, you'd still want to come here. Although it doesn't offer nearly as many products as other malls, it has excellent prices on what it carries, including electronics, books, music, gifts, flowers, coffee, and tea.

Visiting Department Stores Online

Malls and online shopping might be leading to the decline of some department stores, but you can still visit most of your favorite department stores online. That's not to say that you can actually *shop* at them all, because when it comes to online shopping, some department stores are in the dark ages. As of this writing, some of the best-known department stores carry only a limited selection of things you can buy—and in fact, some won't let you buy anything at all. As of this writing, that paragon of luxe and excess, Neiman Marcus, for instance (which a good friend of mine accurately calls "Needless Markup"), doesn't even allow you to order online. Oh, well. There goes the $50,000 toy car I've always wanted to buy for my kids.

On the other hand, some department stores have entered cyberspace with a vengeance and offer some of the best deals and selections you'll find anywhere. Wal-Mart, in particular, at www.wal-mart.com, offers a huge selection of goods, with some of the best prices you'll find online and exceedingly cheap shipping—$3 per order, no matter how many items, with a few exceptions.

Even if you don't plan to shop over the Internet, you might still want to visit your favorite department store's Web site. Some department stores list their current sales and specials online (some even offer online-only specials), some let you browse through their inventory, and many have online store finders that will help you locate the branch nearest to your home.

Finding the online site of a department store is easy. Type www.storename.com to get there in a flash. But is the site worth visiting? Thought you'd never ask. Check out the next section to find the best department store sites on the Internet.

Best Department Stores on the Internet

You'll find a lot of department store sites online—but just because a store slaps up a Web site doesn't mean it's any good. So where to go? Here's the best of the best.

Bloomingdale's

    http://www.bloomingdales.com

For many native New Yorkers, there is only one department store: Bloomingdale's. For them, a trip to the 59th Street and Lexington Avenue store is more than a way to participate in commerce—it is a way to get in touch with their inner shopper. Now you don't have to be a New Yorker to make the trip—you can head there on the Web. You can buy a wide selection of clothing, home fashions, and gifts just like at the real-world store, as you can see pictured here. True, you won't be assaulted by perfectly coiffed women spritzing cologne and perfume on you, but still, it's Bloomie's all the same—where else can you buy New York City subway token cuff links for $50? Your shopping cart is even called the Big Brown Bag, named after Bloomingdale's famous shopping bags.

Macy's

    http://www.macys.com

Macy's, another venerable New York City department store, has made the leap to the Web. The focus, as in the stores, is on clothing, fashion, cosmetics, and gifts.

New Yorkers and others can get in touch with their inner shopper at Bloomingdale's on the Web.

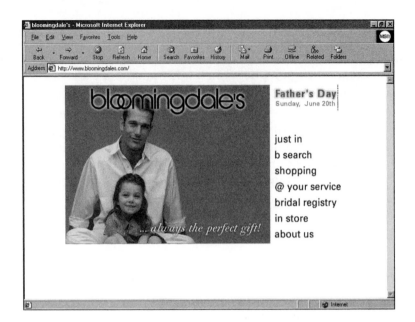

J.C. Penney

http://www.jcpenney.com

This well-known department store has a good online site with a wide variety of stuff you can buy. And this site has a twist—not only can you shop the department store's online site, but you can also order from its catalog. Just type in an item number, and you can order. The site also has a variety of gift registries, so that people can know what gifts you'd like for occasions such as weddings.

Wal-Mart

http://www.wal-mart.com

This site is not just the best department store on the Internet—it's one of the best online shipping sites you'll find. Low prices and shipping costs, big selection, easy to navigate—it's a hard combination to beat. You'll also find a good selection of sales and closeouts.

I Can Get It for You Wholesale: Closeouts and Bargain Hunting Online

Come on, admit it. Nothing gets your blood going like the hunt for a good bargain. Sure, maybe you spent $15 in gas to save $10 on a new pair of slacks, but that doesn't matter—the point is, *you didn't pay retail!* In the culture where I grew up in New York, the cardinal rule of shopping was that you never paid the retail price for *anything*. If you did, you'd no longer be considered a New Yorker; you'd be thrown out of the tribe. The only people we knew who paid the full retail price lived—God forbid!—in Connecticut.

Look for Closeout Areas of Online Malls

Many online malls and shopping sites have special closeout areas. Those closeout areas often offer the best deals on the Internet, so be sure to check them regularly for bargains.

Now no one has to live in Connecticut, because anyone can find bargains online. One way is to find liquidator and closeout sites that sell goods that have been discontinued or overstocked by their manufacturers or by other retailers. Most of these sites sell computer-related equipment, so turn to Chapter 16, "Drive a Hard Bargain on Hardware: Getting the Best Deal on Buying a Computer." When dealing with liquidator and closeout sites, be sure to find out the return policies, including return shipping fees.

Other bargain sites aren't necessarily liquidators, but still sell everything at el cheapo prices. Again, on these sites, check out return policies and return shipping fees. Many of these sites are specialty sites—for example, they might sell only golf equipment. Turn to the chapter that covers specific goods to find bargain sites in that category. In this chapter, I cover general bargain sites.

Many of the best deals are short-lived, one-time deals—sales or specials that take place only for a week or less on a specific site. You'd have to surf to hundreds of sites to track down all those sales and specials. But a number of sites track them for you, reporting on the latest and greatest deals.

Best Closeout and Bargain Sites on the Internet

Where to go for the best bargain hunting online? You want to be sure that the prices are the best and that the source is reputable. So don't be a sucker. When looking for a great deal, check out these best closeout and bargain sites online.

AOL Bargain Basement

KEYWORD BARGAIN BASEMENT

A lot of good deals are available on America Online: discounts, two-for-one deals, and more offers, usually from dozens of different shops. Anyone who shops on America Online and is looking to save money should be sure to stop in.

Andy's Garage Sale

http://www.andysgarage.com

How could anyone not love this liquidator site? It's fun, it's funky, and it's functional, as you can see in the following figure. Andy's features the usual grab bag of items you'd expect at liquidators, which means everything in the world—computers, watches, clothing, radios, lamps, tents, golf clubs, even discounted phone service.

Fun, funky, and functional: Get new stuff cheap at Andy's Garage Sale.

E-Centives

http://www.e-centives.com

Here's a new twist on getting bargains. Sign up at this site and then get discounts at selected stores—both on and off the Web. Just tell E-Centives the kind of goods and services you're interested in. When you do off-the-Web shopping, you print a coupon; when you shop on the Web, you're sent directly to a site that gives you a discount.

Internet Shopper

http://www.internetshopper.com

Internet Shopper is my favorite site for finding bargains and sales on the Internet. You don't actually buy anything on the site itself. Instead, it scours the net for sales and bargains and alerts you to them. Last time I checked in, Internet Shopper found deals on cheap PCs, hosiery, golf umbrellas, sunglasses, and yes, that must-have that you've always wanted: a water fountain for your cat. The site also offers good shopping advice and an email newsletter that highlights the latest deals.

Outlet Bound

http://www.outletbound.com

Yes, I know. There *is* a world of shopping beyond the Web. If you're a fan of discount outlet shops, be sure to head here before you go outlet shopping. This site finds the outlet you want, anywhere. Tell it your location, and it'll give you a list of nearby outlets. It'll give you a description of the outlet, driving directions, and a way to request a brochure online. You can also search for a particular outlet store, and it'll give you a list of them at various locations. And you can even search by a brand; the site will give you a list of outlets that sell that brand. You'll even be able to get coupons for the outlets on the site.

Go Bargain Hunting at WebMarket

Want to find the best bargains online, but don't want to spend your time gallivanting all over the Internet? Try WebMarket at www.webmarket.com. Choose the goods you're looking for, and WebMarket searches through many shopping sites, showing you what it finds—and from there, you choose the best bargain.

Sales and Bargains

http://www.salesandbargains.com

Here's an all-around excellent bargain site. The prices are good, and there's a reasonable selection. It's primarily for clothing, but you'll also find deals on housewares and similar items as well.

The Least You Need to Know

➤ Before buying at an online mall, find out whether you're buying through the mall itself or through a store inside the mall. Each store might have its own return and shipping policies; however, if you're buying from the mall itself, shipping and return policies are likely to be more uniform.

➤ Always check mall shipping prices and return policies on each product—they might vary from product to product.

➤ Check closeout areas of malls for the best prices.

➤ Instead of trying to search the entire Internet yourself for the best bargains, head to a bargain-tracking site.

Chapter 16

Drive a Hard Bargain on Hardware: Getting the Best Deal on Buying a Computer

In This Chapter

➤ How to check out comparative hardware reviews

➤ How to buy direct from the manufacturer; from superstores; and from bargain sites, surplus sites, auctions, and liquidators

➤ The best hardware-buying sites on the Internet

➤ Using hardware-shopping agents to get the best deal possible

➤ Consumer tips for hardware buyers

➤ How to buy refurbished computers directly from the manufacturer

If you're buying hardware the old-fashioned way—in a store—come on, get real. The odds are you're throwing away possibly hundreds of dollars and missing out on great prices and hardware configurations that you won't find in any store. You can find amazing deals on hardware on the Internet that you often won't be able to find in old-fashioned bricks-and-mortar stores. People spend billions of dollars a year buying hardware online and with good reason: bargains.

In addition to finding bargains, you can customize your next computer so that it's exactly the one that you want, not the one that the store tells you that you want. When you shop for hardware online, you can often get only the exact equipment that you specify.

Here's how to use the Internet to research your next hardware buy and to make sure you're getting the absolute rock-bottom price on the best product.

How to Get the Best Deals on Computers and Hardware

The Internet is a computer buyer's paradise. You can use online resources to research your next dream machine so that you'll know you're getting the best computer for your money, and you can comparison shop for the very best price. It's not uncommon to find a piece of hardware for sale at many different prices—and the price spread can be as much as hundreds of dollars. Here's a real-world example: When I was looking for a new NEC 17-inch color monitor, I did a bit of comparison shopping; one site was selling it for $335 while another site was charging $599 for the identical monitor. And that example is only for a monitor. When you buy a complete computer system, you can save even more. Spending a little time doing research can save you some very big bucks.

So read on. I clue you in on how to research your next hardware buy, how to buy it, where to buy it, and how to get the best deal without getting burned.

Step 1: Check Out Comparative Reviews

More print space is probably devoted to reviews of computer hardware than to any other kind of product you will ever buy—and all those reviews are online. You can read reviews online from many computer publishers, such as at ZDNet at www.zdnet.com from computer publishing behemoth Ziff-Davis, which owns magazines such as *PC Magazine, PC Computing, Computer Shopper, FamilyPC,* and many others. You can also read reviews from the C|Net Internet-only site at www.cnet.com and from general-interest newspapers such as the *San Francisco Chronicle* and *San Francisco Examiner* at www.sfgate.com and *USA Today* at www.usatoday.com. I've generally found that the *USA Today* reviews are easier to find than the ones at most other daily newspapers, so you might want to head there if you're interested in what a newspaper has to say about a piece of hardware.

Use Computer Shopper's How to Buy Guides

Computer Shopper at www.computershopper.com is a computer–buying site. One of its great features is the How to Buy section, which offers easy-to-follow comprehensive advice on how to buy any computer system. You don't need to buy a computer from this site to use the guide, so head to the site and click **How to Buy** before deciding on your next system.

The two best places to check are ZDNet and C|Net. That's because both sites put together complete buyers' guides, and, in fact, at ZDNet entire Web sites are devoted to single topics. For example, the DesktopUser site at ZDNet is devoted to helping people decide what kind of desktop computer to buy.

Read the comparative reviews, but keep one thing in mind when reading them—it generally takes several months for an article to get from the writer's hand to the Internet. That means that some prices and models might be slightly out of date. So, follow this rule: Assume that, if anything, you'll be able to get a more powerful computer for a better price than you read about.

You should also be sure that you check more than one magazine, publication, or Web site when reading product reviews. Reviewers are only human. (I've done a fair amount of reviewing myself for computer magazines, and I'm human—or at least, so I've been told.) Authors have their own points of view and prejudices about hardware that you might not agree with. If you check out several sites, you are more likely to get the complete story, not just one person's opinion.

You might come across some sites on the Internet that let you look through current reviews for free, but charge a subscription fee if you want to search through old reviews. In most cases, you won't want to fork over the money. Old reviews are...well, let's face it, they're old. In most cases, they are reviews of products that you can't even buy any more. The only exception is if you can buy a review for a specific computer model without paying an entire subscription fee, which you might want to do if the review is only a few months old and covers a model that is still being sold.

Step 2: Head to the Buying Sites

You can buy hardware at hundreds, and possibly thousands, of sites on the Internet. So which one should you go to? That depends on the kind of hardware you're looking for, how technically proficient you feel (or don't feel), and how much spare change you're willing to spend. Although there are a zillion different hardware-buying sites, they shake down into a few main types. You can buy directly from the manufacturer of the hardware, from a hardware superstore, from an auction site, and from liquidator and surplus sites. You might want to buy—or not want to buy—from one or another kind of site for various reasons. Here are the types of sites, along with their pros, cons, and who should buy there.

Buying Directly from the Manufacturer

Many hardware manufacturers, such as Dell at `www.dell.com`, shown in the figure, sell directly to you on the Web, cutting out the retailer and allowing you to customize your own system. Figure that pretty soon, every computer manufacturer will sell computers directly on the Internet, so buying direct will be an increasingly popular way to buy computers.

Buying directly from a manufacturer such as Dell can be a way to cut out the retailer and to save money.

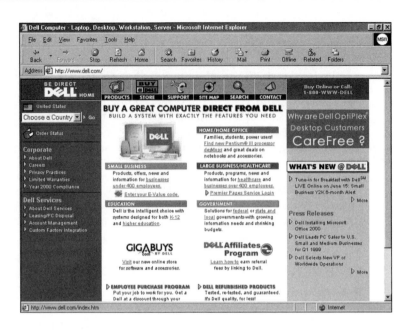

Pros	Cons	Who Should Buy There
You can often save, when compared to buying retail; you are able to customize your own system; you can find out about deals, sales, and specials you otherwise wouldn't know about; you ensure getting the newest and most up-to-date systems.	You're limited to buying a system from a single manufacturer, so you are not able to comparison shop.	Anyone who has decided on a specific system, model, and configuration, or who has an affinity for a particular manufacturer.

Buy Refurbished Computers and Save Money

Some of the better hardware bargains you'll find are used computers—often called refurbished—sold by the manufacturer. Dell at www.dell.com, for example, has an entire outlet store devoted to them. You save hundreds of dollars compared to comparable new systems, and you can get the same kind of warranty as you get when buying new equipment. More information about buying refurbished computers appears later in this chapter.

Buying from a Hardware Superstore

Hundreds of hardware superstores on the Internet enable you to buy many different models of computers and hardware from many different manufacturers. Some sites, such as NetBuyer at www.netbuyer.com, also offer advice and enable you to compare products side by side.

Pros	Cons	Who Should Buy There
Allows you to comparison shop to find the best deal; might offer buying advice; wide selection of computers and hardware.	Can be confusing to find the right computer; might offer many "off-brand" models of hardware and computers; you need to be sure the site is reputable.	Comparison shoppers, people who feel comfortable comparing specifications of computer systems and who aren't wedded to a specific manufacturer.

Buying from Auction Sites

You can buy computers at general auction sites, at computer auction sites, and at auction sections of hardware superstores. At auctions, you bid against others to buy equipment. Turn to Chapter 11, "Sold American! Buying Through Online Auctions," for information about how to buy at auctions.

Pros	Cons	Who Should Buy There
You can get great deals on computers and equipment.	You could get outmoded equipment; pay too high a price because of auction frenzy; and if buying from an individual, rather than the auction site, be the victim of a scam.	People who know enough about computers to know pricing and value of equipment and who are also smart bargainers.

Buying from Liquidators and Surplus Sites

Some sites buy out lots of computers that are overstocked or being discontinued from manufacturers and stores. They then sell that overstocked and discontinued hardware on their sites. Some sites also sell used equipment that they've refurbished.

Pros	Cons	Who Should Shop There
You can get some of the best deals anywhere—for example, computers for $500 or less. There's also often a wide variety of hardware to choose from.	The equipment is often less powerful than what you can buy at other sites You must be careful to understand return policies and warranties.	Bargain hunters who are comfortable with technology and understand warranties and return policies.

Get Written Confirmation of the Warranty

Warranties vary widely at surplus sites. At the same site, some equipment might carry only a 30-day warranty from the site itself; other times, the equipment might carry a year or more warranty from the manufacturer. Surplus sites don't always spell out which warranty you get. For example, at the popular Surplus Direct site at www.surplusdirect.com, all used hardware carries this notice: "Product carries a Surplus Direct 30-day warranty or the manufacturer's warranty as applicable." Nowhere, however, does it say which warranty covers the product being sold.

Step 3: See Whether Shopping Agents Can Get You a Better Deal

With so many places to buy computers and hardware on the Internet, you could spend a good portion of your life trying to get the best buy. You can save yourself some mouse time by sending a shopping agent to do your comparison shopping. Shopping agents work like this: You go to the agent's site, describe the product you're looking for, and deploy the agent. The shopping agent shows you the prices at each store and information about store policies, such as warranty terms and whether overnight shipping is available. Shopping agents can save you tremendous amounts of money and time. For example, I used the CompuCom Computershopper.com site to comparison shop for a 400MHz Compaq DeskPro computer. As you can see in this figure, the difference in prices among sites was enormous—the lowest price was more than $500 lower than the highest price.

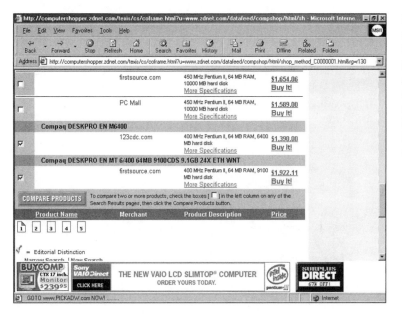

Using a shopping agent such as Computershopper.com can save you money, big-time. A search for a Compaq computer found a difference of more than $500 between the highest and lowest prices for the same computer.

Be aware that not all shopping agents search all sites, so if you really want to be sure to get the best price, use more than one. Here are the best computer-shopping agents you'll find. You can also try the general shopping agents reviewed in Chapter 7, "Shopping Robots, Agents, Search Tools, and Virtual Shopping Assistants"; many of them search for the best hardware prices as well.

Computershopper.com

```
http://www.computershopper.com
```

If you're looking to get dirt-cheap deals on any kind of hardware, head here. The site bristles with flashing ads and buttons of all kinds, but don't be put off—it will go out and find great deals for you. Whether it's complete systems, components, or any kind of computer-related gizmo or hardware you can name, it will find a deal for you. It also has bargain-basement areas, and offers great advice on what to buy and how to buy it.

KillerApp

```
http://www.killerapp.com
```

Here's a solid computer-shopping agent. It's well organized and easy to use, and presents easy-to-read price comparisons. The site is well worth a visit.

PriceScan

```
http://www.pricescan.com
```

PriceScan is another useful computer-shopping agent. It's not quite as easy to use as Computershopper.com or KillerApp, but it still does its job well. The site also offers price comparisons on other products in addition to computers, such as books, movies, sporting goods, and video games.

Figure In Shipping Costs

Some shopping agents, when they scour the Net for the best prices, don't include shipping costs in their price comparisons. Shipping costs vary widely—I've seen some sites that ship for $8 or even for free, whereas others might charge $100 or more to ship a computer. So, when doing your price comparison, include those charges.

Shopper.com

```
http://www.shopper.com
```

This otherwise useful shopping agent makes you work a bit before you get to the nitty-gritty of comparing prices. You'll find yourself clicking through page after page to get to the product you want—and then you might find multiple listings of the same or almost the same product. Still, when you finally get to the price comparison, it will have done a good job.

Step 4: Heed This Advice Before Buying

Buying a computer or hardware is a lot more complicated than buying most other things over the Internet. Not only are you plopping down possibly several thousand dollars in cash, but you're also buying equipment that you hope will last for several years.

Before handing over your hard-earned money for hardware, be sure you follow this buying advice:

➤ **Don't buy anything without a rock-solid, money-back guarantee.** You want the right to return your hardware for any reason, not only if it's defective. Push for a 30-day return period if at all possible.

➤ **Don't buy from sites that charge restocking fees.** Believe it or not, you can end up paying hundreds of dollars if you buy a computer and then return it for any reason. That's because some sites charge a restocking fee for returns. This fee can be up to 20% of the cost of the system—in other words, a whopping $500 on a $2,500 system. Many sites don't charge restocking fees, so never buy from a site that does.

➤ **Check the warranty before buying.** Warranties vary widely when buying over the Internet, especially if you're buying from a liquidator or surplus site. Before buying, know what kind of warranty you're getting and who is issuing it. The issuer might be the site itself or the manufacturer. And be sure you know the length of the warranty as well. You should get at least a one-year warranty.

Check This Out

Get an RMA

When you return a piece of hardware, you must document the return so that you won't be charged for the item. One way to start a paper trail is to get a return merchandise authorization, called an RMA, from the seller.

➤ **Keep a confirmation of your order.** Be sure that you have a record of exactly what you ordered and how much you agreed to pay. Print out your order page and keep copies of it in a safe place. Some sites also email you a confirmation, so print that as well.

➤ **Ask that your credit card not be charged until the product ships.** Sometimes you might buy something that isn't in stock and might take a while to get. Be sure that the site doesn't charge your credit card until the product is actually shipped to you.

➤ **Know your shipping fees.** Shipping fees on hardware vary widely. Some sites ship for free or have exceedingly low fees, as low as $8. That's the exception. Usually, you'll pay at least $50 for the cheapest shipping option and perhaps $150 for the most expensive. Some sites charge a base shipping fee of $5 or so and then charge by the pound. When estimating these kinds of fees, figure that when you buy a computer, the whole thing will weigh about 100 pounds.

➤ **Know exactly what's included before buying.** Some sites sell you a computer, but if you want to buy a monitor, you have to pay extra. Before buying, be sure you know whether a monitor, sound card, speakers, mouse, modem, keyboard, software, and other goodies are included. If not, you have to pay for all that yourself—and it can add up to many hundreds of dollars extra.

Step 5: Head to These Best Computer-Shopping Sites on the Internet

So you're finally ready to buy. Head to these sites on your hardware-shopping expedition. Note that many of these stores sell software as well, so if you're looking for software, they're worth checking into as well.

Apple Computer

http://www.apple.com

If you want to buy a Macintosh, you might want to go to the source. You can buy a prebuilt system or configure your own.

BuyComp

http://www.buycomp.com

BuyComp is a big site that sells all kinds of computers and hardware. You'll find excellent prices on hardware here—in fact, I regularly find some of the best prices on the Internet for computers and hardware. Check this one out.

CompUSA

http://www.compusa.com

The retail computer superstore has an online site, and as you would expect, the selection is huge. In addition to CompUSA's normal offerings, it has factory outlet and clearance areas, where you can find many good deals.

Computershopper.com

http://www.computershopper.com

This huge shopping site offers not just the capability to do comparison shopping but also probably the best consumer advice you'll find online about how to buy a computer. Computershopper has a huge selection of hardware, specials and deals, and a bargain basement for rock-bottom prices. Shopping wizards, such as the one shown here on buying a notebook computer, guide you through the selection process.

Cyberian Outpost

http://www.outpost.com

Cyberian Outpost has a lot of hardware bargains, so if you're going to buy anything computer-related, check it out. You'll also find hardware auctions, and specials, such as free shipping.

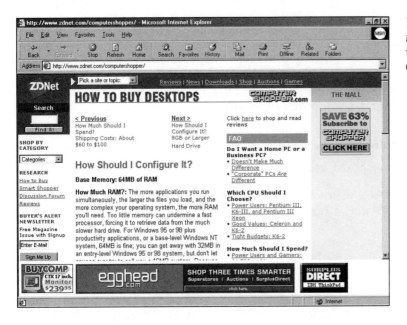

You'll get advice on how to buy any kind of hardware when you visit Computershopper.com

CyberSwap

http://www.cyberswap.com

Those who want to try their hands at getting a good deal at computer auctions should visit this site. The selection is somewhat limited, but some good deals can be found.

Dell

http://www.dell.com

Dell, one of the premier mail-order computer manufacturers, has become the premier manufacturer when it comes to selling hardware over the Internet. You can design your own system, see prices instantly, and check for specials and deals.

MicroWarehouse

http://www.microwarehouse.com

Anyone comparison shopping on the Net has to visit MicroWarehouse—the selection is so massive that if hardware exists, the odds are this place has it. It's also an exceedingly easy-to-use site and spells out in detail the hardware specs.

NECX

http://www.necx.com

What do you get at this site? A massive selection of products and great prices—often the best on the Internet. There are also sales and deals, rebates and coupons, and side-by-side comparisons. NECX is a top spot for comparison shopping.

PC Connection Online Superstore

http://www.pcconnection.com

Here's another monster site with a massive selection of products. It's easy to browse and search, and there's always a host of specials on sale.

Surplus Auction

http://www.surplusauction.com

These sister sites, run by the Egghead software store, might be the best computer auction and surplus sites on the Internet. There's always a big selection at good prices. Unlike some surplus and auction sites, you get a complete, detailed explanation of precisely what you're buying, including a picture. Warranty information is made clear as well, a must at any surplus and auction site.

ZDNet Auctions

http://auctions.zdnet.com

If you're looking for great deals on computer equipment, here's where to go. All kinds of hardware, peripherals, gizmos, and other computer stuff can be had here—and at great prices. A great site to get amazing deals on hardware.

Oldies but Goodies: Buying Refurbished Hardware from the Manufacturer on the Internet

One way to save big bucks on a computer is to buy refurbished hardware (a more polite way of saying used) directly from the company that made it. In contrast to sites that sell all kinds of used or surplus equipment, manufacturers' sites sell only their own refurbished hardware.

When you buy used equipment this way, you're less at risk than if you buy from a liquidator site. That's because when you buy directly from the company, that company has its reputation to uphold. Additionally, the company might also offer the same kinds of warranties and service for their refurbished equipment as they do on their new equipment—for example, the three-year warranty that Dell offers buyers of its refurbished products.

The best way to find out about refurbished computers is to head to the individual computer manufacturers' Web sites. Dell offers a slew of refurbished hardware at its Web site at www.dell.com, for example. Availability of refurbished computers changes daily, so be sure to check back regularly if you are interested in shopping this way.

Keep in mind that when you buy refurbished equipment, you usually won't be able to buy the latest and fastest hardware. So your equipment won't be leading edge—also called bleeding edge by people who have been burned because they've bought new equipment before the bugs were worked out. But you'll get great deals.

Why Buy a PC? You Can Get One for Free

Here's an amazing fact: You can get a free PC from sites such as www.intersquid.com, www.gobi.com, and other sites. These free PCs usually require that you pay a certain amount each month to an Internet service provider for Internet access. For more details on how to get a free PC, turn to Chapter 9, "Great Stuff Cheap! Coupons, Contests, and Free Stuff."

Before buying a refurbished computer directly from the manufacturer, keep these tips in mind:

➤ **Be sure the equipment carries the same warranty as the manufacturer's new equipment.**   There's no reason that a refurbished computer shouldn't carry the same warranty as a new one. Check the warranty on both new and refurbished systems bought on the site. If the used equipment has an inferior warranty, don't buy.

➤ **Find out which software is included.**   Whenever you buy a new computer, you'll typically get hundreds of dollars in free software bundled with the machine. Be sure that when you buy a refurbished one, you get all that software. If you don't, you'll have to buy the software yourself and won't end up saving much money—if you save at all.

➤ **Know which components are included.**   That price on a refurbished computer looks great but does it include a monitor? How about a modem, a mouse, speakers, a sound card, and a keyboard? If not, you'll have to fork out hundreds of dollars extra to buy them.

The Least You Need to Know

➤ Always check hardware and software comparative reviews before buying.

➤ Hardware-shopping agents can help you save hundreds of dollars on a computer.

➤ Never buy from a site that charges restocking fees.

➤ Check the warranty, shipping costs, and return policies before buying.

➤ Buying refurbished computers can save you hundreds of dollars.

Chapter 17

Don't Be a Softie: Getting the Best Deal on Buying Software

In This Chapter

➤ How to download and install software

➤ Checking out comparative software reviews

➤ How to try software for free

➤ How to get totally free software

➤ The best software-buying sites on the Internet

➤ Consumer tips for software buyers

Sometimes it seems that the Internet was designed for the express purpose of letting people buy software. Not only can you research and buy software online—in many cases, you can even get it delivered straight to your computer over the Internet as well, saving you time and money. You save time because you get the software immediately, and you save money because you don't have to pay for shipping.

And here's something more amazing: You can try out most of the software for free before you buy it. That's right. Run the software for about a month, and only if you think it's worthwhile paying for will you have to fork over the money. More amazing still: You can use hundreds of programs for free forever.

So instead of heading to your local computer or software store to buy a new program, go online. Here's everything you need to know.

How Do I Buy Software Online?

In one way, using the Internet to buy software is a unique online experience. That's because you can use the Internet not only to buy software but also to receive it, right over your Internet connection. So, while the way you pay for software over the Internet isn't much different from the way you pay for anything else, the way that you receive that software can be very different.

You can receive software that you buy over the Internet in two ways. One way is traditional: After you pay, the seller ships the box of software to you. As with anything else you buy over the Internet, you have to pay shipping costs. The box of software will reach you in a few days or a few weeks, depending on the shipping method. Nothing unusual about this.

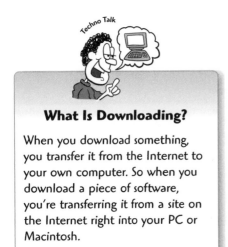

What Is Downloading?

When you download something, you transfer it from the Internet to your own computer. So when you download a piece of software, you're transferring it from a site on the Internet right into your PC or Macintosh.

The second way of receiving software can save you time and money because you can *download* the file from the vendor straight to your computer and then install the software. You get to use the software immediately, as soon as you download and install it, not in a few days or a few weeks.

When software is delivered to you this way, you usually save money—potentially, a good deal of money. You cut out shipping costs: There aren't any. Keep in mind that shipping costs for software can pile up. If you need software fast and request second-day air or next-day express delivery, you can spend $10, $15, or even more. You can save on more than shipping costs, though. You can also save on the cost of software itself—the price of the downloaded version is often $10 or so less than the boxed version of the product. Yes, that's true. The same piece of software costs you less if you download it. You get that savings because the software maker doesn't have to pay for the box, disks, manuals, and other costs associated with traditional retail sales. A little math shows that you can easily save $20 or more on a piece of software when you download it from the seller.

Buying software via download also has a few drawbacks. One is that you don't get a manual, which might or might not matter to you. I, for one, never read manuals and generally find them fairly worthless. However, if you like to read them (can't you find anything better to do with your time?), you might want to get the retail box shipped to you. Another drawback is that if you download the software to your PC, you won't have a copy of the original CD or disks that the software cames on. There are ways around this problem, though. (See the next section, "The Lowdown on Downloading," for how to be sure you have backups of the software that you download.)

The final reason you might want to get software delivered to you via mail rather than via download is that you have an odd, unreasonable attachment to brightly colored boxes. In that case, I can't help you. Just realize that you'll be paying through the nose for your weird obsession.

The Lowdown on Downloading

If you choose to download software from the seller, you should know a few things before using it. Downloaded software comes in as a single, large file. Figure that the file will be anywhere from 2 megabytes all the way up to 25 megabytes—in other words, this baby can be a whopper. You can expect the download to take anywhere from 15 minutes all the way up to several hours, depending on the size of the file, the speed of your connection, and the speed of the Web site delivering the file.

Virus Check All Files That You Download

A possibility exists—remote, but still a possibility—that a file you download could contain a virus. Viruses can delete files from your computer, and harm your computer so badly it won't be able to run. To keep your PC safe, get virus-checking software and always use it. My favorite is Norton AntiVirus. Buy it on any software-buying site on the Internet (see later in the chapter for a list) or directly from Symantec's site at www.symantec.com.

After you download the file, you're going to have to install it. Most Web sites provide instructions for doing that. In case they haven't, however, here's a simple rundown.

Write down the location on your computer of where you downloaded the file—for example, you might use C:/DOWNLOAD as the directory.

Now find the file. In almost all cases for the PC, the filename has an EXE extension, such as NEWSTUFF.EXE. (One exception is if you're downloading a demo, shareware, or trialware version of the program, in which case, it might end in a ZIP extension. See the "Try Software Before You Buy It" section later in this chapter on how to handle those kinds of files.)

Then double-click the file to run the installation program. Now just follow the onscreen instructions. Voilà! You've just downloaded and installed the program.

Top Tips for Handling Downloaded Software

As I mentioned before, downloading software has some drawbacks. But buying software this way is perfectly safe; I've done it quite a bit myself. Just be sure to follow this advice:

- ➤ **Keep a copy of the file you downloaded.** You want to be sure that if something goes wrong with the program after you installed it, you have a backup. So after you install the software, don't delete the actual file you downloaded. Instead, keep a copy on your hard disk.

- ➤ **Copy to a floppy.** If the file you downloaded fits on a floppy disk (if it's less than 1.4 megabytes), copy it to a floppy disk and keep the disk somewhere safe. That way, you always have a backup if, God forbid, your hard disk crashes.

- ➤ **Print your order page and put it in a safe place.** If for some reason you need to get another copy of the software, having a hard copy of your order page will be proof that you paid for the software.

- ➤ **Keep a copy of your email confirmation.** Some sites send you an email confirmation when you order. Keep a copy of the confirmation message, both on your computer and printed out, so you can get another copy of the software if something goes wrong.

- ➤ **Bookmark the Web page from which you downloaded the software.** If you need to redownload the file for some reason, you'll be able to get it directly from that page.

How to Get the Best Deals on Buying Software Online

Okay, I've already told you about a dozen times that you can get great software deals online. So how should you go about buying software using the Internet? Follow these steps to get the best deals possible.

Step 1: Check Out Comparative Reviews

What do the experts say about which software you should buy? It's easy to find out. As I detailed in Chapter 16, "Drive a Hard Bargain on Hardware: Getting the Best Deal on Buying a Computer," you'll find lots of help online. Head to the same sites for software reviews that you do for hardware reviews—notably ZDNet at `www.zdnet.com` and also ClNet at `www.cnet.com`. When you're at ZDNet, also be sure to check out the message boards—many are devoted to discussions about software.

In particular, head to the SoftwareUser section of ZDNet at www.softwareuser.com. You'll find hundreds of software reviews, as well as columns and hands-on advice about what to buy. ZDNet is owned by Ziff-Davis, the company that publishes top computer magazines such as *PC Magazine, FamilyPC,* and *PC/Computing.* You get to read all the reviews from the magazines for free online at the SoftwareUser site. Shown here is the reviews-at-a-glance feature of the site.

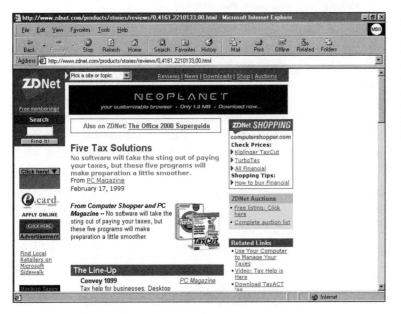

For advice on which software to buy, head to the SoftwareUser section of ZDNet at www.softwareuser.com. Here's a roundup of what many magazines have to say about tax preparation software.

Daily newspapers also often review software. From my point of view, *USA Today* at www.usatoday.com is the best place to find software reviews. Check out its tech section.

When reading the reviews, be sure to look at the version number that's being reviewed. Software is always being rewritten and rereleased, and you want to be sure that the review you're reading refers to the most current version of the software available.

What's a Version Number?

Software is constantly being rewritten and revised. Each time a new version of a particular piece of software is released, it gets a new *version number*. The first version is always 1.0. When the software is significantly rewritten and then released again by the publisher, it gets the next higher number, for example, 2.0. However, sometimes companies make only minor changes to the software, and in that case they put out what's called a *point release*. The first point release after version 2.0 of a piece of software is version 2.1. The second point release is version 2.2. When a major upgrade follows a point release, it jumps to the next digit—in this case, 3.0.

Always check out more than one magazine, newspaper, or Web site for software reviews. That's because you want more than a single point of view about a particular piece of software.

Some Internet sites let you read the newest reviews for free but then charge you to read old reviews. In general, old reviews aren't worth the money. In many cases, those old reviews cover versions of the software that aren't even being sold anymore.

Step 2: Try Software Before You Buy It

Imagine this: You want to buy a new car, but you'd like to test drive it for a month before deciding whether to fork over the moolah. Or you'd like to use a new refrigerator for two weeks before deciding whether to turn over your cash. Sounds crazy, yes?

Well, when it comes to software on the Internet, this idea's not so crazy. In fact, you can get free, fully working, test-drive versions of most software to use for a month or more before deciding whether you want to buy it. So let me get this straight, you're no doubt asking, I can try out software for free, no questions asked, for at least 30 days before deciding whether to buy it? Is that true? Is there some kind of catch here?

Yes, it's true, and there's no catch. Some people call try-before-you-buy software *demo* software, some call it *trial* software, and some call it *shareware*. I just call it a great deal. You'll find tens of thousands of programs such as this all over the Internet—everything from powerful programs from companies such as Microsoft and Symantec to games from big game companies such as Sierra Online. The software is available at a number of sites, such as the ZDNet Software Library at `www.hotfiles.com`. You can also head directly to the manufacturers' Web sites to see which software you can download and try out for free.

Here's how it works. You go to a site that specializes in this kind of software, such as the ZDNet Software Library at `www.hotfiles.com`, shown here. Then you download the software to your computer, install it, and try it out. If you like it, go ahead and buy it. If you don't like it, no problem; you don't have to pay a penny for it.

To use the software, you first have to download it, which means transferring it over the Internet. You usually click a **Download** button or link—then just follow the site's instructions.

Use "Freeware" Instead of Commercial Software

Many companies give away their software for free forever, which means you can save big bucks. This software is perfectly useful and is often as good as software you have to spend money on. Sometimes, this software is from small companies you've never heard of. But not only small companies give away freeware. The biggest software company on the planet, Microsoft, gives away its Internet Explorer browser, and Netscape gives away its Navigator browser. The big download sites, such as `www.hotfiles.com`, have good selections of freeware.

When the software has been saved, you have to install it. One important thing to keep in mind is that often, but not always, the software has been *compressed* in some way—shrunk in size so that it doesn't take so long to download. However, you can't run the program in its compressed form, which is bad. First you have to uncompress it. Here's where things get a bit sticky.

If the PC file has been compressed, it ends in an *extension* with the letters ZIP, like this: DEMOFILE.ZIP. *ZIP* refers to a compression method that uses a program called PKZIP. So you're going to have to unzip the program before you can use it. (No unzipping jokes here, please. This is a G-rated book, after all.) Unzipping a program uncompresses it and puts it into a form that you can use.

To unzip any program, get a copy of a program called WinZip. It's the easiest-to-use and all-around best program for unzipping files. Get it at the WinZip site at `www.winzip.com` or at a software download site such as `www.hotfiles.com`.

Best place on the Internet for finding try-before-you-buy software: the ZDNet Software Library at www.hotfiles.com.

So you've downloaded the file, you've unzipped it, and you're ready to try it out for free. What next? You'll have to install it. Some files unzip into a single file. Other files unzip into many files. In either case, after you unzip the program, you have to install it by running an install program. Typically, the install program is called INSTALL.EXE, SETUP.EXE, or something similar. Just run that file by double-clicking it and then follow the instructions. Voilà! You can now try out the software for free.

You can usually use the free program for about 30 days. (Sometimes you can use it for less time, and sometimes more.) After that trial period, you can buy the program. Almost always you'll be able to buy it online. A list of the top sites on the Internet for buying software online appears later in the chapter.

If you're a member of the small but hardy band of Macintosh users, the situation is slightly different after you download software to your computer. Typically, the files have been compressed in the Stuffed, BinHexed format (hey, who said the Mac was easier to use than the PC?) and so have to be uncompressed. The best way to uncompress them is to use a program called StuffIt Expander. You can get the free program at www.macdownload.com or many other download sites on the Internet. After you uncompress the downloaded files, install them as you do any other Mac files. You can then try out the program for free and buy it on the Internet.

Another reason to check out the software download sites such as the ZDNet Software Library at www.hotfiles.com is that major software companies at times give away their software. Microsoft, for example, was giving away its excellent personal information manager and email package, Outlook, when it was launched. Microsoft did that, hoping to create a buzz around the product at launch. It happens fairly frequently.

222

Step 3: Heed This Advice Before Buying

So you finally decided on which software you want to buy. The hard part of your shopping is done, right? No, wrong. Here are some shopping tips you should keep in mind before buying software over the Internet:

➤ **Check out the site's return policy.** If you want to return software that's been shipped to you, often you have to return it within 30 days after ordering it—and only if you haven't opened the box. In the case of software you've downloaded, you might have to deal with different return policies. Check before buying.

➤ **Consider buying the download-only version of the software.** As mentioned earlier in this chapter, you can save money by buying this way.

➤ **Ask about free or low-cost upgrades.** Software companies sometimes agree to give their customers the next, upgraded edition of certain software for free or at a reduced cost. Call the software maker to see whether they offer these deals.

➤ **Ask about competitive upgrade offers.** Software companies fight hard for your dollar. Sometimes they give cut-rate deals to people who own competing versions of certain products—for example, Microsoft giving WordPerfect owners a half-priced deal on Microsoft Word. Again, call the software company to see whether it has any offers like that. If you own a previous version of the product, see whether a special deal exists for current owners—there almost always is.

Take Advantage of Online Rebates to Get Software Free

It's often possible to get high-quality software free—if you keep an eye out for special online rebates. Software selling sites such as Beyond.com at www.beyond.com gather together rebate offers from software companies, and then kick in special rebates of their own, often offering rebates that equal the selling price of the software. That means you essentially get the software free. You have to buy the software, and then send in the forms for the rebate. I've done it often, and it's one of the world's best deals. When I last checked in at Beyond.com, you could get a free copy of Microsoft's excellent Encarta encyclopedia because of the rebates offered by Microsoft and Beyond.com. Just be sure to read the fine print on the rebate offers.

➤ **Be sure that you're buying the current version.** You don't want to get stuck with an older version of software. Check the publisher's Web site for the latest version before you buy.

➤ **Keep the confirmation of your order.** Keep a record of what you ordered and what you paid. Print it out and keep it in a safe place. If you've been sent email confirmation, print that out and keep it.

➤ **Be sure that your credit card isn't charged until the software is shipped.** The product might be out of stock, and it could take the seller a while to get a copy of the software you want. Be sure your credit card isn't charged until the seller ships the software to you.

Step 4: Head to a Software-Buying Site

If you're gotten this far, now you're *really* ready to buy. You can head to a software-buying supersite or directly to the publisher of the software. Here's the lowdown on each.

Buying from a Software Supersite

Mostly, you'll want to buy software from a software supersite. Many hardware sites, covered in the previous chapter, also sell software, so be sure you check them as well. Software supersites, such as Beyond.com (www.beyond.com) shown here, carry a huge selection of software, sell software for less than software companies themselves do, and often have special deals that you won't find elsewhere.

Beyond.com is one of the biggest software supersites you'll find on the Internet.

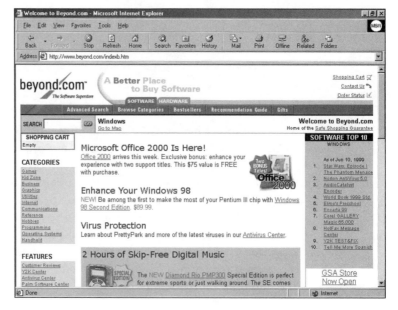

Buying Directly from the Software Company

Many software companies, such as Symantec at `www.symantec.com`, sell their software directly on the Internet. When you buy from a site such as this, you usually pay more than if you buy from a software supersite. But you often find deals and promotions on these sites that you don't find elsewhere on the Web. For example, Symantec has a Tell a Friend promotion on its Web site. If you get people to buy Symantec products, you earn points toward free software and other goods from Symantec. And when you buy directly from the software company, you know you're getting the latest version of the software. Of course, that site sells only its own software, so the selection is limited.

Best Places to Buy Software on the Internet

Most of the hardware-buying sites mentioned in the last chapter sell software as well, so be sure to check them out before buying. Here are the best of the best software-buying sites, some of which also sell hardware.

Beyond.com

> `http://www.beyond.com`

Beyond.com is the best software-buying sites I've come across. It has a great selection of just about any title; you can buy some software by downloading it directly; and you get descriptions of all the products you buy. Browsing and searching are easy. The prices are good and they often have software that you essentially get free. You get rebates from the manufacturer and from Beyond.com that add up to the purchase price.

BuySoft

> `http://www.buysoft.com`

BuySoft is a solid site for buying software. It has a good selection, often has good specials, and makes it pretty easy to find what you're looking for. BuySoft is a companion site to the BuyComp.com computer-selling site.

CompUSA

> `http://www.compusa.com`

The retail computer superstore sells software online. No great surprise: The selection here is huge. You'll find hardware on sale as well.

Check This Out

Here's How to Find a Software Publisher's Web Site

It's a breeze to find a software publisher's Web site. Just type the publisher's name between the www and the .com. For example, Brøderbund's Web site is `www.broderbund.com`.

Cyberian Outpost

http://www.outpost.com

Neon colors, animated graphics, blowout sales—you might think you accidentally wandered into Times Square. However, the selection and deals here are good. Cyberian Outpost sells a lot of hardware as well.

Is this Times Square or a software store? Check out the deals at Cyberian Outpost at www.outpost.com.

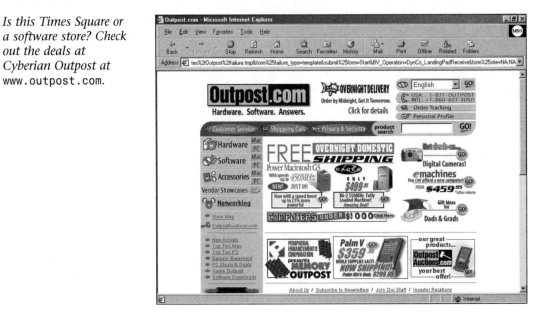

DownloadWarehouse

http://www.downloadwarehouse.com

DownloadWarehouse isn't particularly pretty or glitzy—in fact, it's one of the more boring sites you'll come across—but it features a good selection of software. It often has hard-to-find software but tends to be skimpy on some of the better-known names. DownloadWarehouse is a companion site to the MicroWarehouse hardware site at www.microwarehouse.com.

Egghead

http://www.egghead.com

There was a time when Egghead software stores were all over the country. No longer. Now if you want to buy software from Egghead, you have to do it on the Internet. There's a huge selection of software here, and it's all easy to find.

PC Connection Online Superstore

http://www.pcconnection.com

This site, which sells software as well as hardware, features a reasonable collection of software. The drawback is that it's hard to find what you're looking for. Still, it's worth checking out the prices.

Softmania

http://www.softmania.com

Softmania is a great site for games, entertainment, and home software, but not as good for business-related software and utilities. Finding what you want is easy, and the top 10 list in each category is useful if you want to know what other people are buying.

Software-Buying Sites Usually Don't Let You Try Software Free First

If you go to a software-buying site expecting to try out software free, you'll be disappointed. With few exceptions, those sites won't let you try before you buy. You need to go to a site that specializes in try-before-you-buy software, such as the ZDNet Software Library at www.hotfiles.com, or a software company's Web site, to get a trial version.

Software BuyLine

http://www.softwarebuyline.com

This site offers a lot of software at decent prices. More than other sites, it also offers the capability to download products directly to your PC. You'll find lots of files from little-known publishers here, as well as well-known software.

> ## The Least You Need to Know
>
> ➤ Always check software comparative reviews before buying.
>
> ➤ Downloading software over the Internet can save you time and money.
>
> ➤ Using freeware instead of buying software can mean big savings.
>
> ➤ Check for competitive and upgrade offers before buying any software.

FAT!

Chapter 18

How to Buy Consumer Electronics

> ## In This Chapter
>
> ➤ Where to get advice on consumer electronics
>
> ➤ What kinds of online stores sell consumer electronics—and which are the best for you
>
> ➤ Things you should know before buying consumer electronics over the Internet
>
> ➤ Best sites for buying consumer electronics over the Internet

If you like gear, gadgets, and gizmos, as well as TVs, radios, and stereos—in fact, if you like anything to do with consumer electronics—you'll find a whole lot of help on the Web. You'll be able to find the best products by checking out consumer advice and review sites. Then you'll be able to search and compare the best products to find the best prices online. So read on, gadgeteers, whether your pleasure be pagers, PalmPilots, or portable players of all kinds.

Great Guides to Gear, Gadgets, Gizmos, TVs, and More

The Internet is a great tool to research your next electronics buy. Even if you don't plan to buy your favorite electronics and gizmos over the Web, you can still use the Internet to find the best product at the best price. You'll be able to find reviews and shopping guides, comparison lists, how-tos, and backgrounders. Whether you're a gearhead or a technophobe, there's help for you online. Before buying any piece of electronics, check out the reviews and buying guides.

Catch Up on the Latest News About DVD

DVD is an electronic techie's dream—but it's often tough to get news about the technology or to find out what the newest releases are. To get the latest, head over to etown at `www.etown.com` and then click **DVD Central**. Not only do you get news about DVD, but also you get a list of currently available movies and movies that soon will be out on DVD.

Start at etown at `www.etown.com`. It's the place to keep coming to again and again for great backgrounders on any piece of electronics equipment. Click the **Buy Guide**. Want to know the most important features to look for when buying an 8mm camcorder—and the price you should be paying? It's in there. How about the most important things to keep in mind when buying a surround-sound speaker system for your TV? Yup, it's in there, too. How about the three most important things you should know when buying a new cordless telephone? You guessed it...etown has it.

You'll also find reviews of individual electronics products and a great gear finder, shown here, that asks questions about what you're looking for and then guides you to the right product reviews. Not to be missed are the site's message boards (click **Town Hall**) where you can talk about anything to do with electronics, from where to find the best price on a product to which product to buy.

Looking for gear? etown helps you find what you need, using its gear finder.

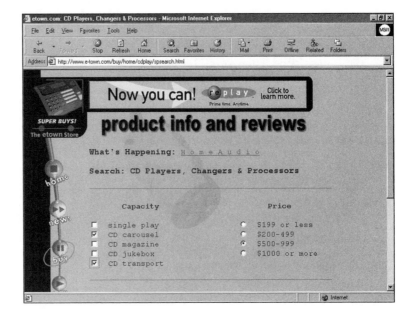

The GTE ConsumerGuide at www.consumerguide.com is another place worth stopping. While it won't give you nearly as good a background or overview of different kinds of electronic products as etown does, this site does something that etown doesn't: ConsumerGuide makes specific suggestions on which makes and models to buy and gives best buys for each kind of electronics products, such as DVD players. It also lists the retail price—but better yet, this site tells you the range of the lowest prices you should find for that product.

Get Free Advice from Electronics Techies

Need help understanding the specs of a DVD player? Want to know the difference between satellite TV services? The Roxy electronics-buying site at www.roxy.com promises to answer any questions you have about electronics products within 24 hours. Just send email to askthetech@roxy.com, and you'll get an answer.

For detailed product comparisons, head to CompareNet at www.comparenet.com. In addition to finding good help about various categories of electronics products, you'll be able to do side-by-side comparisons of specific makes and models.

Do you consider yourself an audio snob? Does the slightest imperfection in sound set your teeth on edge like chalk scraping across a blackboard? Do you have to have the best, the latest, the utmost in audio gear? If so, you'll find a home at the AudioReview pages at www.audioreview.com. That's where you'll find more than 5,000 reviews from the most persnickety people on the planet when it comes to audio gear. Visitors to the site do the reviews, rather than professional reviewers. And these people know their stuff. Don't believe me? Okay, here's a sample section of a review of a phonograph cartridge: "The ATOC9 tracks marvelously on the Telarc Omnidisc tracking test going beyond 35 seconds before distortion. However, the channel separation is poor when tested with my Ortofon test disk. It never reaches 25db!" Huh? Want to run that by me again? You'll also find bulletin boards here for talking about audio, but as you can tell by the reviews, you better be well informed before you pipe up.

Where Can I Buy Consumer Electronics Online?

The Web has an abundance of places where you can buy consumer electronics. If you have the money, they have the goods. Following are the kinds of places at which you'll be able to buy consumer electronics.

Malls and Department Stores

Any self-respecting mall or department store has an electronics department or section. Check out Chapter 15, "Mall Fever: Department Stores, Malls, Closeouts, and Bargain Hunting," for more information on how to shop at these sites and on the best malls and department stores on the Web. You can expect to find a reasonable selection of mainstream electronics products, often at very good prices. But don't expect much high-end equipment or the widest selection—for that, you'll have to head to online electronics specialty stores.

Computer Stores

Many online stores that sell computers and software also sell consumer electronics. They're worth checking out because, in some instances, the prices are excellent and the selection can rival that in electronics specialty stores. Check out Chapter 16, "Drive a Hard Bargain on Hardware: Getting the Best Deal on Buying a Computer," and Chapter 17, "Don't Be a Softie: Getting the Best Deal on Buying Software," for more information on ordering at computer stores and where to find the best ones.

Electronics Specialty Stores

Be sure to check out these stores, even if you find something you like in a mall or department store. They offer the biggest selections (Audiosource Pre One Preamplifiers, anyone?) and the best prices. Specialty sites often provide useful help, advice, and articles, as well as bulletin boards where you can talk to other people buying similar equipment.

Online Auctions and Classified Ads

One of the best ways to get consumer electronics at el cheapo prices is to buy them at auction and classified sites. You'll often find used and refurbished equipment as well as new. In fact, auction and classified sites are absolutely stuffed with this stuff—it's their bread and butter (or is that their camcorders and CD players?). For advice on how to buy at auctions and for the best auction sites, turn to Chapter 11, "Sold American! Buying Through Online Auctions." For classified ads, check out Chapter 10, "Classified Information: Getting the Most Out of Classified Ads on the Internet." Later in this chapter, you'll also find auction and classified ad sites that specialize in consumer electronics.

Shopping Agents

Shopping agents are Web sites that go out and find the best bargains by checking prices all across the Internet. Unfortunately, there aren't any top-notch agents that find the best prices on consumer electronics for you. But the shopping agent at Excite does help you find product reviews and has links to some of the best electronics-shopping sites online. Just be sure to check for the best prices yourself instead of relying on the agent. Turn to Chapter 7, "Shopping Robots, Agents, Search Tools, and Virtual Shopping Assistants," for more information on using shopping agents and for a list of shopping agents.

Use an Internet Escrow Service When Buying Electronics Equipment from Individuals at Classified and Auction Sites

When you buy electronics equipment from an individual at classified and auction sites, you might have no recourse if you receive defective equipment—goods sold this way rarely carry a manufacturer warranty or return privileges. Protect yourself by paying through an Internet escrow service. Instead of paying the seller directly, you pay the service. After you receive the goods and are satisfied with your purchase, you authorize the escrow service to pay the seller. If the goods don't check out, the escrow service refunds your money. There are a number of escrow services, including TradeSafe at `www.tradesafe.com`, I-Escrow at `www.iescrow.com`, and Trade-direct at `www.trade-direct.com`. Turn to Chapter 11 for more information about escrow services.

Closeouts and Liquidators

Some of the best deals you'll get on electronics are on equipment that is being discontinued or that has been overstocked. You'll find this kind of merchandise at closeout and liquidator sites. Head over to Chapter 15 to get the lowdown on these kinds of sites and to find good general ones.

Consumer Advice for Gearheads

Okay, I know you're salivating over that 35-inch Trinitron Sony TV, but hold on a second before sending your credit card number over the Internet. You still need to know a few things about buying consumer electronics.

Let's start with the basics:

➤ **Check out the warranty before buying.** This step is especially important if you're buying from liquidators or closeout specialists because their warranties might be more restricted than those from traditional stores—and in some cases might be nonexistent. Turn to Chapter 4, "How to Be a Cybersavvy Shopper," for more information on warranties.

➤ **Find out whether the equipment is new or used.** Sounds basic, doesn't it? But if you're buying from an auction site, a closeout specialist, or a liquidator, you might be buying refurbished equipment.

Read the Fine Print About Shipping Charges

For consumer electronics, you might end up paying more for shipping than you bargained for. For example, bulky large-screen TVs and tower-style speakers might incur extra shipping charges. And in one instance, I found fine print that said a shipping surcharge would be added if the TV had to be carried up more than four flights of stairs. So check the shipping charges for every item you buy—don't just rely on the general shipping charges posted on the site.

➤ **Figure in shipping costs.** Shipping charges, especially on big-ticket or over-size items, can add up—up to $100 or even more. Find out the cost of shipping before you buy. Again, turn to Chapter 4 for more information on shipping costs.

➤ **Know the return policy.** Do you have the right to return something you've bought—for any reason? How long do you have to decide whether to return it? And who pays the shipping charges? These policies vary greatly from site to site. Crutchfield at www.crutchfield.com, for example, has a no-questions-asked, 30-day return policy—and pays the return shipping.

➤ **Find out about toll-free technical support.** You've just bought a new double-freebish technode A-908Z1A. But now you can't get the thing to work (or even figure out what it's supposed to do). Whom do you call? No, not the Ghostbusters. The truth is, you probably don't know whom to call. Find out whether the seller offers toll-free technical support to help you set up or use what you've just bought. Few do. Again, Crutchfield is the exception; it offers that kind of support.

Best Sites for Researching and Buying Consumer Electronics

To help you find the site you want, I've divided them up into sections: sites to help you decide what to buy and sites that sell the merchandise. Keep in mind, though, that you might be able to buy electronics products at some sites that primarily offer advice and you can get advice on some sites that are primarily for shopping. So it's a good idea to check both kinds of sites, whether you're just researching or ready to go on a buying binge.

Sites for Consumer Advice and Reviews

You know you want to buy something—maybe it's a DVD player or a new stereo or a big-screen TV. But you're not sure exactly what to buy. Not to worry. There's a lot of help for you on the Internet. If you're like most gear, electronic, and gadget junkies, you think that researching is at least half the fun of the whole buying process. So check out these sites before buying. You might even want to browse through them just to read the reviews and fantasize about the dream home-entertainment system you can't afford to buy.

AudioReview

```
http://www.audioreview.com
```

Hang out where the audiophiles hang out—and read reviews written by what might be the pickiest people on the planet. Head here only if you really care about high-end equipment. But if you do, you'll probably never leave. AudioReview is an audiotech's heaven.

CompareNet

```
http://www.comparenet.com
```

CompareNet is the place to turn when you want to compare specs of different electronics products. You get side-by-side comparisons of features and prices, as well as helpful background information. There's also a classified section, where you can buy and sell electronics.

ConsumerGuide

```
http://www.consumerguide.com
```

Here's a place that names names—for just about every kind of consumer electronic product, ConsumerGuide gives specific recommendations on makes and models. It also tells you the lowest prices you can expect to pay and provides some good background information on the various technologies.

Head to the Equip Web Site at www.equip.com to Get the Latest on Electronics, Gadgets, and Geek Goods

You'll find articles about the latest and the greatest; reviews, techie notes, news from gadget freaks, and get the latest info at the Equip Web site (www.equip.com).

etown

http://www.etown.com

Here's the place to start your online research. Buying guides, reviews, articles, the latest news, discussion areas—here's where you should head when trying to decide what to buy. You'll find great information detailing exactly what you need to know about all kinds of consumer electronics before buying. There's also an area on the site where you can buy equipment as well.

Where to Head When It's Time to Buy

So you've done your research, you've checked your bank account (or maybe your credit rating), and it's finally time to put the cash down on the barrelhead. Where should you buy? Here are the sites you should head to when you get your next electronics hankering.

AudioWeb

http://www.audioweb.com

Here's a great place to buy audio equipment through classified ads and auctions. Lots of items are on sale, and you can find many good deals. AudioWeb also has newsgroups so that you can talk to others about what to buy and what not to buy, good articles, and links to other audio-related Web sites as well. There are also reviews of equipment taken from www.audioreview.com, written about earlier in this chapter.

Consumer Direct Warehouse

http://www.consumer-direct.com

Although this site concentrates on consumer electronics, you'll find all kinds of equipment here. It has an amazingly large selection of products, including a lot of stuff that would be hard to find elsewhere. I mean, when there's a selection of universal remote controls that range in price from $15.00 to $54.95, you know the site has a lot to choose from.

Crutchfield

http://www.crutchfield.com

Crutchfield is a great site for buying any kind of consumer electronics. It has a huge selection of products, good prices, good product descriptions, helpful articles—in short, anything you could want from an online electronics store. With its policy of paying return shipping fees and its toll-free tech support, Crutchfield is always a solid bet for electronics buying. It even has helpful interactive product finders, as you can see pictured here.

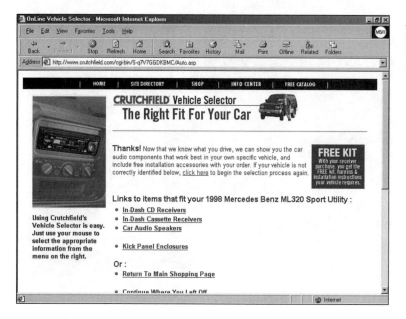

At Crutchfield, a product finder helps you determine which car audio equipment fits into your car.

NetMarket

http://www.netmarket.com

NetMarket is an all-around mall that deserves a mention here because its excellent electronics section is better than that of many electronics-only stores. NetMarket has a big selection, low prices, classifieds, and auctions; it's a great all-in-one site.

rec.audio.marketplace *and* rec.audio.misc

Go to rec.audio.marketplace and rec.audio.misc with your newsgroup reader.

You can barter, sell, and buy almost any piece of electronics equipment at these two newsgroups. The rec.audio.marketplace features more classified ads, and rec.audio.misc has more talk, but both places have great deals and lots of buying advice as well.

Sharper Image

http://www.sharperimage.com

What's the coolest electronics catalog in existence? Sharper Image, of course. Where else can you get James Bond–like devices such as voice-activated phone dialers or bizarre products such as a personal cooling system (essentially a tiny fan that wraps

237

around your neck)? Don't believe me? Check out the following figure. There's all that and more at the Sharper Image online.

Looking for a personal cooling system? Look no further—you've found it at the Sharper Image online.

Shopping.com

http://www.shopping.com

Here's another all-around mall with a huge electronics section. Shopping.com features more products than most electronics-only stores and makes it easy to search for the precise product you want.

Tek Gallery

http://www.discountwarehouse.com

Shortwave radios, minidisk players, electronic keyboards, radar detectors, stereos, TVs, DVD players...okay, I'll stop now because I think you get the idea. This site has lots and lots of stuff. Be sure to stop here on your comparison shopping expedition.

The Least You Need to Know

➤ The best place to start your electronics buying research is at www.etown.com.

➤ Check warranties, shipping charges, and return policies before buying.

➤ Read the fine print in shipping policies to see whether you have to pay extra for oversized equipment.

Chapter 19

Come Fly with Me: How to Get the Best Travel Deals

In This Chapter

➤ How to find the lowest-priced airline tickets

➤ How to book tickets online

➤ Ways to get extra frequent-flier miles

➤ Finding the best hotel rates

➤ Best travel sites on the Internet

You like exotic destinations? That's what I figured. You like convenience? I thought so. How about saving money? No great surprise. And making it easy to make travel plans? Of course. There's no better way than the Internet to research your next trip to help find the best airfare at the best price, get reservations at the best hotels, and to find out the best places to vacation. Whether you're heading to Timbuktu for a month-long trek, to Disneyland for a week, or to your mother's house for the week-end, the Internet helps you shop for the best travel deals—and enables you to buy them as well.

You'll be able to research your travel plans online, whether or not you actually book the travel over the Internet. You can also buy tickets, book hotel rooms and rental cars, and get extra travel perks, such as frequent-flier miles. And bargain-conscious travelers will be pleased to know that they can get great deals on the Internet that aren't available anywhere else. So be sure to head online for the sites before you visit the sights.

Getting the Best Deals on Airplane Tickets

I have a hard-and-fast rule about travel these days: I never go on a trip without checking the Internet first. Sometimes I go online to find the cheapest fare. Other times it's to find a hotel, to learn about travel destinations, or get maps. I can't tell you how much money and time I've saved and how many vacations I've salvaged by using the Internet.

So whether or not you book your travel online, the first thing to do is head to the Internet to do travel research. Here's how to do it.

How to Research Airfares Online and Find Bargains

If you do nothing else when making travel plans, at least research flights and airfares on the Internet. It's exceptionally easy to do and won't cost you a penny. If you're uncomfortable buying tickets over the Internet, that's no problem. After you find the flight information, call the airline and book it yourself. By doing things this way, instead of relying on calling one or two airlines, you can save yourself hundreds of dollars.

Follow These Tips for Getting the Cheapest Airfares

Although finding the cheapest airfare often feels like finding a needle in a haystack, following a few travel rules can help you get the best deal. If you stay over on a Saturday night, you usually reduce your ticket price, sometimes significantly. Book midmorning or late-evening flights; those are the cheapest. Travel on a Tuesday, Wednesday, or Saturday (unless you're staying over Saturday night) and avoid traveling on a Monday, Friday, or holiday. And be sure to buy your ticket more than 21 days in advance.

Any major travel site, such as Expedia at www.expedia.com, Preview Travel at www.previewtravel.com, or the Internet Travel Network at www.itn.com, lets you research your own travel flights and fares. It's easy to do it. Here's how.

Most sites ask that you first become a member before checking their flights. You won't have to pay, so don't worry about joining; all you have to do is make up a username and password. You'll be asked for your email address, and often you'll be asked whether you want to receive special offers via email. I always say no—I get enough junk mail as it is. Many sites are happy to send you email announcements of great travel deals, so if you don't mind getting mail, then sign up.

After you register, you can check for fares. All the sites work similarly. Fill in information about your travel plans, such as when you're leaving, when you want to return, and whether you have preferred airlines. I suggest at this point not limiting your search to specific airlines because you might miss out on the best possible price.

After you fill out all your travel information, you get to see the flights and their prices, as shown here in a screen from Expedia at `www.expedia.com`. This information is for a round-trip flight between Boston and San Francisco—a route you can often find me on. The flights are usually shown with the least expensive at the top to the most expensive at the end of the list.

Tracking down the cheapest airfare from Boston to San Francisco on the Expedia site.

As you can see, spending a few minutes online checking for flights can save you hundreds of dollars. The cheapest round-trip flight from Boston to San Francisco is more than $80 less expensive than the next cheapest flight—and the cheaper flight goes through Denver, while the more expensive flight requires you to make a connection in Las Vegas. And, of course, if you're flying through Las Vegas, you could lose a good portion of your money on the slots if you're not careful—and yes, there are slot machines in the Las Vegas airport. Lots of them. Take it from one who's lost his share of money there.

Create a Traveler Profile for Quicker Service

Some travel sites, such as Expedia at www.expedia.com, let you create a traveler profile. That way, whenever you book travel, all your pertinent information is already filled in and you are able to make travel plans more quickly. You include information such as your seat and meal preferences and your home airport. Perhaps most importantly, you also put in the name and numbers of your frequent-flier plans so that whenever you book travel from the site, your miles are automatically credited.

Be very careful to note all the pertinent information when checking flights that you book over the Internet. Is the flight nonstop? Is it a stopover or do you have to change planes? How long is the layover between planes if you're catching a connecting flight? All this information might not always be immediately apparent, so read the fine print everywhere. In fact, I suggest printing out the pages and reading them off the Web as well as on the Web. By the way, no great surprise: The cheaper flights are rarely nonstop and often have longer layovers. Also, be sure to check for any restrictions on the flights and what kind of penalty you'll pay if you cancel your tickets—or if you can cancel them at all. Again, lower-cost flights often charge higher cancellation fees.

Family travelers, note: You should also check how often the flight is on time versus how often it's delayed. Many travel sites, such as Expedia, tell you how often each leg of the flight arrives on time. Speaking from personal experience, few events in one's lifetime are more harrowing than being delayed at an airport with young children demanding to know "Are we there yet?" when in fact you haven't even boarded your flight. You'll be surprised at the huge variance in on-time arrivals among different airlines and different cities. Taking the Boston to San Francisco trip as an example, Expedia reports that when returning from San Francisco, the connecting flight to Las Vegas is on time only 50% of the time.

Most flight information also tells you whether a meal is served on the plane. In these days of continuing airline cutbacks, not all flights serve food. Of course, if you're like me and believe that most airline meals aren't really food anyway, the food situation might not be a big deal.

After you find the flight you're interested in, if you're not comfortable buying online, print the itinerary information. Then call the airline and make the reservation over the phone. That's what I often do. And when I travel on business, before calling my company's travel agent, I always check the flights myself over the Internet and then tell the agency which flights to book.

If You Order by Phone, Demand the Same Deal You Found Online

Sometimes you'll find a great deal online, but you've decided that you'd rather pay over the telephone instead of online. When you call in to pay, though, the operator might not offer the same deal you found online. Be firm: Tell them that you found the deal online, and even give the Web page if you have to. They'll generally agree to give you the same deal. I found a great deal online on Miami-to-Los Angeles round-trip tickets that was about $1,000 cheaper than the second less-expensive fare. My parents, who lack an Internet connection, called the airline to buy the tickets. At first, the operator balked, but after a few minutes, agreed to book the fare.

Another way to search on a site for airfares is to search only for the lowest published airfares. When you choose that option, put in the pertinent information, just as you would for your regular flight checker. You'll then be shown the lowest published fares between cities. You'll also be shown a good deal of fine print, describing all the various restrictions, caveats, excuses, folderol, and hoops you'll have to jump through to get those fares. Print the folderol. Read it if you can. Then call the airline, tell the reservation agent the fare you want to get, and book your flight.

How to Buy Tickets Online

After you decide on your travel plans, you can buy your tickets right online—you can save yourself time, and possibly get extra frequent-flier miles or other bonuses for buying tickets this way.

All the usual caveats apply when buying tickets over the Internet. You'll be asked for your credit card number and other information when booking a flight. Because air travel is literally a big-ticket item, be sure that you're buying from a secure site. Turn to Chapter 4, "How to Be a Cybersavvy Shopper," for information on how to do that. All the major travel sites on the Internet, including the airlines, are secure sites.

Free Perks When You Buy Online

You'll want to research flight information at Web sites such as Preview Travel at `www.previewtravel.com`. However, after you decide which flight to book, consider buying instead at the airline's Web site. Many Web sites, such as American Airlines at `www.aa.com`, give you perks such as extra frequent-flier miles when you book through them online.

After you pay for your ticket, you'll often have a choice of how to get it delivered. Usually, delivery is free via normal mail—that is, if anything about the U.S. Postal Service can be called normal. You'll often be given the option of paying extra for an overnight express service, and in some instances you'll be able to instead pick up the ticket yourself at a local travel agent.

An increasingly popular way of booking travel is called the e-ticket. Think of an e-ticket as a virtual ticket because, in fact, the ticket itself doesn't exist. Instead of getting a ticket delivered to you, you get a confirmation number. That confirmation number becomes your ticket. So be sure to print it out, as well as copy it down and keep it in a safe place. A single confirmation number covers all the passengers in your party, so if you're traveling as a family, everyone uses the same number.

When you buy an e-ticket, you'll also get an email that includes your itinerary and flight information, including meal information (yum!) and which movies, if any, will be shown on the flight.

When you show up at the airport, you don't need to go to a ticket counter. Instead, just head to the gate for check-in. Give your confirmation number and show a photo ID. That's all there is; then head onboard.

By the way, if you want to use frequent-flier miles for booking your flights, you won't be able to do that online. Instead, you'll have to contact the airline directly.

The Frugal Flyer: How to Get Rock-Bottom Airfare Prices

Here's one of the traveling world's biggest secrets: You can use the Internet to get absolutely rock-bottom prices on airline tickets. You won't be able to find better deals anywhere else.

One way to get these deals is to subscribe to email newsletters that alert you to one-time offers—or to visit Web sites that specialize in listing them. Another way is to visit the auctions and broker sites that offer steep discounts on airline seats. In both instances, you won't have the same kind of choice of destinations and departure and arrival times as you have when you pay full freight. Still, if you're flexible and looking for some great deals, you won't believe the bargains you can get. Here's how to do it.

How to Save Big Bucks on Last-Minute Plane Tickets

The airlines are always looking at ways to squeeze as many people as possible into as small a space as possible—and so to squeeze out as much profit as possible. So they've come up with a way to fill seats that at the last minute would otherwise be empty—and that means you can save big bucks.

Every week, many major airlines—notably American Airlines—send out a free email alert to people looking for deals, telling them of last-minute price breaks. The airlines see what flights have a good number of empty seats that aren't likely to be filled for the next week and drop the prices on those seats drastically. For example, one time when I checked, I could fly from San Antonio, Texas, to Mexico City for $149 round-trip, even though the usual inexpensive price on that route was $325. That's some serious saving.

Travel in the Fall to Get Top Discounts

The time of year you travel determines how high your ticket prices will be. The fall is often a slow travel season, and so starting near the end of August, airlines start offering discount prices.

As you might guess, there's a catch. These last-minute deals are really last minute. The emails on domestic flights are typically sent out on a Wednesday afternoon, and the prices are good only from that day through the weekend. International flights are usually posted instead on Monday and are good through the weekend. And the deals are available only on selected flights to selected cities—from Chicago to Atlanta one week, from Boston to Seattle the next. So if you're interested in these kinds of deals, have your bags packed and be ready to go—and pack your bathing suit as well as your down jacket because you could end up heading to anywhere from Maine to Southern California.

These kinds of last-minute deals are generally available only on the Internet—you won't find them any other way. Head to the individual airline sites to sign up for the alerts.

Of course, sorting through all that email could become a pain. Fortunately, two Web sites have sections devoted to helping you find these last-minute deals. Go to WebFlyer at www.webflyer.com and click on **Deal Watch**. You'll be able to look at the city you're flying from to see what deals are available that week. If you prefer to receive a weekly email alert clueing you in to all the deals from all the airlines, surf over to 1travel.com at `www.1travel.com`, click **Last Minute Deals**, and sign up. Both sites, by the way, also let you find similar deals offered by hotels across the country. I cover that topic later in this chapter.

Getting El Cheapo Prices from Ticket Auctions

Another way to get inexpensive tickets is from so-called ticket-auction sites. These aren't at all like the normal kinds of Internet auctions because you don't do the bidding. Instead, travel agents and others bid against one another to give you the lowest ticket price.

Right now, two slightly different ticket-auction sites are available on the Internet: PriceLine at `www.priceline.com` and TravelBids at `www.travelbids.com`.

At PriceLine, you choose where you want to travel to and from and the dates you would like to arrive and depart. Then you head to the site and fill in that information about your trip. You also fill in a price that you're willing to pay for a ticket. Agents and other travel pros then try to match your price. If they match your price, you have to pay for the ticket; if they don't, no money changes hands.

One thing to keep in mind about PriceLine is that if you're willing to leave and depart from several airports—not just the one closest to your home—you improve your chances of getting a ticket at the price you want. Shown here is a page that let me choose which airports I'd be willing to leave and arrive from.

At PriceLine, you name the price, and travel agents or airlines have to meet it; or you don't buy the ticket.

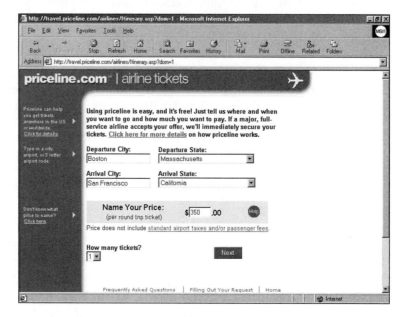

The other thing to realize is that the more outrageously low the price you ask for, the less likely you are to get a ticket. So don't expect to get any round-trips to Paris at $59 (but on the off chance that you do, could you please take me along?). Your best bet is to go to one of the major travel sites such as Expedia, find the cheapest ticket to your destination, and then chop some off that for your asking price. Oh, and one final thing to keep in mind: If someone meets your price, you have to buy the ticket; you can't back out or get a refund. So be really sure you want to go.

TravelBids works a little more like a traditional Internet auction. You start off by finding the lowest-price ticket to your destination; then you call the airline to make a reservation—but don't pay for the ticket. Instead, ask the reservation agent to hold the ticket for you. Sometimes the airline holds it only for a day; sometimes longer. Right after you make the reservation, head to the TravelBids site and put in the exact details of your ticket—the airline you're flying, the arrival and departure time, in other words, the whole nine yards. Travel agents then bid on giving you a lower price than the airline did. If someone can give you a lower price, you pay that travel agent instead of the airline, and he or she takes care of getting your tickets for you. If a travel agent can't give you a lower price, call back the airline and buy the ticket—or simply decide not to go to Acapulco and, instead, bank the money.

Fly and Fly Again: Using the Web to Get More Out of Frequent-Flier Plans

Nothing is more satisfying than getting something for nothing, like when you get a free ticket or an upgrade to first class through your frequent-flier club. You can use the Web to make those miles add up more quickly.

Best Sites for Frequent Fliers

So where should you go when you want to earn more frequent-flier miles? Head to these three best sites for getting the most out of frequent-flier clubs—and for earning bonus miles.

> *Check This Out*
>
> **Earn Frequent-Flier Miles by Staying in Hotels**
>
> Many hotels give you frequent-flier miles when you stay there, especially if your stay is in concert with an airplane flight. Whenever you check in, ask whether you can earn frequent-flier miles for your stay.

ClickRewards

http://www.clickrewards.com

Here's what this site promises: Use your mouse to earn frequent-flier miles. It's a pretty straightforward offer. Whenever you buy a product or use a service from a site that has a deal with ClickRewards, you earn extra frequent-flier miles. Each

ClickReward point equals one frequent-flier mile. You can earn miles by doing things such as buying software, toys, CDs, and other products online and by opening an online banking account.

WebFlyer

        http://www.webflyer.com

Here's the best site on the Web for getting the most out of your frequent-flier plan—and for getting bonus miles as well. I mean this site has everything, absolutely everything you'll ever need to know about frequent-flier plans. There's news, advice, comparisons of different plans, online enrollments, the capability to check your accumulated mileage, and much more. But probably the best part of the site is its coverage of special deals and bonuses for frequent-flier miles. It reports, for example, on the top 10 special ways for getting frequent-flier miles. These are short-term deals that otherwise you never would have heard about, things such as earning 10,000 miles for signing up for a Diner's Club card. And the site also lists the top five frequent flier bonuses—things such as being able to get a free ticket on Midway Airlines for 15,000 instead of 25,000 miles.

The site does much more as well. It also helps you find deals on last-minute plane tickets, get deals on hotels and car rentals, and lets you research travel plans. Make this one a must-visit site.

Book It! How to Get Hotel and Car Reservations Online

Just as you can use the Web to book flights and find great deals on airfares, you can do the same for getting hotel reservations and car rentals. All the major travel sites (reviewed later in this chapter in "Best Travel Sites Online") let you research hotels and rental cars and also let you book car rentals.

Get Hotel and Car Rental Discounts

Little-known fact: Many organizations you belong to can get you discounts on hotels and car rentals. For example, the American Automobile Association and the American Association of Retired Persons have many deals that give you these discounts. Whenever booking a room, mention your memberships and see whether you can get a special discount.

Finding hotels or car rentals is pretty straightforward, and most sites generally work the same. Fill in the city you're planning to visit, and you'll get a list of hotels and car-rental firms. You'll get descriptions, prices, and generally more information than you'll ever need. When you find the hotel or car-rental place you want, you can either call the company directly or instead place a reservation online. It's that simple.

How to Get Special Deals and Rock-Bottom Prices on Hotel Rooms

In the same way that the Web can get you rock-bottom airline prices, it can get you great deals on hotels and car rentals. For great discounts, you can visit Web sites that specialize in heavy-duty discounts, or you can watch for last-minute deals where hotels are trying to book rooms that would otherwise be empty. In contrast, you can often find normal discounts well ahead of time. Most of the discount sites listed in this chapter are the plan-ahead kind, rather than those that offer last-minute deals.

You'll get last-minute deals only from hotels that need to fill up their rooms, often in the off-season, or out-of-the way locations—although that isn't always the case. Even prime locations sometimes offer these last-minute deals, but you might not know about them until the Wednesday before the Saturday they're available. So you'll have to be willing to fly off at a moment's notice. In general, you won't find last-minute deals on car rentals; it's usually hotels that offer last-minute deals.

Check the Weather Before You Travel

Heading to San Diego for the weekend? Should you pack a sweater, a raincoat, or something heavier? Before traveling anywhere, head to the Weather Channel's site at www.weather.com and get the local weather for your destination.

Hotels also have longer-lasting seasonal promotions. The first place to check is the hotel-chain Web sites. Some post their specials there, and others also offer email alerts when they have deals. For example, when I checked the Westin chain at www.westin.com, I found a slew of specials, including rooms for under $80 in some cities, and a $100 coupon that could be credited toward another stay in a Westin.

Instead of trying to hit every hotel chain on the Web, you can head to Web sites that give you the lowdown on all the deals from all the chains. WebFlyer at www.webflyer.com does that, as does 1travel.com at www.1travel.com. Just head to those sites and look for the hotel discount areas.

Best Travel Sites Online

The Web hosts dozens, and more likely hundreds, of travel sites. Here are the best of the best.

Expedia

http://www.expedia.com

Book flights and hotels, find out special deals, get the latest travel news, find out special vacation bargains, get maps of where you're heading, read travel articles—it's hard to beat this all-around site. As with most travel sites, you'll have to register to get the most out of it, but registration is free.

Hotel Discounts

http://www.hoteldiscounts.com

Here's the place to go for hotel discounts of all kinds, as well as last-minute bargains. You can even subscribe to an email newsletter with all the latest bargains. Using the Internet can't get any easier: Click the city where you want to stay and fill in a form detailing the days you're staying, how many people will be staying, and similar information; in return, you get a list of available rooms. Then click a hotel to book the room. You're done.

Don't Get Lost When You Travel

There's nothing worse than getting lost in a strange city. You don't have to get lost anymore. Check out the interactive maps at MapQuest at www.mapquest.com. Type any location in the United States as a starting point and then your destination; you'll get detailed driving directions, complete with a map, that you can print out and take along.

Internet Travel Network

http://www.itn.com

You can do more than book travel at this site. It also includes links to getting travel directions, to an online travel bookstore, to a very busy, useful discussion area (about every aspect of travel from general travel to specific areas, such as the Caribbean, to traveling with bicycles, getting airline tickets, and many more), and to articles on travel.

1travel.com

```
http://www.1travel.com
```

Here's an excellent site if you're looking for bargains and discounts. You'll find discounted airfares and hotel rooms as well as the latest short-term bargains.

Preview Travel

```
http://www.previewtravel.com
```

Another superb all-around travel site that helps you get the lowest prices on tickets, hotels, and car rentals. There's news, a vacation area, a section for business travelers, and great ways to find the cheapest prices. The site is shown in the following figure.

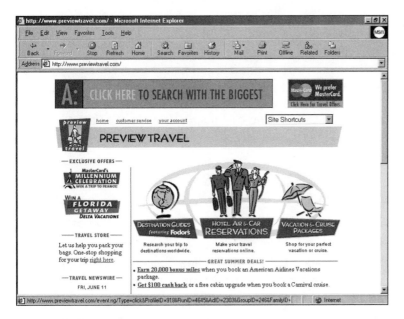

Preview Travel: A great all-around travel site.

TheTrip.com

```
http://www.thetrip.com
```

Here's a great all-in-one travel site that lets you research and book flights, hotel rooms, and rental cars. The site is beautifully laid out with a wealth of information and booking help. You can get information about the city and country you're traveling to, and can even track the progress of a flight, so you can see whether it's been delayed or is scheduled to arrive on time.

Check Newsgroups for Travel-Related Information

Internet newsgroups can be a great source of information about everything having to do with travel, from buying air tickets to great destinations. Two newsgroups worth checking out are `alt.travel` and `rec.travel.misc`.

Travelocity

`http://www.travelocity.com`

Although this site isn't quite as simple to use or as attractive as sites such as Expedia or Preview Travel, you'll still find it helpful for researching travel and finding flight times and booking flights. You can also find specials on vacation packages and cruises, as well as bargains on last-minute air tickets.

Travelscape

`http://www.travelscape.com`

This is a solid, useful travel site that lets you book airline tickets, hotel rooms, and car rentals. Especially helpful is that it also lets you search for combined air/hotel package deals, which can offer big savings.

Travel Web

`http://www.travelweb.com`

As with the other major travel sites, Travel Web enables you to find and book flights and hotel reservations. This site also has good areas for finding short-term bargains and an interesting price ticker that shows you cheap fares being booked through the service.

The Least You Need to Know

➤ Always turn to an Internet travel site to compare prices among different airlines before buying a ticket.

➤ When checking for the cheapest fares, read the fine print—see how many connections are required, what kind of cancellation penalties are in force, and how often the flight is delayed.

➤ Consider using e-tickets instead of traditional tickets as a way to save time and to avoid the risk of losing paper tickets.

➤ If you're looking for last-minute inexpensive airfares, start checking online on Wednesday afternoon, when the special fares are announced—or subscribe to a free email alert service.

➤ Check hotel-chain Web sites and discount sites to find short-term and seasonal special room-rate offers.

Chapter 20

Food, Glorious Food: Groceries, Wine, and Gourmet Foods

In This Chapter

➤ Different kinds of grocery sites

➤ Best grocery sites on the Internet

➤ What you should know before buying gourmet foods and wines

➤ Best gourmet food and wine sites on the Internet

Stalking the wild (or domesticated) asparagus? Are you looking to find the best bottle of under-$10 Bordeaux? Want a roast suckling pig for your next party? Or would you like to have groceries brought right to your door so that you never need step into a grocery store again (well, almost never)? In addition, you might not have to pay for delivery, and you'll often get a discount over normal grocery shopping.

You are able to do all that and more over the Web. Whether it be bird, beast, or fowl; vegetable, fruit, or legume; wine, beer, or the harder stuff, you are able to use the Web to order just about anything you can consume. And more than that, you are also able to get information about any kind of food or drink. So the next time your dinner companion asks, "What do you think of the wine?" instead of answering, "Well, it's wet and cold," you'll be able to rattle off a sentence such as, "Ah yes, an excellent, full-bodied Chardonnay, tasting of ripe fruit, and with a pleasing, well-integrated oak influence." And you'll actually know what you're talking about.

Please, Sir, May I Have More? Ordering Groceries and Food Online

All kinds of foods are for sale over the Internet—just about anything that can be eaten or imbibed. But what you can buy really boils down to two categories. The first category is day-to-day foods, the stuff of survival, the breads, the milks, the fruits, the vegetables, and if you live a 1950s' kind of life, the Jellos and the cream of mushroom soups—basically your weekly shopping list. The other category is the specialty or harder-to-find items, such as wild mushrooms, broccoli da rape, wines, organic vegetables, and, if your name happens to be Trump, Rockefeller, or Gates, the caviars.

You need to know different things before ordering food from those two categories; so let's start with the stuff of survival—ordering groceries online.

Your Weekly Shopping List: Ordering Groceries Online

Unless you actually enjoy grocery shopping (I've heard a rumor that such people exist), you'll find that the Internet is a big timesaver. You save time because you don't have to drive back and forth to the grocery store, push an unwieldy cart down the aisles, or stand in an endless checkout line. On the Internet, just point your browser to the right site, fill up your virtual shopping cart, and depending on the site, your groceries will be delivered to you the next day or within several days.

Don't Overload Your Cart

One thing that you might want to watch out for when shopping online: You might be tempted to buy more than you can really eat. When adding something to your grocery cart is a simple matter of clicking on the screen, instead of taking it off a shelf and schlepping it with you over half of creation, you might find your impulse buying going up. So think before you click: Do I need this food?

Some online stores have limited selections—for example, some of them don't carry milk and dairy products, or anything perishable. But other sites, such as HomeRuns at www.homeruns.com (the online grocery service that I use all the time and can vouch for) have selections that rival large grocery stores and have far more substantial offerings than small, neighborhood grocery stores.

Some grocery sites, such as NetGrocer, are centralized sites, and they ship your order via express mail. (These sites don't ship perishables.) Others, such as HomeRuns, route your order to a local branch, so your food is delivered from a local warehouse. The advantage of these local services is that they let you order produce and perishables.

As you can probably tell by now, all grocery sites aren't created equal. Before placing your first order, here's what to think about:

➤ **What are the delivery options?** Some sites, such as Peapod at www.peapod.com and HomeRuns at www.homeruns.com, deliver groceries the old-fashioned way: A delivery person drives them to your door and carries them into your house. You can also schedule the time of delivery (at least within an hour or two). Other sites, such as NetGrocer at www.netgrocer.com, deliver groceries via an express delivery service such as Federal Express, so you can't schedule a specific delivery time. Generally, the groceries are left outside if you're not at home.

Forget About Groceries and Cooking. Order Takeout Instead!

There are times when the last thing you want to do is order groceries online—what you really want is a good meal from a restaurant, without having to leave home. Solution: Order takeout food from local restaurants via the Internet. Just head to Food.com at www.food.com and follow the directions. After registering, you'll be able to order food from many different kinds of restaurants—Pad Thai, anyone?

➤ **Does the site charge for delivery?** Some sites, such as Peapod and HomeRuns, waive a delivery fee if your order is over $60. Others, such as NetGrocer, charge a delivery fee for any size order and may tack on an extra delivery fee for orders over a certain amount.

➤ **Does it carry a full complement of foods?** Not all grocery sites carry all kinds of foods. Shop around to see which one carries the kinds of foods you order most. NetGrocer, for example, doesn't carry any perishable foods such as fruits and vegetables, whereas Peapod and HomeRuns do.

➤ **Does it have low-cost brands for commodity items?** One way to save money when grocery shopping is to buy low-cost brands for commodity items such as paper towels, garbage bags, milk, and so on. Some sites, such as HomeRuns, carry a low-cost brand (Hannaford's) at substantial savings over well-known, national brands.

➤ **Is it available in your area?** Unfortunately, not all grocery Web sites deliver to all areas of the country. Peapod and HomeRuns are available only in certain parts of the country, whereas NetGrocer is available everywhere.

➤ **Can you order from a catalog as well as on the Web?** Face it, there are times when you just don't want to go online—or maybe you can't get online because your Internet service provider won't let you connect. Check whether the site has a print catalog for ordering.

➤ **How do the prices compare to your local grocery store?** You're not only looking for convenience when you order online—you would like to save money as well. Price the goods available on the Web site and compare them to your local grocery store—and to one another. If you're paying a premium for online ordering, you might decide it's not worth the extra cash you'll have to lay out every week.

➤ **Can you return foods at no cost—or get credited for them?** Let's say you ordered fresh vegetables and the mushrooms were mushy, the tomatoes tortured, the peaches putrid. Can you get a credit for them—or do you have to eat the cost? (You're certainly not going to eat the vegetables.)

➤ **Does the site accept coupons?** Coupons can save you money big-time (for details on how to get grocery coupons online, turn to Chapter 9, "Great Stuff Cheap! Coupons, Contests, and Free Stuff"). Check whether the site accepts coupons.

➤ **How easy is it to shop and fill up your shopping cart?** Online grocery shopping is better than having to do it in a store, but that still doesn't mean it's a whole lot of fun. You want a site that's well-organized, allows you to find what you want fast, and makes it a snap to fill up your shopping cart.

➤ **Can you create a standing shopping list?** Filling up a virtual shopping cart on the Web can be a laborious process—and so you would like to be able to set up a standing shopping list with your regular order, which you can modify each time you place an order. That's a huge timesaver. Better yet, you would like to have more than one standing list—a weekly list, perhaps, as well as a monthly list. The following figure shows a list from the HomeRuns site.

Look for Links to "Instant Coupons"

Some shopping sites such as NetGrocer do more than just accept coupons. They put links on the site to "instant coupons" on their site, and list all the coupons offers they have. Look for them—it can be a big money saver.

Qty for Cart	Brand	Description	Size	Price	Unit Price	Create A List: Named List 1
0	Eggo	N/A Minis Waffles - Eggo KD	ct	$2.69	$16.81/100 CT	☐
	Arnolds	Country White Bread - Arnolds KD	oz	$2.59	$1.73/LB	☑
	Hellmann s	Mayonnaise - Hellmanns Ⓤ	16 oz	$1.99	$1.99/qt	☐
	Heinz	Ketchup - Heinz Ⓤ	20 oz	$1.49	$1.19/lb	☐
	Cabot	Unsalted Butter Quarters - Cabot Ⓜ	oz	$2.99	$2.99/LB	☐
	Pampers	Unscented Baby Fresh Wipes, Alcohol-Free, Refill - Pampers	168 ct	$5.79	$3.45/100	☐
	Lenders	Plain, Big & Crusty Bagels - Lenders ⓊPᵥ	ct	$1.49	$29.80/100 CT	☑
	Joy	Antibacterial Ultra Liquid Dish Detergent - Joy Ⓤ	14.7 oz	$1.39	$12.11/GAL	☐
0	Bold	N/A Powder Detergent Plus - Bold	36 oz	$3.39	$1.51/	☐
	Reynold s	Aluminum Foil, Heavy Duty 18 inch - Reynolds	75 ft	$3.19	$4.26/100sqf	☐
	Hannaford	Drawstring Tall Trash Kitchen Bags (13 gal) - Hannaford	20 ct	$2.49	$12.46/100	☑
	Hannaford	Clear Trash Bags w/Flap Ties (30 gal) - Hannaford	20 ct	$2.99	$14.96/100	☐
	Minute Rice	Instant Long Grain Rice - Minute Rice K	14 oz	$1.99	$2.27/lb	☐
0	Perdue	N/A Perdue Fresh Done-It Chicken Nuggets	14 oz	$3.89	$5.19/lb	☐
	Hannaford	2% Milk, Plastic - Hannaford	1/2 gal	$1.59	$3.18/GL	☐

Cut your online shopping time by creating a standing grocery list. Here is a list at HomeRuns at www.homeruns.com.

➤ **What kind of giveaways can you get?**   Online grocers want your business. And they'll do almost anything to get it. Be on the lookout for freebies and giveaways. Last time I visited the NetGrocer site, for example, it was giving away a copy of the trivia game *You Don't Know Jack* to anyone who placed an order.

Best Grocery Sites on the Internet

When it comes to grocery shopping online, only the big three are worth considering: HomeRuns, Peapod, and NetGrocer. Here's the lowdown on each.

HomeRuns

```
http://www.homeruns.com
```

Here's my favorite grocery-shopping site on the Web. It has a great selection of foods and produce (including organic fruit and vegetables if you're a health food nut; Stonyfield, my favorite brand of nonfat yogurt; and a substantial selection of meat and poultry). Delivery on orders of over $60 is free. We use this service all the time at my house and have found delivery reliable—one driver even delivered to us in the midst of a thunderous snowstorm and apologized for being a few minutes late. The private-label brand products are lower priced than you'll find in the supermarket, and the shopping is easy. The site lets you create several standing shopping lists so that each time you order, you won't have to start from scratch—you start with your basic shopping list already filled out and customize it as you need. HomeRuns isn't available everywhere, but if it's in your area, here's the site you should buy from.

Peapod

http://www.peapod.com

Here's another good grocery service. Order online—including produce as well as other nonperishables—choose a time when you want delivery, and your goods show up. It's that simple. The main complaint I have is that the site requires special software—to use Peapod, you have to install software from its Web site. Otherwise, though, Peapod is a great service. It isn't available everywhere, so check out the Web site to see whether Peapod is in your area.

NetGrocer

http://www.netgrocer.com

This popular grocery Web site, shown in the following figure, offers a big selection of nonperishable goods (no produce or dairy), many of them at prices comparable to those in a grocery store. It also sells a whole lot of other things, such as software and books. Although shopping is easy here, if either Peapod or HomeRuns is available in your area, you'll do better there. NetGrocer ships from a central location, unlike Peapod and HomeRuns, which have locations around the country. Delivery by Federal Express can take up to four days, and you can't schedule a specific delivery time. Still, if Peapod, HomeRuns, or WebVan isn't in your area, NetGrocer is a good place to go.

Lots o' food: shopping online at the NetGrocer site.

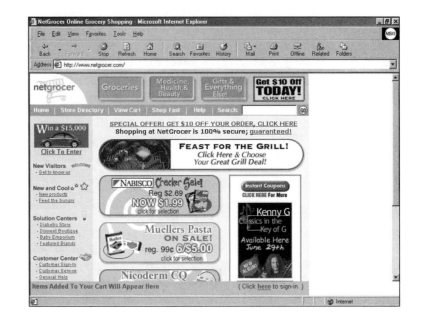

258

WebVan

`http://www.webvan.com`

Like HomeRuns and Peapod, WebVan delivers fruits, vegetables, and other perishables, not just nonperishable items. Their selection isn't as large as HomeRuns or Peapod, but if those services aren't in your area, it's worth checking out. WebVan also has a selection of prepared foods, and offers free delivery on orders over $50.

The Surfing Gourmet: Buying Specialty Foods and Wines on the Internet

Maybe your tastes are a bit more rarified than what you can buy in the standard grocery store. Perhaps you absolutely have to have honey made by bees that supped on the nectar of eucalyptus trees. Or maybe you're looking for something a bit more down-to-earth, such as chocolate truffles, organic foods, or good wine. No matter your food or drink craving, you can satisfy it on the Internet. But before you buy, here's what you need to know:

➤ **How are the foods shipped?** If you're ordering perishables, such as meats or other foods that need refrigeration, find out in detail how they'll be kept cold during shipping—and how long a time will elapse before the food gets to you. The meat-lovers' site, Omaha Steaks at `www.omahasteaks.com`, provides a complete description of how it refrigerates the food en route—and even includes a diagram of the refrigerated shipping carton, shown here.

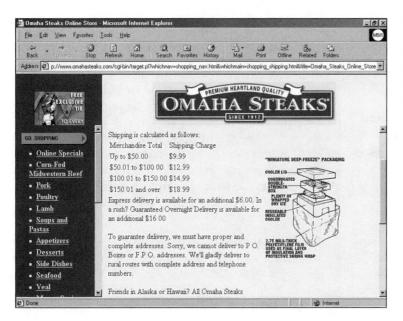

Keep it cool, man. Be sure any perishables you buy are delivered in refrigerated containers. Here's how Omaha Steaks ships its meat.

259

➤ **Be sure you pay only one shipping charge per order.** At some specialty sites, you are in fact ordering from multiple gourmet grocers—herbs from one and oil from another, for example. Be sure that when you put an order together from a site such as this, you're charged only one shipping fee. Greatfood.com, for example, charges only a single shipping charge for each complete order, even though you might be ordering from five different stores. And even if it is only one shipping charge, find out how much it is.

➤ **Find out the return policy.** Especially with any kind of perishable food, you'll want to be sure that you get a no-questions-asked return policy on the food.

Learning About Gourmet Foods on the Internet

The Internet is a great source not only for buying gourmet foods but also for learning about gourmet foods and getting recipes. So for all you would-be gourmands or existing gourmands, here are the sites to check out.

Epicurious Food

```
http://food.epicurious.com/
```

If you're looking for information about gourmet food, for great recipes, or any other kind of information about gourmet food, check here. It includes information from the gourmet magazines *Gourmet* and *Bon Appétit*.

Even Nonperishable Food Might Need to Be Refrigerated When Shipped

Perishable foods such as meats aren't the only kinds of food that needs refrigeration when they ship. In warm weather, chocolate, for example, might need to be refrigerated when it ships—otherwise, instead of pretty Godiva chocolates, you'll end up with a big, gunky mess.

Food & Wine Magazine

```
http://www.foodwinemag.com
```

This excellent food and wine site is the online outpost of *Food & Wine* magazine. In addition to recipes and articles, there's also a very helpful section titled "What's Fresh at the Market," which is the most useful part of the site for food shoppers. It tells you—well, as you can tell by the name—what's fresh in the markets these days. And it gives advice on how to buy that food—for example, a watermelon should sound hollow when you rap on the rind.

foodwine.com

```
http://www.foodwine.com
```

Here's another great site for finding out about gourmet foods. You'll find columns, articles, recipes, and resources. Worth checking out is Kate's Global Kitchen, a daily column with recipes such as grilled portobello mushrooms and lemon-pepper coleslaw.

Specialty Food and Wine Sites on the Internet

With hundreds of specialty food and wine sites on the Internet, merely listing the best would take up countless pages. So here is a brief sampling of great specialty food and wine sites, including several that specialize in ethnic foods. I've also included some sites that specialize in several types of specialty foods. A great way to find specialty and gourmet food sites is to head to the shopping areas of Yahoo!, Excite, and Lycos.

3E Market

```
http://www.3emarket.com
```

If you love Mediterranean cuisine, check out this site, which has Mediterranean olive oils, pastas, spices, specialty vegetables, cheeses, and much more.

Cajun World

```
http://www.cajun-world.com
```

You want gumbo? You want crawfish? How about chicory coffee, more hot sauces than you can count, gumbo file, remoulade sauce, or any other kind of food that comes from that foreign land otherwise known as Louisiana? Then head here. In addition to buying food, you'll also find recipes and more. *Laissez les bons temps rouler!* (For you non-Cajun folks and fans, that means, "Let the good times roll!")

Dean & Deluca

```
http://www.dean-deluca.com
```

This well-known SoHo gourmet shop has a Web site—and it has a great selection of goods you can buy online, including truffles, smoked fish, baking ingredients, desserts, dried nuts and fruits, herbs, oils, cheeses—the whole shmear as they say in New Yawk.

Godiva Chocolates

```
http://www.godiva.com
```

If you can resist a Godiva chocolate, you're a better person than I. Yes, I know they're overpriced. And, yes, I know that the elegant shapes might be a little too precious-looking. But I also know how they taste—and so I know that if you're on a diet, avoid this site. Otherwise, it's a great place to satisfy your chocolate craving.

Greatfood.com

http://www.greatfood.com

From specialty cheeses to olive oils, chocolates, coffees, dried fruits and nuts, exotic meats and beyond, you'll find a wide variety of gourmet and similar foods at this site. Although you order from many different specialty stores, you pay only one shipping fee per order. It's a great site for great food.

KosherGrocer

http://www.koshergrocer.com

Where are the pickle barrels of my youth—the neighborhood delis where you reached into a huge barrel swimming with dill pickles and picked out a nice crisp one? Where can I get some nice pastrami? And the most pressing question of all: Just where can I get a good knish? If you're looking for New York deli-style foods and kosher foods of all sorts, here's the place to go. I have only one complaint about this site: It doesn't carry Cel-Ray soda, a soda flavored like, you guessed it, celery. When I was a kid, no place considered itself a self-respecting deli without it.

Mo Hotta Mo Betta

http://www.mohotta.com

Serious lovers of hot sauces and foods, look no further; you've found your home on the Internet. From habanero hot sauces and chilies to pepper sauces, Jamaican jerk, and all kinds of hot foods (including hot pickles and even hot cinnamon toothpicks), you'll find it all here.

Omaha Steaks

http://www.omahasteaks.com

You like meat? I mean rare, red steaks dripping with juice? Corn-fed Midwestern beef? Pork, lamb, poultry, and anything else on four legs—or at least that used to be on four legs? Then you'll like this site. It's a meat-lover's paradise. Just don't try to buy sissy-looking vegetables here, because Omaha doesn't have them.

thefoodstores.com

http://www.thefoodstores.com

This site has a huge selection of hard-to-find specialty and gift foods. Here's where to go the next time that you need to order that 40-pound suckling pig. An unbelievable variety of other kinds of specialty foods is available as well—gourmet honey, olives, oils, Italian foods, cheeses, and almost anything else.

Get a Different Microbrewed Beer Delivered Every Month

Do you like beer? I mean real beer, not the swill you see advertised on football games? If so, then you'll want to join one of the several Internet-based micro-brewery beer-of-the-month clubs. Just sign up, and you get a different micro-brewery beer delivered each month. Check out 1-800-Microbrew at www.800-microbrew.com and Hog's Head Beer Cellars at www.hogshead.com. I haven't joined any yet, but I'm considering it. How else will I be able to try a beer with the name of Screaming Lobster Lager?

Shore to Door

http://www.shoretodoor.com

Maybe you're not lucky enough to be living near one of the coasts, and so it's hard to get your hands on fresh seafood—or perhaps you live on one of the coasts and crave seafood available only on the other. In either case, head here. You'll be able to order fresh fish as well as smoked fish. Because the availability of fresh fish is so variable, what you can buy here might change a bit from day to day. Fresh fish is shipped in insulated containers, with ice, and arrives in a day.

Virtual Vineyards

http://www.virtualvin.com

You want wine, you go here. It's that simple. Whether you're a long-time oenophile or don't know a Chardonnay from a zinfandel, Virtual Vineyards is the place to go. You'll get a great selection of wines; advice on what wine to buy; tips about wine; and a great column by the "Cork Dork," who answers questions such as how to open a bottle of wine and whether red wine should "breathe" for a while after you open it; and suggestions for great wines at great prices. And yes, to the relief of us all, the site also answers the most common wine questions: which wines go best with which foods, and which wines are dry, semidry, and sweet.

In Some States, It's Illegal to Have Wine Shipped to You

It's great and easy to buy wine over the Web—but depending upon what state you live in, it might be illegal as well. Ever since Prohibition was repealed in 1933, it's been up to the states to regulate the sale of alcohol. And many states make it illegal to ship wine across state lines, which means in many states, it's illegal to have wine shipped to you from out of state. The wealth of laws are confusing at best, and no one—including law enforcement personnel—seems to pay any attention to them. Still, the laws are on the books.

The Least You Need to Know

➤ Check whether grocery sites will schedule delivery dates and times.

➤ Check whether grocery sites carry low-cost brands on commodity items such as paper goods and milk.

➤ Try to find a grocery site that lets you keep standing shopping lists for easy shopping.

➤ Before ordering any perishable goods, get details on how they'll be shipped—and how long they'll take to get to you.

➤ Find out whether food sites will give you refunds or accept returns on food, especially perishables.

Chapter 21

It's the Money, Honey: Shopping for Financial Services Online

In This Chapter

➤ Researching and trading stocks, bonds, and mutual funds online

➤ Finding the best deals on loans and mortgages and applying online

➤ Using the Internet to do your banking

➤ Finding insurance information online

Show me the money!

Well, okay, I will, if you're going to be like that about it. There's only one thing, though. It's on the Internet.

These days, you can shop for all kinds of financial services online. And more than just shop for those services, you can perform many types of financial transactions as well. From trading stocks to banking, to applying for loans and getting life insurance, the Internet is a great way to get the most out of your money.

Keep in mind that you can use the Internet to research stocks, loans, banks, and insurance without actually doing the trading or buying online. So the Internet is a great tool for handling your finances even if you don't do any financial transactions online.

Taking Stock of Your Finances: How to Research and Trade Stocks, Mutual Funds, and Bonds

Stocks. Mutual funds. Bear market. Bull market. Bonds. Buying on margin. Whether you're an experienced investor looking to get hard-core investment advice and information and hoping to save money on your trading, or you're a newbie to the financial world (What is a stock anyway? Do the bulls and bears ever fight? Can I really buy futures in pork bellies—how disgusting!), the Internet is your best way to deal with the stock market, mutual funds, bonds, and other investment vehicles. (*Investment vehicles*—kind of sounds like buying an old VW Beetle in the hopes that it'll go up in price some day.) The Internet has transformed the trading world and has put into the hands of individual investors the kind of information that only insiders used to have. In fact, using the Internet is the easiest way to become an investment insider.

Generally, you can use the Internet in several different ways when it comes to investments. You can use it to get as much investment information as you can so that you'll make the smartest investments possible. You can use the Internet as an information-gathering tool whether or not you actually invest online. You can also use the Internet to make trades—and potentially to save hundreds or even thousands of dollars a year in brokers' fees because you pay only a minimal fee per transaction. You can use the Internet to track your portfolio, which not only tells you how well your finances are doing, but also gives you early alerts to let you know when you should buy or sell.

So what are you waiting for? There's money to be made. Here's what you need to know about getting investment information and investing online.

What Kinds of Investing Sites Are There?

The hundreds of investment sites on the Internet generally fall into four categories. Keep in mind, however, that any one site might have elements of the other kinds of investment sites. But these sites are primarily one of these four kinds.

Check This Out

Type Personal Information Only If You're on a Secure Site

Many financial sites ask you for personal information, especially if you're opening up an account, trading online, applying for a loan, or banking. Never enter that kind of information unless you're sure the site is secure. You'll know you're in a secure site when you get a warning that you're entering one and when a small icon of a locked lock appears at the bottom of your browser. For more information about knowing when you're in a secure site, turn to Chapter 4, "How to Be a Cybersavvy Shopper."

➤ **Investment research sites**   These sites provide information about investments; one example is Informed Investor at www.informedinvestor.com. You won't do the buying at these sites, so if you're leery of investing online, it'll still be worth your while to go here. Investment research sites offer an enormous amount of information: articles, advice, financial reports, fast-breaking news, tips, message boards to talk to other people interested in investing, and much more. For beginning investors and serious investors alike, these are great places for getting the lowdown on the market so you don't get burned. Some of the investment research sites are free, others charge a fee, and some offer a combination of a free site combined with a value-added for-pay area.

➤ **Stock-trading sites**   Surprise! You don't need a broker anymore to trade stocks—and you don't have to pay outrageously high fees for trading. Dozens of sites on the Internet, such as E*TRADE at www.etrade.com, enable you to place trades yourself for amazingly low fees—sometimes less than $10 a trade. Most of these sites also offer a wealth of investing information, although some offer much more than others do. Some of these sites also have added services, such as an alert that tells you when a given stock reaches a certain price level.

➤ **Portfolio-tracking sites**   These sites allow you to track your portfolio online. You tell the site the stocks, funds, and other information you want to track, and it automatically updates the information for you, live on the site. Some portfolio-tracking sites can create a scrolling ticker so that you can track your stocks when you're not on the site. Many financial-advice and stock-buying sites include portfolio-tracking features.

Use the Gomez Advisers Site at www.gomez.com to Find the Best Stock-Trading Sites

This site rates the stock-trading sites and lists the top 20. The rankings include information about cost, ease of use, onsite resources, and similar factors. Especially useful are the rankings by the kind of investor you are, such as Life Goal Planner, Hyperactive Trader, and Serious Investor. That way, you can match your needs to the best stock site for you.

➤ **Sites of individual investment companies**   Mutual fund companies such as Vanguard at www.vanguard.com have set up sites on the Internet where you can get information about their mutual funds and investment services. Some companies allow you to buy funds online; others don't. Most only allow you to buy their funds—although the financial giant Fidelity at www.fidelity.com runs a complete online investment site, including stock trading on any stock or mutual fund. Many individual investment companies let you track your account online as well. They're good sites to visit when you're trying to decide whether to buy a particular fund or if you've already invested and want to track your fund's performance.

What You Should Know Before Visiting Investment Sites Online

No matter the kind of site you're planning to visit, there's a lot you should know about the site, about getting financial information online, and about investing online. Here's the lowdown:

➤ **What price does a stock-trading site charge per trade?**   There's a wide range of prices here. Be sure you know what you'll be charged before deciding whether to use a site.

➤ **Does the site charge a membership fee? If so, what do you get for it?** Some stock-trading sites and research sites charge fees for using part or all of the site. These fees might gain you access to special reports and research, features such as stock alerts, message boards, and similar information. Find out what the fee is and check what you get before you buy—and be sure to look at competing sites, too; another site might provide the same services for free.

➤ **How comprehensive is the investment research at a trading site?** Information is not just power—it's money as well. The better information you have about the market, businesses, and the financial climate, the more money you'll make. So when choosing a trading site, see what kind of valuable investing research and information it provides. It's usually worth paying a few dollars extra per trade if the site contains great information.

➤ **Does the investing site offer email alerts when stocks hit a certain price or level of trading?**   You might want to know when a stock hits (or dips to) a certain price, reaches a certain volume of trading, or reaches a particular price-to-earning ratio. Some sites offer email alerts that let you know when those events occur.

➤ **How good is the quote service on the site?** You want one that's easy to set up and use and that can easily be altered. Ideally, you'd like a quote service that sits on your computer whenever you're on the Internet, not just when you're on the site. And you want to be sure that the site offers *real-time stock quotes*. Many sites offer free quotes, but those quotes are delayed 20 minutes. To get real-time quotes, you usually have to become a member. If you're going to do any trading, you need real-time quotes.

➤ **If it's a trading site, how easy is it to move money from your bank account to make a trade?** Ideally, you'd like to be able to move money and make trades with a click or two. The trading sites vary greatly in how easy they are to use.

Use E*TRADE's Smart Alerts to Warn You When It's Time to Buy or Sell a Stock

E*TRADE at www.etrade.com offers a Smart Alert service: an email alert that tells you when a stock reaches a certain price, level of trading, or price-to-earnings ratio. Click on Smart Alert. (You must sign up for an account to use this service.)

➤ **Does it provide high-quality research, such as company profiles, investment guides, IPO alerts, and more?** Any investment site worth its salt gives you in-depth financial information. You have many sites to choose from, so compare the quality of their information before deciding on which to use. (By the way, for the uninitiated, an IPO stands for an Initial Public Offering—it's when a company first goes public and issues stock. Often, there's a lot of money to be made—or lost—in investing in IPOs.)

➤ **Does it match your investing style?** Do you invest for the long term, or are you looking for short-term gains? Are you investing for your retirement, or to make as much money as you can in the next year? Try to match the services of a site to your investment style.

➤ **Does the site have message boards where you can talk to other investors?** Often, the best source of financial information is other investors. Look for a site that has wide-ranging, busy message boards.

➤ **Does it offer extra financial services?** Increasingly, online trading sites are offering banking and other financial services. If you want a one-stop online financial shop, see what extra services it offers.

Best Investment Sites in Cyberspace

Hundreds of sites offer investment advice or enable you to trade online. Check out the following sites; they won't lead you wrong.

Don't Make an Investment Based Primarily on What You're Told in Message Boards

You check out a message board at an investment site, and someone is touting a stock that he or she claims is about to go through the roof. Based solely on that advice, you pour your money in, only to see it vanish. You've been had! Never make an investment based primarily on what you read on a message board. People have been known to post false claims and statements as a way to push up the price of a worthless stock—and they then proceed to sell all the stock at the high price, making a mint and leaving you holding the bag.

Charles Schwab

http://www.schwab.com

The well-known brokerage house Charles Schwab has an excellent online investing site. You'll get everything you expect—the capability to buy and sell, investing advice, and a way to customize the service to your own needs.

CNNfn

http://www.cnnfn.com

The online site of the CNNfn cable financial network is excellent for people who want breaking news about the stock market. You'll get up-to-the-minute reports on the market (it was the site I checked most regularly during the market crash in late August 1998). You won't get a lot of background information or in-depth investing advice, but if you want breaking financial news, here's where to go.

Discover Brokerage Direct

http://www.discoverbrokerage.com

This trading site, owned by the giant financial services firm Morgan Stanley Dean Witter, is excellent. It features low-cost trading, is exceedingly easy to use, enables you to create a customizable home page available whenever you log in, and provides very good charting and research information.

DLJDirect

http://www.dljdirect.com

Here's one of the best trading sites online. DLJDirect has everything an investor could want: low prices, comprehensive investing advice, a stock quote ticker, news, and a portfolio tracker. Be forewarned, though: I tried to use this site and found its customer service and level of help thoroughly worthless. It was so bad, I ended up transferring my money elsewhere.

E*TRADE

http://www.etrade.com

This very popular trading site is one of the best on the Internet: It's easy to use, offers low-cost trading, and provides great advice and investing tools. One outstanding feature is Smart Alert email that tells you when a stock hits a certain price, level of trading, or price-to-earnings ratio. You can set up an online portfolio, get market analysis, and find much more here as well. It also offers loans, insurance, and credit cards—and possibly at some point online banking as well.

Fidelity.com

http://www.fidelity.com

The giant financial services company Fidelity has an online financial site, and it's an excellent one. You can buy and trade stocks and funds, plan for your retirement, get information about fidelity funds, and much more.

Gomez Advisers

http://www.gomez.com

What are the best stock-trading sites online? Which one has the best prices, the easiest-to-use services, or the best research information? Based on the kind of investor you are, which one is best for you? This site answers all those questions. It prepares a scorecard on the best trading sites online and lists the top 20—and includes details on each, as you can see in the following figure. Before signing up with any online trading firm, check here first. Gomez also rates online banks, travel sites, auction sites, and many more online shopping sites.

Which stock-trading site is best for you? You don't need to check them all out. Instead, head to the Gomez Advisers site at www.gomez.com, *which lists the top 20 sites every month.*

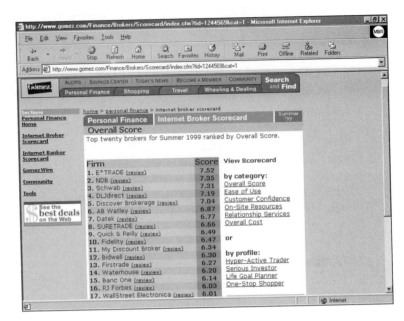

Informed Investor

http://www.informedinvestor.com

The name of this site pretty much says it all—it's a very good site for getting investment information. You'll find excellent, in-depth reports about individual companies; articles that offer investment tips, strategies, advice, and techniques; message boards where you can talk to other investors; interactive calculators; and more.

Some Investment Sites Give You the Inside Track on IPOs

When a company decides to issue stock and go public, its first offering of stock is called an *Initial Public Offering*—IPO for short. IPOs can be quick ways to make (or lose) a lot of money, because the initial offering price is often given only to certain investors, and the price might go up from there. Some online sites such as E*TRADE, though, allow their customers to participate in IPOs. Be aware that IPOs can lose as well as make money, so if you participate in one, be prepared to gamble.

MoneyCentral

http://www.moneycentral.com

This comprehensive financial site run by Microsoft covers everything to do with money—not just investing, but saving, insurance, banking, and financial planning. There's information about investing and a helpful area for aiding you in finding a discount broker. And its market report, updated throughout the day, is an excellent source of timely information about the stock market. You don't trade on this site; it's for getting information only.

The Motley Fool

http://www.motleyfool.com

On America Online, KEYWORD FOOL

If you like solid investment advice along with humor, wit, news, and many people to talk to, check out the Motley Fool site on America Online and the Internet. You'll find articles, sample portfolios, investment recommendations, and useful message boards. The Fools have become media stars and have books and radio shows, but they still show up here, which is where it all started.

Quote.com

http://www.quote.com

Here's a solid site for getting financial information and tracking your portfolio. The free portion of the site offers financial news and information; the for-pay area offers quote tracking and other useful features. The one complaint I have about this site is that its news isn't always up to the minute. For example, when I checked it during the August 1998 crash, its lead story at 3:30 in the afternoon had news about the market conditions for that morning—and in a crash, old news is no news.

TheStreet.com

http://www.thestreet.com

TheStreet.com is a heavy-duty subscription-only site for the serious investor. How heavy-duty? One of my friends made his living for a good part of a year doing nothing but trading stocks on his own using the Internet—and he relied on this site day in and day out. You get a daily newsletter with business news, market development, and other important information. You get analysts' insights, in-depth reports, online bulletin boards, and much more. The following figure shows TheStreet site.

If you're serious about making money using the stock market, head to TheStreet at www.thestreet.com.

Check This Out

Learn About the Stock Market and Win Prizes at Investing Sites

Many investing sites offer monthly investing contests in which you get a certain amount of imaginary money to invest. The person who makes the most in a month gets a prize. It's a great way to learn about investing—and to win some serious prizes. Giveaways include cash, computers, Palm organizers, and more.

Using the Internet to Help Find Loans and Mortgages

You're buying or refinancing a house. Or you're buying a car. Or you need money to fix up your house. Or you're looking for a way to consolidate your credit card debt (a debt, no doubt, brought on by all the shopping you've been doing online lately). Heck, maybe you just want a loan so you can vacation in Sri Lanka for the month. No matter the reason, you can use the Internet to find the best loan for you. You can use the Internet to compare the deals you can get from various banks, and then you can contact the bank directly. But you can also apply for loans on the Internet.

Taking out a loan this way can save you money because at some sites you'll save in loan application costs compared to applying for a loan at a bank. Here's how to use the Internet to find the best loans and mortgages.

How to Use the Internet to Research Mortgages and Loans

Using the Internet to research mortgages and loans is easy. Just head to one of the many mortgage and loan sites (listed later in this chapter, in the "Best Mortgage and Loan Sites on the Internet" section). From there, you'll be able to compare loan rates at many banks. You'll find contact information as well. Just choose the lowest price and then contact the bank offline to take out a loan. Simple.

Some of the sites, though, help you even more. They also help figure out how much of a loan you qualify for, do a search, and list the banks that offer that kind of loan. You just fill in information about the loan, and the site does the rest.

How to Take Out Mortgages and Loans on the Internet

Taking out a loan on the Internet is very much like doing it in the real world—the only difference is that you apply online rather than through a loan officer. At some sites, you can save on loan application fees by doing things this way.

Use an Interactive Mortgage Calculator to Compare Different Kinds of Mortgages

How much will you pay extra per month if you take out a 10-year instead of a 30-year mortgage? How much will you save in interest costs? When will you start paying more in principal than interest with your 15-year loan? Would you be better off taking out a larger loan for a longer term or a smaller loan for a shorter term? You can get answers to these questions at Karl Jeacle's Interactive Mortgage Calculator at `http://www.jeacle.ie/mortgage/`. *Sliders* (little onscreen devices) let you alter the size, interest rate, and term of a potential mortgage. You then get to see a graph charting the loan, along with all kinds of information—everything from the monthly payment to the total interest you'll pay. Just change anything about the loan with the sliders, and everything is automatically recalculated.

To take out a loan or mortgage online, visit one of the online loan or mortgage sites (listed later in this chapter, in the section titled "Best Mortgage and Loan Sites on the Internet"). Then fill in information about the kind of loan you're looking for. You'll get a list of potential mortgages. Choose the best for you and fill out the application form online. You'll be sent information in the mail, which you'll need to sign; from that point on, the loan is handled in the same way as normal loans. That's all there is to it. Note that at some sites, when you fill in all the required information (such as your salary, the amount of a loan you want, and similar information), you'll get a list of loans for which you qualify. You can then click a link to email the bank, asking for a qualifying letter in the mail, even before your loan goes through. Sometimes the seller of a house asks for this kind of letter as part of the deal to ensure that you're a qualified buyer.

Best Mortgage and Loan Sites on the Internet

It's time to finally take the plunge and take out a loan. Here are the best mortgage and loan sites on the Internet. Note that many home-buying sites also have mortgage areas or links to mortgage sites, so if you're looking to take out a mortgage, head to Chapter 22, "Shelter from the Storm: Finding Houses and Apartments Online," to check out home-buying sites. And many new car and used car sites also offer loan areas or links to loan sites. Check out Chapter 12, "Hot Wheels: How to Research and Buy New Cars Online," and Chapter 13, "Avoiding Clunkers and Lemons: Using the Internet to Help Buy a Used Car." Note that I haven't listed individual banks here because your best bet is to compare rates at many different banks. Happy hunting!

Bank Rate Monitor

http://www.bankrate.com

Looking for the best rate on a mortgage, car loan, or other kind of loan near you? Then head to this site. It'll list for you the rates in your area and provide contact information, including a phone number, and in some cases a Web link to the bank. Bank Rate Monitor has other features as well, such as mortgage and loan calculators, useful articles and tips about loan shopping and home buying, and an alert service that sends you news about loan rates. For comparing rates of different bricks-and-mortar banks, this is the place to go to on the Web.

E-Loan

http://www.eloan.com

Here's an excellent site for anyone who wants to take out a loan or a mortgage online. It's remarkably easy to use. You fill out information about the kind of loan that you want. The site then searches through dozens of banks and shows you the different rates and terms. Choose the loan you want and then apply. The site also offers extra services, such as loan calculators. You can even use the site to track the progress of a loan you've applied for.

Get Smart

http://www.getsmart.com

Here's another site where you can compare loans of all kinds: mortgages, auto rates, and others. However, these loans are available only over the Internet, so if you're not interested in this type of deal, don't bother coming here. One problem with the site is that it forces you to fill out many screens of information before it shows you any loan rates.

Mortgage.com

http://www.mortgage.com

As the name of this site suggests, you'll get mortgages here. Check out and compare rates, apply online, and get the mortgage. That's what you'll do, and it's easy.

Quicken.com's Mortgage and Loan Areas

http://www.quicken.com

Click **Banking and Credit** for loans and **Home and Mortgage** for mortgages.

Quicken.com might be the best personal finance site on the entire Internet—it's the one I always check for anything to do with money. So, it's no surprise that the mortgage and loan areas should be excellent. Both areas ask you to fill out a brief form describing the loan you want; in return, they provide a list of banks and loan rates, with detailed information about each loan. You get contact information as well, so you can call the bank. For those banks that allow you to apply online, you can do that as well. The Quicken.com site also offers online banking, insurance information, investing news—anything you need to know about money is here.

Like Money in the Bank: What You Need to Know About Internet Banking

The days of marble entranceways, hushed lobbies, and a sense of importance and occasion when you walked into a bank are long behind us. Today, for most people, a bank is little more than an ATM location and a name.

Increasingly, though, banks will become not just ATM locations, but Web sites. Today you can bank directly over the Internet with many banks. Note that when I talk about Internet banking, I'm not talking about the services that many banks offer where you can use special software to dial into them. I'm talking about doing your banking business right over the Internet—paying bills, checking balances, and the like. Some bricks-and-mortar banks such as Wells Fargo at www.wellsfargo.com have already gone into Internet banking big-time. And some banks, such as the Security First Network Bank at www.sfnb.com, exist solely on the Web.

If you're interested in banking over the Internet, here are the questions you need to ask:

➤ **Can you send electronic payments automatically for your mortgage, utilities, and loans?** One of the big plusses to electronic banking is that you can pay your recurring bills easily and automatically, without having to write out checks every month. If an Internet bank doesn't offer this service, walk away. Find out how much, if anything, you'll be charged per payment.

➤ **Can you write checks that are printed and automatically sent out via mail, can you still use regular paper checks, and how much does it cost?** Not everyone accepts electronic payments. Be sure that you can write traditional checks and that you can make payments online that are then printed out and mailed for you. And find out how much these alternative services cost.

➤ **Will you get monthly statements?** If an Internet bank doesn't offer monthly statements so that you can see your account activity, don't bank there.

➤ **Can you use a local ATM network to get cash—and does it cost you anything?** In this electronic world, we all still need cash. And we all get cash from ATM machines. Be sure that your Internet bank lets you withdraw money from local ATM machines and that those withdrawals are free. The $1 charges can add up quickly.

Is Online Banking Safe?

As long as you protect your username and password in the same way as you protect your ATM card and password, online banking is as safe as real-world banking. Online banks have the same level of protection as real-world banks (in fact, many online banks such as the Internet-based Bank of America are branches of real-world banks).

➤ **What rates does the Internet bank pay for savings accounts, checking accounts, certificates of deposit, and similar accounts?** If the rates are lower than what you'd get from a real-world bank, why bother?

➤ **Is a toll-free customer service number available—and does anyone answer the phone?** If you have a question or problem, you'll want to know that it'll be resolved. Before going with an Internet bank, test out the toll-free number several times by calling and seeing how quickly it's answered.

Internet Banking Sites

A fair number of banks do business on the Internet—both Internet-only banks as well as traditional banks that have set up shop online. Here's a list of banks and banking sites to check out when looking for an Internet bank.

Bank of America

`http://www.bankamerica.com`

This big bank, based in San Francisco, offers an excellent Internet bank. You can pay bills electronically, use the bank's ATM network, and take advantage of a host of financial services.

Bank Rate Monitor

`http://www.bankrate.com`

If you're looking for a list of Internet banks—and would like reviews of them as well—then head to this site. It's a very good site for information about Internet banking. An added benefit is that it includes information about bricks-and-mortar banks as well, with information such as checking-account fees and ATM fees nationwide.

Do the Services Offered by Online Accounts Differ from Those Offered by Traditional Accounts?

Most online accounts offer the same services as traditional accounts, although you might find some slight differences. For example, some online accounts enable you to pay your bills such as mortgages, loans, and utility bills automatically and electronically every month, something that traditional accounts don't let you do. However, with some online accounts, you'll have to pay a fee every time you use an ATM machine—a fee that traditional accounts don't charge.

Gomez Advisers

`http://www.gomez.com`

Here's the best site to visit if you want to find the best Internet bank for you. Gomez rates Internet banks, picks the top 20, and then ranks them in order, in the same way it ranks stock-trading sites (see the review earlier in this chapter). Gomez also offers the details to back up its ranking.

Security First Network Bank

http://www.sfnb.com

This Internet-only bank offers excellent services and prices, such as 20 free electronic payments every month, interest on your checking account if you maintain a minimum balance of $5,000, and credit cards.

Telebanc

http://www.telebanc.com

The Internet-only Telebanc offers a host of services, such as being part of the national Cirrus ATM network. It's been bought by the online stock site E*TRADE, so at some point expect the services of the two to merge.

Wells Fargo

http://www.wellsfargo.com

This venerable old bank has entered the 21st century with its Internet banking presence—and it's a good one. The online branch of Wells Fargo offers the usual banking services you would expect, and it has a leg up on many Internet-only banks because it has a huge network of ATM machines you can use at no cost.

Better Safe Than Sorry: Using the Internet for Insurance Information

Time to think about the unthinkable. Yes, you guessed it. I'm talking about insurance. It's one of those things in life that you need to have, but you hope you never use. Whether it's life insurance, home insurance, car insurance, or some other kinds of insurance, you can use the Internet to help get you the best deal at the best price. You'll be able to compare policies of different companies, and in some instances, you'll be able to apply online as well.

However, there's an old saying in the insurance industry: Insurance isn't bought; it's sold. Translated into English, that means that insurance agents can't wait to get their hooks into you, to sell you as much insurance as possible. Therefore, you won't find the same wealth of information about insurance online—especially life insurance and home insurance—as you will about other financial products such as mortgages and loans. In many instances, you'll have to talk directly to an insurance agent to get a quote (I shudder at the mere thought). On the other hand, when it comes to auto insurance, you'll get all the information you need. That must be because you deal with banks, rather than with insurance agents, for auto insurance.

Best Insurance Sites on the Internet

If you're looking for insurance, check out the following sites. I don't list sites run by individual companies. Instead, I list sites that enable you to compare policies from many different companies. Note that many home-buying sites also have home insurance areas or links to home insurance sites, so if you're looking for home insurance, also check Chapter 22 for home-buying sites. And many new car and used car sites offer insurance areas or links to insurance sites. Check out Chapter 12 and Chapter 13 for new and used car sites.

Insuremarket.com

```
http://www.insuremarket.com
```

Head to the best insurance site on the Internet when you want help finding the lowest-cost and best insurance policies. Insuremarket is exceedingly easy to use. Fill out forms describing the kind of insurance you want and, in the case of life insurance, provide information such as your age, height, and weight. You'll then get a list of policies that you can compare. For some policies, you get vital information such as the cost and what the policies cover. For other policies, you have to send an email request (by clicking on a button); information is then sent to you via email. Alternatively, you can get a list of agents and then call an agent directly. In addition to providing insurance quotes, this site also offers many articles to help you choose insurance wisely.

InsWeb

```
http://www.insweb.com
```

This site is excellent for comparing insurance policies and rates, whether you're looking for life insurance or home and rental insurance. Click on the kind of insurance you're interested in and then fill out a series of forms (for example, for home insurance, you have to enter all kinds of information about your home). You'll then receive information about insurance quotes—often, you'll have to contact the insurance company, or have it contact you, for more information.

InstantQuote

```
http://www.instantquote.com
```

If you're looking for an easy site for finding life insurance quotes, head here. Fill out a quick form, and you'll then see a list of companies that issue policies, along with the price and policy information. To apply, click a link and fill out a form. It's that simple.

Life Insurance Analysis Center

```
http://www.underwriter.com
```

Here's a good site to head to when you're looking for life insurance. It offers advice on what kind of policy and how much insurance you need. It'll also give you a quick estimate of how much you'll have to pay for life insurance, based on your height, age, weight, and health history. An insurance agent may contact you for a follow-up detailed quote.

QuickQuote

```
http://www.quickquote.com
```

If you're looking to apply for life insurance online, here's a good place to go. Fill out a simple form with information such as your height, weight, age, and health history, and you'll then get a list of quotes from several insurance companies. To apply, simply fill out a form. From that point on, getting life insurance is the same as if you applied in person.

The Least You Need to Know

➤ When visiting a financial site, never give out personal information unless you're sure the site is secure.

➤ Try to find an investment site that suits your investment style.

➤ Never make an investment based primarily on what you read on message boards—someone could be trying to manipulate the price of a stock.

➤ When looking for a loan or a mortgage, check a site that compares many products.

➤ Before deciding which Internet bank to use, find out whether it has local ATM machines—and whether you'll be charged to use them.

➤ When looking for insurance, check a site that compares different policies.

Shelter from the Storm: Finding Houses and Apartments Online

In This Chapter

➤ What apartment-hunting sites offer that daily newspapers don't

➤ What to know before looking for an apartment online

➤ The best apartment-hunting sites on the Internet

➤ What to know before using house-hunting sites

➤ The best house-hunting sites on the Internet

Where do we spend most of our lives? Where we live—in our houses and apartments. Nothing could be more basic than housing; nothing could be worse than having to *find* that housing.

The Internet, though, offers hope. It's a great source of information on finding the best housing...and getting financing if you're buying a house. You can use it to go apartment hunting; to go house hunting; to find out about the town or city, and neighborhood, you're moving to; and in general to make your housing search a pleasant experience. And even better than making your search a pleasant experience...the Internet can help you get the right apartment or house at the lowest cost. How do you do all that? Read on. I clue you in first on how to search for an apartment and then on how to find and buy a house. For information about finding mortgages, turn to Chapter 21, "It's the Money, Honey: Shopping for Financial Services Online."

Dear Landlord: How to Use the Internet to Find an Apartment to Rent

What's one of the most unpleasant chores you face in life? Yes, even worse than going to the dentist? Even worse than eating overcooked chicken and half-cooked baked potatoes at your mother-in-law's home? Bingo...you've got it: going apartment-hunting. You spend endless hours ruining your eyes by poring over the tiny type in classified ads that use arcane language such as "Hrv, ht/hw, w/d hkups, hwf, ww, d&d." (Hey, sounds just like the place *I* want to rent, how about you?) You'll get lost several times en route to the "convenient" location that happens to be located about seven miles from the nearest grocery store or other inhabited building...and is right across the street from a toxic waste dump. And what you'll usually find at the end of your search is a tiny, cramped apartment populated by dust bunnies, with a view of a nearby parking lot and a beady-eyed owner sizing you up to see just how desperate you are and how much money he can extract from you on the spot.

There must be a better way, you think.

Yes, in fact, there is a better way. You can use the Internet to find your next apartment. You'll be able to get help finding the apartment you want in the neighborhood you desire, at the price that you want. (Yes, I know, sounds like an ad, but it's all true.) Whether you're moving to an apartment in the same town or you're relocating across the country, you'll find help. Here's how.

What Can Apartment-Hunting Sites Do That Newspapers Can't?

Good question. You may think that all you really need to do is use your local newspaper. But apartment-hunting sites offer a lot more than your local paper does. They're especially useful for people who are relocating to another city and need basic information about neighborhoods, services, and schools, as well as rental listings. One thing that apartment sites don't yet offer is more listings than their newspaper counterparts. Still, when you're looking for a new apartment, they're great places to go. Here's a quick rundown of the benefits that apartment sites online offer:

➤ **They can make it easier to search for listings.** Looking for a two-bedroom apartment with air-conditioning, a health club in the vicinity, and wall-to-wall carpeting, in a specific town, for $1,500 a month? When looking through a newspaper, you'll have to search through page after page of tiny-type listings. Online, just tell the site that's what you're looking for, push a button, and you'll get a list of apartments that fit the bill. Keep in mind, though, that not all sites offer search capabilities. Look for ones that do; they're easy to use.

➤ **They give you information about the neighborhood you're moving to.** Many apartment sites include detailed descriptions of the neighborhoods in which apartments are located, including how close they are to conveniences such as grocery stores and post offices.

> ### Check Local Online Apartment Listings in Addition to National Listings
>
> In addition to the big, national apartment sites, many local sites are devoted to helping people find apartments in only a certain region. Some of these sites are superb and are better than national listings when looking in your area, such as the MetroNet site for rentals from San Francisco to San José at www.metronet.com. Other sites, however, offer decidedly slim pickings, sometimes offering fewer than two dozen listings. Your best bet is to check local, as well as national, rental sites.

➤ **They give you a more detailed description of the apartment than newspaper ads.** The better apartment sites give you an amazing amount of detail about your new apartment, including, in some cases, floor plans and photographs. Try finding *that* in your local classified ads.

➤ **They can give driving directions.** How many times have you gotten lost trying to find an apartment to check out? Many apartment sites online give you driving directions, including a map, that you can print out.

➤ **If you're relocating, they give you the lowdown on everything about your new town.** Want information about local schools, how to register your car, what the crime rate is? Apartment sites can give you that information and more.

How Do I Use Apartment Sites?

Most apartment sites are easy to use, and they all work similarly. First, you fill out a form detailing in which city, town, or region you're looking for an apartment. Sometimes you'll fill out several forms so that you can search through the precise area you're interested in. Next, in the better sites, you give the specifics of the apartment you're looking for: size, price, amenities, and so on. After that, you get a screen full of listings. Depending on the site, these listings may be detailed or brief. For more information about any listing, click on it.

When you click on a listing, you get a detailed description of the apartment, often including a floor plan and sometimes a photograph. Sometimes you can click a button for driving directions and a map to the apartment. When you find a listing you're interested in, you have several options. In some sites, you call a phone number, in the same way that you would through a newspaper—so the contact and renting is handled exactly as it's handled in classified ads. In other instances, you click on an email link or send a message to an email address. The owner will then get in touch with you. And some sites even let you fill out a rental application online—but don't worry, just filling out the application doesn't mean you have to take the apartment; it just means that some of the paperwork is already taken care of.

Different Kinds of Apartment-Hunting Sites

Three kinds of sites handle apartment listings: general classified sites; local classified sites, such as those run by daily newspapers; and sites that specialize in apartment hunting. Here's the lowdown on each:

➤ **General classified sites** Some general classified sites carry listings for apartments. In general, these sites aren't the best places to look for apartments because the listings are so skimpy and because they don't offer the same kind of comprehensive services as do the apartment-hunting sites. And general classified sites usually don't offer many details about the apartments. However, some large classified sites, such as Classifieds2000 at www.classifieds2000.com (click on the **Rentals and Roommates** section), have deals with apartment-hunting sites, so that when you search on the classified site for an apartment, you're actually searching the apartment-hunting site.

➤ **Local classified sites** These sites are often run by local newspapers and tend to have a significant number of apartment listings (because the apartment listings that normally run in the newspaper also run online). *The Boston Globe*, for example, has an excellent listing of apartments for rent on its Web site at www.boston.com. The downside is that local classified sites usually don't offer the comprehensive services that national apartment-hunting sites do. And local sites usually give very little information about the apartment for rent; their listings usually just reprint the paper listings.

➤ **Apartment-hunting sites** These sites offer the most comprehensive services, such as information about neighborhoods, schools, and crime; give the most detail about the apartment, often including floor plans and photographs; and are generally quite easy to use. They also often offer mapping services, email alerts, information about relocating, and much more help. The only downside is that they tend not to offer as many listings for a particular area as local classified sites do. Still, these specialized sites are your best bet for apartment hunting online.

What You Should Know Before Going Apartment Hunting Online

You've gotten this far in the chapter, so no doubt you're ready to start your apartment search. But before heading to the sites to find your next apartment, heed this advice about what to look for in a site when apartment hunting online:

➤ **How detailed are the listings on the site?** Does it include comprehensive details about the apartment, such as whether there's a dishwasher, a fireplace, air-conditioning, and other extras? Does it show you a detailed floor plan...and ideally a photograph as well?

Don't Send Personal Information About Yourself over an Unsecure Internet Link

Some apartment sites let you fill out a rental application online. That application, though, might contain personal information, such as your current employer, salary, and where you do your banking. Never send this type of information over an unsecure Internet link, where prying eyes can see it. You'll know an Internet link is secure because of warnings telling you that you're entering a secure site and because a tiny locked lock icon appears in your browser. Turn to Chapter 4, "How to Be a Cybersavvy Shopper," for more information about how to know you're using a secure site or secure area of a site.

➤ **Consider the source—where does the information come from?** Most apartment-hunting sites (and almost all, if not all, major national sites) are very much like classified ads. Property owners pay a fee to list their apartments, and potential renters browse for free. In a less-common kind of site, the person looking for an apartment pays a fee to use the site, and owners place their listings for free. The final kind of site is run by a large apartment complex or real-estate firm; all units listed on these sites are owned by the company.

➤ **Does it include information about the neighborhood?** Sure, a three-bedroom apartment with air-conditioning, hardwood floors, and a gym in the complex for $800 sounds great. But what if it's in a neighborhood where you hear gunshots at night and where you feel as though you need an armed guard every time you walk outside? The best apartment-hunting sites include information about the neighborhood, not just the apartment.

➤ **Does it include a mapping service?** Getting lost en route to an apartment isn't any fun...and if you're late, you could lose out to someone else. Is there a mapping service that gives you directions and a map?

➤ **Does it offer an update service via email?** Great apartments rent fast. You'd like to be sure that you know when one comes on the market.

Some sites offer update services that send you email whenever an apartment that matches what you're looking for comes on the market.

➤ **If you're thinking of moving to a new town, does the site give you the complete rundown on the town?** What's the crime rate where you've moving? What are the schools like? In general, what kind of town is it? These are some of the questions you'd like answered about any town you're moving to. Some of the better apartment sites give you that kind of rundown about every town where apartments are listed.

➤ **Does it offer advice on moving, and does it provide extra moving services?** Some sites offer moving checklists and helpful articles and services such as moving insurance. If these things are important to you, be sure to find a site that offers them.

The Best Apartment-Hunting Sites Online

So now it's time to actually hunt for an apartment. Where should you go? Following are the best national apartment-hunting sites. Also check your local newspaper's Web site; newspapers often offer the best local classified sections.

Make It Easy to Notify People, the Post Office, and Businesses When You Change Your Address

One of the biggest hassles about moving is that you need to send your new address to everyone. The SpringStreet site at www.springstreet.com offers two change-of-address services that notify everyone for you when you move. Click on **Change of Address** when you're on the site and follow the instructions.

Apartments.com

```
http://www.apartments.com
```

Here's a useful site to check when searching for an apartment. Its services aren't as comprehensive as SpringStreet, and it was a little harder to search, but still, it's worth a visit when you need to find a new place to rent.

Apartments for Rent Online

```
http://www.aptsforrent.com
```

Apartments for Rent Online is a no-frills apartment-hunting site. It might not cover the area you want (for example, when I checked, it had no listings at all for the entire state of Massachusetts), but it's worth checking.

Rent.net

```
http://www.rent.net
```

Rent.net is a very good site for apartment hunting...and for moving in general. In addition to apartment listings, this site offers many moving services, including furniture and truck rentals.

SpringStreet

```
http://www.springstreet.com
```

Here's what I think is probably the best apartment site in all of cyberspace. It has a very good selection of listings; you get exceedingly detailed information about the apartment, neighborhood, and town the apartment is located in; and searching for the exact apartment you're looking for is easy. The site also offers a wealth of special services, such as getting information about renting trucks and finding movers, getting rental insurance, finding out about local schools, and much, much more. When looking at a listing, you can even get information about the nearest grocery store, bank, restaurants, post office, and other useful places.

Give In to Your Nesting Instinct: Using the Internet to Help Buy a Home

It's finally time: You've decided to buy a home for the first time, or you're selling your existing home and are buying a new one. Hey, relax: Buying a house is only one of the biggest decisions you'll ever make, affecting everything from the quality of your life to your kids' education to your family's finances. Seriously, though, if you use the Internet, you'll go far toward ensuring that you buy the best house at the best price...and you can also make the process of buying a house a little easier. Here's everything you need to know.

*The inside skinny on
your next apartment: an
apartment listing at
www.springstreet.com.*

*The inside skinny on
your next apartment: an
apartment listing at
www.springstreet.com.*

What Can House-Hunting Sites Do That Newspapers Can't?

Hhmmm. That question sounds familiar. Check earlier in the chapter for information about what apartment sites offer that newspapers don't. Most of what you'll find there applies to house-hunting sites as well. In addition, house-hunting sites offer the following advantages:

➤ **You might see the taxes that you'll be paying.** Some house-hunting sites list the property taxes you'll be paying on your new home...something that newspaper classified sections don't do.

➤ **You get comprehensive guides to buying a home.** Especially for the first-time buyer, purchasing a new home can be a daunting task. Many sites offer simple, step-by-step instructions on what you need to know before you buy.

➤ **You get links to mortgage sites.** Finding a house you want to buy is only half the battle—you still have to find a mortgage. Many sites include links to mortgage sites to help you get financing. (Turn to Chapter 21 for more information about shopping for mortgages.)

➤ **You get advice on how much home you can afford.** You make $65,000 a year. You have $50,000 saved toward a mortgage. You're carrying $200 a month in car loans. So how much home can you afford to buy? Many sites include calculators that tell you how much house you can afford...and how big a mortgage you can afford to carry.

➤ **You can find out how much more—or less—the cost of living is in the part of the country you're moving to, as compared to where you now live.** Some of the sites have salary calculators that show you how much money you need to live in the same manner if you're moving from one part of the country to another.

➤ **You can get information about crime rates, local schools, and other vital information.** When you buy a home, you're buying more than a house—you're buying a town, a neighborhood, a school district, and an entire way of living. The better house-hunting sites give you ample information about towns and neighborhoods.

How Do I Use House-Hunting Sites?

House-hunting sites are exceedingly simple to use. Tell the site where you're looking to buy a home. Then fill in more information, such as the price range of the home, how many bedrooms you want, and similar information. After you do that, you'll be shown brief listings that match what you're looking for. For the complete listing, click on it. You'll then get much more comprehensive information, usually including a photograph and a detailed description of the house. There might also be a mapping service; information about the town, neighborhood, and schools; and similar material.

Get the Lowdown on Every Aspect of Your Move at HomeFair.Com

How much will moving to your new home cost? What's the cost-of-living difference between where you live now and where you're moving? For what size mortgage will you qualify? If you're looking for answers to questions like these—or just about anything else to do with moving to your new house—check out this site at www.homefair.com.

If you find a home you're interested in, contact the seller. You can call the seller directly or send email. (The site should have the necessary email link.) At that point, the home-buying process is the same as if you had seen the ad in a newspaper.

Different Kinds of House-Hunting Sites

You can head to three kinds of house-hunting sites: general classified sites; local classified sites, such as those run by daily newspapers; and sites that specialize in house hunting. Here's the lowdown on each:

➤ **General classified sites**   You'll be able to find homes to buy at some general classified sites. Usually, they're not the best places to find a new home because the listings are limited and the sites don't offer extra services. Some large classified sites, such as www.classifieds2000.com, have deals with house-hunting sites so that when you search for a house, you're really searching the house-hunting site.

Use Realtor.Com at www.realtor.com to Find a Realtor

Maybe you'd like someone to help you with the buying process and would prefer to deal with a person rather than the Internet when looking for a home. In that case, you're looking for a realtor. But how to find one? Go to www.realtor.com. There you'll be able to search for a realtor in the area where you're looking to buy.

➤ **Local classified sites**   These sites usually offer the most homes for sale because they're often run by local newspapers. The papers simply take their own print classified ads and put them online. But these sites rarely offer the kinds of services that house-hunting sites do and rarely provide much information about the house.

➤ **House-hunting sites**   These dedicated sites provide the most comprehensive services, such as information about the home-buying process; links to mortgage sites; and information about neighborhoods, schools, property taxes, and crime. They offer more details about the houses for sale than classified sites do, but tend not to offer as many listings as local classified sites. Still, they're a great bet for finding your next house, even if you use them only for getting information about the town you're thinking of moving to.

What You Should Know Before Going Online to Get Help Finding a House

Buying a house is a big decision—one that requires a great deal of time. Before heading online, here's what you should know.

➤ **Does the site offer comprehensive information about the house—including taxes?**   You want a full rundown on what the house looks like, how many bedrooms it has, and any amenities. And you especially want to know the property taxes.

➤ **Can you use the service to sell your house as well?**   If you already own a house and are buying a new one, you're going to have to sell your old house. Some sites offer one-stop shopping—they'll help you sell your old house as well as buy a new one.

Use the SchoolReport to Find Out About School Districts

If you have children, perhaps the most important thing about the town you're thinking of moving to is what the schools are like. At www.theschoolreport.com you'll get basic information about the school system, such as class size and student–teacher ratio—as well as a comparison to nearby school systems. You can also fill out a form online to request a more comprehensive report.

➤ **Does the site offer a mapping service?**   You'd like to be able to get directions to the home you're thinking of buying, and you'd also like to see where it's located. Some sites offer mapping services that give directions and maps to their homes.

➤ **Does the site offer comprehensive information about your prospective new town and neighborhood, including schools, crime, and nearby amenities?**   Ask any realtor to tell you the three most important things to keep in mind when buying a home, and here's the answer: location, location, and location. You'll want to know everything about where you're moving to. The best house-hunting sites give you that kind of information. One site that specializes in providing this kind of information is the SchoolReport at www.theschoolreport.com, shown in the following figure.

293

Get school information at www.theschoolreport.com.

The School Report for Middlesex county, MA - Microsoft Internet Explorer

File Edit View Favorites Tools Help

Back Forward Stop Refresh Home Search Favorites History Mail Print Offline Related Folders

Address http://www.theschoolreport.com/cgi-bin/WMNSRS?countyid=9&county=&state=MA&submit=Go

The school report.com — County Statistics

iCreditReport™ click here

Redefine Search
Middlesex, MA

Free: **School Info**
County Statistics
The School Report
Child Care
School Maps
Free: **Moving Info**
Community Content
Find a Home
Property Analysis
Low Mortgage Rates

SPECIAL OFFERS
$1000 toward moving expenses
Relocation Reward$ (win a new PC!)

Middlesex County, MA Districts	Total Student Population	Average Elementary School Population	Student Teacher Ratio	Average Class Size - Grade 1	Average Class Size - H.S. Math	Computers in Elem. Classroom
Acton	2159	431	22	24	22	K
Arlington	4104	363	17	22	25	K
Ashland	1918	485	17	22	18	2
Ayer	1175	615	12	17	21	-
Bedford	1890	445	15	23	25	K
Belmont	3561	374	17	20	19	K
Billerica	6109	537	19	22	17	K

Start W M. T. M. Address 7:58 PM

➤ **Does the site give a full explanation of the buying process?** Especially for first-time buyers, finding and buying a new home can be an overwhelming experience. The best home sites don't just offer listings—they lead you on a step-by-step process to help you find a new home.

➤ **Does the site offer other extra services?** Some house-hunting sites offer a host of other services as well, such as help with moving, links to mortgage and insurance sites, and email alerts. Look for sites with the most comprehensive services.

The Best House-Hunting Sites Online

Take a deep breath. Now another. Now another. Time to make one of the biggest decisions of your life—buying a house. It needn't be so hard, though. Here are the best sites online for helping you find a home.

Cyberhomes

```
http://www.cyberhomes.com
```

Cyberhomes is a good house-hunting site with a good set of extra features, such as a mapping service and links to helpful information such as local schools. The main problem with the site is the same one that other sites have: insufficient listings.

Get an Email Alert When a Home You're Interested In Comes on the Market

The HomeAdvisor site at www.homeadvisor.com offers an excellent service for home buyers: an email alert whenever a home that you'd be interested in is listed. Click on **HomeTracker** and then fill out a form describing the kind of house you want. Whenever such a home is listed, you'll get an email alert.

HomeAdvisor

http://www.homeadvisor.com

HomeAdvisor is a superb site to check when you've decided it's time to buy a new home. It provides clearly detailed, easy-to-follow instructions on everything you'll need to do when buying a new home, from selecting a neighborhood to getting a mortgage. You'll get help on deciding what kind of home to buy and where to buy it; you'll find information about towns and neighborhoods, including crime and schools; and you'll get help on everything else having to do with buying a home. Where the site falls down is in the actual listings—each time I've checked, there simply weren't very many of them. But still, visiting this site is worthwhile because it's so helpful in every other way.

HomeNet

http://www.homenet.com

This site is an all-in-one site for anyone buying or selling a home. You can search the listings for a house to buy; for $49 you can list your house for sale; you can learn about home renovations; you can get information about mortgages and insurance; and you can link to moving and storage companies.

Homes.com

http://www.homes.com

Here's an excellent all-around house-hunting site that offers more than just listings. It also has mortgage calculators, a link to mortgage-buying information, and more.

iOwn.com and HomeScout

http://www.iown.com and http://www.homescout.com

These sister sites are great places to go when looking to buy a home. iOwn is a comprehensive site for help with everything from financing to finding the home itself and more. HomeScout specializes in listings, so it's the place to go when you want to search in a specific area for a home to buy.

Figure Out How Much House You Can Afford to Buy

Let's say you make $60,000 a year, you have $25,000 saved toward a down payment, and you spend $100 each month on a car loan. How much house can you afford? Head to HomeScout at www.homescout.com and click on **How much can you afford?**. After you fill out a brief form, you get an estimate of how much house you can afford to buy.

Realtor.com

http://www.realtor.com

Here's a house-hunting site with a twist: In addition to finding a home to buy, you can also find a realtor to help you buy it. In addition, you'll find information about mortgages, including rates; real-estate news; and a helpful resource center for information about insurance, moving, and other similar topics.

The Least You Need to Know

➤ Apartment-hunting sites offer many more services than newspaper classified ads—but newspaper classified ads often have more listings.

➤ Look for apartment-hunting sites that offer extra services such as email alerts, driving directions, and neighborhood information.

➤ See which apartment-hunting sites include detailed descriptions of the apartments for rent, including floor plans and pictures.

➤ Look for a house-hunting site that provides information about the city and neighborhood you're thinking of moving to, including crime rates and data about the schools.

➤ Try to find a house-hunting site that shows the property taxes for the listings.

➤ Even if you use your local newspaper to find a house, go to house-hunting sites for their step-by-step help and advice on buying a house.

Chapter 23

Pump It Up: Sports, Recreation, Leisure, Health, and Fitness

In This Chapter

➤ What kinds of sites sell sports, health, recreation, and fitness goods

➤ What to know before buying

➤ Best sports, health, recreation, and fitness buying sites on the Internet

What are you doing in front of your computer? Pump it up! Get that blood circulating! Time to go outside and play baseball, golf, swim, jog, bike, and generally tire the heck out of yourself. Or head to your own indoor gym to pump some iron or work out on a stair climber. Oh, and while you're at it, why don't you pop some nutritional supplements and antioxidant vitamins? Your body will thank you...if you don't keel over first (just kidding).

Use your computer to help get in shape or to enjoy sports and recreation. The Internet is a great place to buy sports, health, and fitness products and equipment. Here's how to do it.

Where to Buy Sports, Health, Recreation, and Fitness Goods

You can buy sports, recreation, health, and fitness goods at many different kinds of places. Here's the lowdown:

➤ **Specialized sites**   Many sites specialize in selling these kinds of goods, such as Fogdog at www.fogdog.com, shown in the following figure. These sites often offer the largest collection of goods, especially if you go to a very specialized site such as the International Golf Outlet at www.igogolf.com. They might not necessarily offer the greatest discounts, but they'll often offer advice on what to buy and possibly offer articles and help on using the products and keeping yourself in shape.

➤ **General Internet malls and shopping sites**   Many general Internet sites and stores offer sports and health equipment—and often at solid discounts. For example, Shopping.com at www.shopping.com, Wal-Mart Online at www.wal-mart.com, and the shopping sites of the major search engines at www.yahoo.com, www.excite.com, and www.lycos.com all have very good areas for finding this kind of equipment. They often offer good prices. But they don't offer the same breadth of equipment and goods that the specialized sites do. Turn to Chapter 15, "Mall Fever: Department Stores, Malls, Closeouts, and Bargain Hunting," for more information on what to look for when buying at these sites and for a list of malls and general shopping sites.

From boxing gloves to putters to running shoes to knee braces, you'll find anything to do with sports at Fogdog at www.fogdog.com.

Use an Internet "Escrow" Service When Buying Sporting Goods and Leisure Equipment from Individuals at Classified and Auction Sites

Be careful when buying sporting goods and leisure equipment from an individual at classified and auction sites. If you're buying a big-ticket item and you're burned, you could lose your money. Consider using an Internet escrow service. When you use an escrow service, you pay the service for the goods rather than the individual. Then, after the goods have been delivered to you and you verify that they're not damaged, the service sends the money to the individual. If the goods aren't delivered or are damaged, the escrow service returns your money to you. A number of escrow services operate on the Internet, including TradeSafe at www.tradesafe.com, I-Escrow at www.iescrow.com, and Trade-direct at www.trade-direct.com. Turn to Chapter 11 for more information about escrow services.

➤ **Auction sites and classifieds sites**   Auction and classified sites on the Internet, such as eBay at www.ebay.com and Classifieds2000 at www.classifieds2000.com, offer the best places to find the best deals on sports, recreation, and health goods. The downside of these sites is the limited goods you'll find there. Because you'll often be buying from individuals at these sites, rather than from the site itself, you need to check the seller's credentials. See Chapter 10, "Classified Information: Getting the Most Out of Classified Ads on the Internet," and Chapter 11, "Sold American! Buying Through Online Auctions," for more information on what you should know when buying through those kinds of sites, and for lists of auction and classified ad sites.

➤ **Product comparison sites and shopping agents**   Buying sporting goods and leisure equipment can be confusing. Do you really know everything you need to know about exercise bikes or snowboards? If not, check out a product comparison sites or shopping agents, such as the excellent CompareNet at www.comparenet.com. There you'll get help in deciding the right equipment for you, and you'll also be able to compare makes and models. Turn to Chapter 7, "Shopping Robots, Agents, Search Tools, and Virtual Shopping Assistants," for more information on using these sites and to find sites to check out before you buy sporting and leisure goods.

➤ **Online sites of department stores**   Many online department stores offer a limited selection of sporting and leisure equipment. They generally carry popular, big-name mainstream products but shy away from the more esoteric equipment. However, they often have goods on sale, so if you're looking for a well-known, brand-name product, department stores are a good place to head.

What You Should Know Before Buying Sports, Health, Recreation, and Fitness Goods

Before you buy that gut-buster exercise machine or those sci-fi-looking new running shoes, you'll want to know about the site you're buying from. Here's what to know before you buy:

➤ **What are the return policies?**   You might *think* that size 8D Adidas running shoes are the right size for you...but can you really know before trying them on? Of course not. So be sure that any place you buy from allows returns.

➤ **What are the shipping fees?**   Shipping fees on a Louisville slugger bat probably won't run you too much money. But how about that recumbent exercise bike that takes up half your living room—think the seller's going to eat the shipping costs on that baby? Probably not, although some sites do pay shipping costs. Check out how much you'll pay before forking over your credit card.

Subscribe to Email Alerts for Good Deals

Some sites will alert you via email when they have good deals on sporting goods. Sometimes you get more than an alert: Subscribe to the alert, and you might get a discount on what you buy on the site.

➤ **What kind of warranty do you get?** Bad things can happen to good equipment. Handles can crack. Bats can break. Rowing machines can snap in half while you're in them, crushing your body into little tiny bits...well, maybe that's an exaggeration. Anyway, the point is that anyone who's ever used sports gear knows that things can go wrong. Find out what kind of warranty the site offers—and whether the warranty comes from the site or the manufacturer. That way, you'll know where to turn if something goes wrong. In general, manufacturers are better at handling warranty issues than are sales sites, so you should always try to get a manufacturer's warranty.

Best Sites for Sports, Recreation, Health, and Fitness

It's time to buy those new hourglass-shaped skis that you've been eyeing since last snow season or to get a new baseball glove, golf driver, or Nautilus equipment to help you build up your abs and add to your muscle mass. But where to go? Check out the following sites when you're starting your online shopping expedition.

Bike World

http://www.bikeworld.com

If you're looking for a plain-Jane 3-speed or 10-speed bicycle, don't come here—you won't find a thing to buy. But if you're looking for high-end components for fancy, expensive bikes, it's the place to go. You can even get a watch that tracks your racing times, hooks up to a computer, and transfers data.

Classifieds2000

http://www.classifieds2000.com

Classifieds2000 is the best classified site on the Internet—and has an excellent section for buying sporting goods. When I last checked, dozens of categories were offering products for sale—everything from bicycles to fishing equipment to skateboards, and even rugby equipment and well beyond. If you're in the market for buying (or even selling) any kind of sports or leisure goods equipment, you'd do well to turn here and look for bargains.

Body Trends

http://www.bodytrends.com

If you have a thing for home exercise equipment and crave things such as stair climbers, exercise cycles, treadmills, gravity boots (gravity boots?), inversion therapy products (don't ask), and any other kind of product to improve your body, you've got a friend here. Body Trends has anything you can name, including old-fashioned medicine balls for those who prefer their aerobics with a retro twist.

Fitness Zone

http://www.fitnesszone.com

Here's another site, like Body Trends, that specializes in fitness equipment. You'll find strength-training equipment, cardiovascular devices, clothing, and even steam rooms and saunas you can install at home.

Fogdog

http://www.fogdog.com

Pick a sport, any sport. Now pick a piece of equipment they use in that sport. Got it? Good. You can buy it here. Don't believe me? Okay, in addition to the usual suspects in all the usual sports, here are some of the things you can buy at Fogdog: lacrosse sticks, polo balls, volleyball sets, and that most necessary of all sports equipment, a glove pounder. What is a glove pounder, you ask? A wooden device that you pound into your baseball glove to "soften and shape" it, says the site.

Head to the GoSki Site for In-Depth Reviews of Skiing Equipment

Want honest, clear-eyed reviews of skiing equipment—anything from skis to bindings, boots, snowboards, and more? Head to the Gear section of the GoSki site at www.goski.com. You'll find great reviews of any kind of skiing equipment. Definitely head here for advice before buying.

International Golf Outlet

http://www.igogolf.com

I'll admit this up-front: I think golf might well be the stupidest game ever invented, except for the ball games the Aztecs played in which the losers had their hearts ripped out and eaten (talk about needing motivation for winning!). Still, if you enjoy whacking a tiny ball around to no apparent purpose, you'll probably want to head here. You'll find discounts on just about any golf equipment you can name.

Check Internet Newsgroups for Product Advice

Internet newsgroups are worldwide public bulletin boards where people discuss every topic under the sun. Many, many newsgroups are devoted to sports, leisure, and recreation. Participants often discuss specific products and sometimes offer used goods for sale. To find a complete list of newsgroups, head to the Deja.com Usenet site at www.deja.com. Then either browse the newsgroups by category or else type a word that describes what you're looking for. Deja.com will then show you which newsgroups to check out, and you can read the newsgroups straight from the site. For more information about newsgroups and how to use them, turn to Chapter 8, "Have I Got a Deal for You!"

Online Sports

http://www.onlinesports.com

Here's a huge site with about a zillion (that's a scientific calculation; I counted every item) things for sale. In addition to sporting equipment, there are also collectibles here such as photographs and baseball cards. It's not as easy to shop here as at Fogdog, but if you're comparison shopping, I suggest heading to this site as well as to Fogdog.

Use Excite's Golf-Shopping Agent to Find the Best Golf Products at the Best Price

Looking for the perfect driver, putter, or wedge at the best price? You don't need to surf all over the Internet to find it—check into Excite's golf-shopping agent. This agent has two parts. First it helps you find reviews of golf equipment— just type what you're looking for, and you'll get links to product reviews. Then, when you have a better sense of what you want to buy, type the equipment (including the specific manufacturer if you want). The agent gives you links to places on the Internet where you can buy and shows you the prices so that you can find the best product at the cheapest price. To get there, go to Excite Shopping at www.excite.com/shopping and then click **Sports and Leisure**. When you're on that page, you'll see the golf-shopping agent and review and product finder.

Sporting Auction

http://www.sportingauction.com

Sporting Auction is a big auction site that specializes in sports. The products are offered for sale by the site itself, so you won't be dealing with a private seller. In addition, many of the products carry a warranty, something that you won't get when you buy products from individuals at classified sites.

Sports and Leisure Section of Excite Shopping

http://www.excite.com/shopping; then click **Sports and Leisure**

Here's one of the best sites online when you're shopping for sports or leisure equipment. It's about as comprehensive a site as you'll find. There are links, by category, to

303

Check This Out

Use CompareNet for the Best Sports Comparison Shopping on the Internet

CompareNet at `www.comparenet.com` lets you compare the features and prices of different kinds of goods—and the sports equipment area is excellent. Head there for information before buying any sporting good.

shopping sites for every possible kind of sports and leisure equipment—from archery to wrestling and everything in between. You can also click on links to CompareNet product finders that help you choose the right equipment. You'll find a shopping agent for helping you find the lowest-cost golf equipment, as well as links to classified ads for sporting and leisure goods. In short, Excite Shopping is a great place to start when you're shopping for sports and leisure goods.

Tennis Warehouse

```
http://www.tennis-warehouse.com
```

The name of this site pretty much says it all—it's a huge online warehouse that sells tennis equipment. Name a kind of product, name a manufacturer, and the odds are great that you'll be able to buy it here.

What's truly exceptional about this site, though, is that it also offers honest, no-holds-barred reviews of tennis products—reviews that are free of hype and clearly describe a product's problems as well as strengths. For example, here's a comment about the Prince ThunderStrike Titanium Longbody racket: "The high power level of this racquet limits the number of players who can use it and the lack of maneuverability limits the number of players who will want to use it." Honest, yes? Tennis Warehouse clearly is not running a racket at its site.

Check This Out

Head to the Sports Fan Site If You're Looking for Sports Stuff from Your Favorite Teams

Do you like to watch? Are you a sports fan who can't get enough of your favorite team's logos on clothing, hats, watches, and just about anything else? Then head to `www.sports-fans.com` and get your credit card ready. You'll find officially licensed goods from professional baseball, basketball, football, and hockey teams and leagues, as well as from college teams.

Pharmacies and Vitamins Online

Part of ensuring your health is the proper use of vitamins and nutritional supplements—and getting the right treatment if something goes wrong. A slew of pharmacies have sprung up online, as have sites where you can buy vitamins and nutritional supplements. Keep in mind that in order to get prescription drugs from an online pharmacy, your doctor will have to notify them first, or you'll have to send them your current prescription.

Here's where to go for pharmacies and vitamins.

Drugstore.com

http://www.drugstore.com

You need anything from a drugstore, just go here. From vitamins to personal care products, to prescriptions and anything else, you'll find it. Especially useful are the various wellness guides and resource areas. And you'll be able to get the complete rundown on any prescription medication as well.

From vitamins to personal care products to prescription drugs, you'll find them all at drugstore.com.

PlanetRX.com

http://www.planetrx.com

Personal care, beauty products, medications, vitamins...it's all here. When I last checked in, they were running a special, giving you three products for free, just for trying out the site. If you head here, check out eCenters with helpful information on things such as men's health, baby's health and care, weight loss, and women's health.

Head to DrKoop.com for Health Advice

One of the best sites for health advice on the Internet is associated with the popular former Surgeon General of the United States, Dr. Koop. Go there to get any information about just about any kind of medical condition you can name, and great data on prescription drugs.

Soma

http://www.soma.com

Here's yet another excellent online pharmacy. Like the others, you'll be able to buy everything from personal care good to prescription medications. And like the others, you'll find help and advice on a wide variety of subjects. When I last checked in, you could get $25 off on your first order.

Vitamins.com

http://www.vitamins.com

You'll find a whole lot of vitamins at this site, as the name suggests. The site is confusing to use, and not as helpful or as well laid out as the VitaminShoppe, reviewed next.

VitaminShoppe

http://www.vitaminshoppe.com

You want vitamins and nutritional supplement? This site's got 'em—more than 1,700 products, from Angelica to zinc lozenges. If you can't find it here, it doesn't exist. The site even has a frequent buyer program—the more vitamins you buy, the more money you save.

GreenTree

http://www.greentree.com

Here's another good site for vitamins. Like the others, there's a whole lot you can find here. It even has wild oats. For what medicinal purpose could anyone need wild oats? If you've sowed them in your youth, you should know. This is a G-rated book, so I'll leave it to your imagination.

The Least You Need to Know

➤ Specialized sites offer the greatest variety of sporting goods, but sometimes general shopping sites offer better discounts.

➤ To find very low-cost and used sporting goods, try auction and classified sites.

➤ Check warranties, shipping fees, and return policies before buying.

Chapter 24

Home Sweet Home: Home, Garden, Flowers, and Gifts

In This Chapter

➤ Kinds of sites that sell home-related products

➤ Tips for buying home-related products

➤ What to look for when buying from garden sites

➤ Advice for buying flowers online

➤ What you should know before buying gifts online

➤ Best sites for buying home-related products, flowers, gardening products, and gifts on the Internet

Work, work, work. Sometimes it seems that for many people that's all there is to life—and for some people, that's all there is to the Internet.

But you can use the Internet to do much more than just work, work, work—if you've gotten this far in the book, you know it's also a great place to buy, buy, buy. And as you'll find out in this chapter, it's a great place to buy things for your home and garden—and also a great place to buy flowers and gifts.

You might be surprised to find out that you can buy anything for your home and garden over the Internet—anything from kitchen sinks to vegetable seeds. And you can buy flowers for next-day delivery, as well as a remarkable variety of unique gifts, not only from gift outlets, but from places such as museum stores.

So read on. In this chapter, I clue you in on how to shop for home and garden goods, as well as how to shop for flowers and gifts. And I tell you about the best shopping sites for your home and garden, the best sites for buying your sweetie (or other loved ones) sweetheart roses, and the best sites for buying anyone the perfect gift.

Home Is Where the Shopping Cart Is: Buying Home Products Online

So you're looking to buy a small appliance, or a bookshelf, or something to decorate your home. One of the Internet's great secrets is that you can buy all kinds of home products online. In this section, you learn what kind of sites sell home products, what you should know before you buy, and which sites are the best for buying home products online. So before buying your next microwave, wall paint, or chintzy little plaster figurine (sorry, I know you really wouldn't buy one of those—but maybe a plaster flamingo for your front lawn?), read this section.

What Kinds of Sites Sell Home Products?

Home products are available at many different kinds of sites on the Internet—at general shopping sites; at sites that specialize in general household goods; at very specialized sites, such as those that focus on kitchen appliances; at sites of individual products; and finally, at shopping "agents" that go out and find the best price on a product for you. Here's the lowdown:

➤ **General shopping sites**   Most general shopping sites and Internet malls, such as Shopping.com at www.shopping.com, have a section, and often a sizable one, for home-related products, such as for the kitchen and bath, hardware, and similar products. If you're not looking for anything unusual and don't need a large selection—especially any unusual or specialized ones—these sites are often a good bet. However, for any kind of specialized goods, you'd do better to head to a dedicated home-product site. General shopping sites also often don't give shopping advice, whereas some of the dedicated sites do. Turn to Chapter 15, "Mall Fever: Department Stores, Malls, Closeouts, and Bargain Hunting," for listings of general shopping sites.

➤ **General-interest home-product sites**   A number of sites, such as HouseNet at www.housenet.com, shown in the following figure, specialize in home-related products. These sites often do more than just offer goods for sale—they also offer helpful articles about home improvement, decorating, and similar subjects. No surprise: They also usually offer a wider range of this type of merchandise than do the general shopping sites. They're often your best bet for buying, although you should also check the prices at general shopping sites, which might offer lower prices on some products.

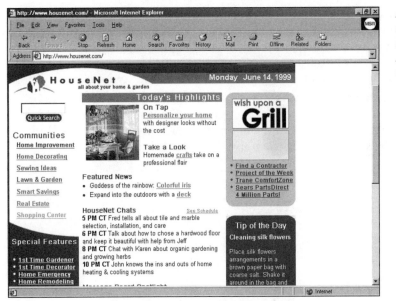

Buy house-related products and get advice on how to use them at HouseNet (www.housenet.com).

➤ **Manufacturer sites**   Right now, very few manufacturers of home-related products own Web sites that sell their products online. However, I figure that someday—possibly by the time you read this—manufacturers will decide to sell on the Web. In either event, their sites are still worth a visit, especially for the most up-to-date product information. These sites might also tell you about any special deals that are available.

➤ **Specialized home sites**   Want to buy a new food processor? The best place to go might well be to a kitchen site, such as The Internet Kitchen at www.your-kitchen.com. These sites carry the greatest variety of goods for any kind of specialized purpose—but if you want to also buy something else there, say, a screwdriver, you'll be out of luck (and no, there is no site www.your-screwdriver.com—at least not yet). So when you're buying a single product, they're worth a visit; when buying several not in the same specific category, they're not the best bet.

➤ **Shopping agents**   Shopping agents go out and find the best deal for you on a particular product or make and model. However, only a few agents are available for home-related goods.

What to Do Before Buying Home Products

Buying a home product online isn't as simple as buying a book or a CD. Issues such as warranties, shipping costs, and return policies become much more important. So before you buy, here's what you need to do:

➤ **Price-shop at different sites.**   Because some home products are relatively expensive, you can save real money by comparison shopping. Even when you find something at a specialty site, be sure to check a general shopping site before buying. Sometimes sites run specials, so you want to be sure you've covered the waterfront (or at least surfed the Internet) before spending your money.

➤ **Find out about shipping costs.**   Some items, such as small appliances or other goods that cost a fair amount of money, can run up serious shipping charges—costs of $15 or so are not uncommon. So before buying, check shipping costs and be sure to include them in your comparisons.

When Shopping at Home-Product Sites, Be Sure to Check Out Shipping Costs and Rules for Each Item You Buy

Some sites, such as HouseNet at www.housenet.com, sell items from many different catalogs, and the shipping costs and rules vary for each catalog. At first glance, you might not know which catalog you're buying from. So when shopping at a home-product site, always be sure to check the shipping information before you buy—it could be different for each item. Some sites charge by size, others by the amount of money you spend, and still others charge a flat fee. Know before you buy.

➤ **Check out the return policy.**   You'll want to know how long you have to return products—and who pays the shipping costs. If you pay the shipping costs for defective products, that means you'll be paying shipping costs twice—once for getting it and once for returning it to the site.

➤ **Find out whether your returns are for exchange, credit, or cash.** Sometimes, home-product sites won't let you return your goods for cash—they'll give you only a store credit or an exchange. If possible, stay away from those sites and buy where you can get a refund.

➤ **Visit the manufacturer's site.**   Manufacturers are always coming out with the newest, the latest, and the snazziest. Before buying a small appliance or similar product, check out the manufacturer's Web site to see whether what you're buying is the newest model. If it's not, either demand the newest model from the site you're buying from, ask for a discount, or buy from another site.

➤ **Check out the warranty.**   Is there a warranty? What are the terms? Who gives the warranty—the manufacturer or the Web site?

➤ **Find out whether the item is rebuilt, refurbished, used, or discontinued.**   Some bargain sections of home-product sites might sell equipment that's used or that's being discontinued by the manufacturer. Know what you're buying, especially because these kinds of goods might not be covered by warranties or might be covered by a lesser warranty than new goods.

Best Home-Products Shopping Sites Online

So where should you buy that microwave, food processor, or other home-related product? Check out the following sites. Also, as I mentioned earlier in the chapter, be sure to check general shopping sites, which often have many home products for sale as well.

Benchmark BeHome

http://www.behome.com

Buy furniture over the Internet? You must be kidding! No, I'm not. Head to this site, and you can buy all kinds of big-ticket and big-size items such as sofas, recliners, chairs, dining room furniture—pretty much the whole nine yards and more. Delivery is via the national delivery service Bekins, and delivery people help set up what you've bought. (Delivery can easily add $100 or more to the cost of what you're buying.)

Home and Garden Section of Excite Shopping

http://www.excite.com/

(Click **Shopping**, followed by **Home and Garden**.)

For one of the best directories of where to buy home-related goods online, head here. You'll find stores in many categories, ranging from appliances, to bed and bath, home decor, rugs and carpets, and more. A great feature of the site are its product finders that help you decide which product to buy in certain categories. Just click the kind of product you want, such as refrigerators or cordless drills, and you'll be led through a set of steps that help you decide which particular product to buy.

HouseNet

http://www.housenet.com

Here's a good site for getting information about home-related products and doing home improvements, as well as information about gardens. You'll find many useful articles, links, and a relatively small shopping area. You'll mainly come here for the articles and to spend a little time browsing through what's for sale.

The Internet Kitchen

```
http://www.your-kitchen.com
```

Cookbooks, cookware, cutlery, small appliances, vacuum bottles (vacuum bottles? yes, vacuum bottles)—you'll find everything you need for your kitchen here. This site features many products from top manufacturers. This site is a good place to go when you need to buy something for your kitchen.

Home Area of NetMarket

```
http://www.netmarket.com
```

(Click **Complete Home**.)

This excellent product-comparison site has a great home section. It doesn't just link you to products to buy—it also gives you advice on what to buy and offers step-by-step instructions on how to choose a home-related product.

Find a Contractor Online

Need to find a contractor to do work on your home? Good luck—contractors are at a premium these days. But you can use the power of the Internet to find the names of certified contractors who will do everything from remodeling to plastering, plumbing and more. Head to either ImproveNet at www.improvenet.com or ContractorNet at www.contractornet.com. Then detail where you live and the kind of work you need done; the sites will spit back a list of contractors who can do the work. ImproveNet is the better of the two sites because it offers much more specialized searching. Still, both sites are worth a visit to get a list of local contractors. Now you just have to find a way to get them to show up on time! Sorry; the Internet can't help you there.

Sears

```
http://www.sears.com/
```

Rev up your power tools, big boys (and big girls). Here's the place to go online when you have a yen for a circular saw, router, screwdriver, or toolbox. You can now buy the Sears Craftsman line of tools online. When I last checked in, thousands of tools were available—everything from hand tools to power tools to tool sets and much more. And it's not just power tools that are available here. You'll also be able to buy appliances and other household items as well. And you can buy parts for just about any kind of appliance you can name—the site boasts over 4 million parts, accessories, and owners' manuals.

Home Section of Yahoo! Shopping

```
http://shopguide.yahoo.com/
```

(Click **Home & Garden**.)

Here's a good place to find sites that sell a variety of home products. You'll find sites for home improvements, bedding, and much more.

It's Easy Being Green: Buying at Garden Sites

How does your garden grow? No matter how it grows, you can probably make it grow better—or at least for less money—if you buy garden products on the Internet. Whether you're looking for seeds, plants, or gardening equipment, you'll find sites and help online.

Buying gardening goods online isn't hard, but you should know a few things before you make a purchase. Here's the rundown:

➤ **When are the goods shipped?** It'll do you no good if those tulip bulbs you ordered early last winter don't arrive until midsummer—you'll have missed the season. Be sure there's a guarantee that whatever you buy arrives in a timely fashion.

➤ **Are there special discounts for ordering out of season?** At garden.com, for example, you can get a 15% discount when buying certain garden products out of season. It's a way to save a lot of money.

➤ **If you're ordering live plants, how are they shipped?** A good deal of damage can be done to plants shipped through the mail. Look for and read the site's information about how live plants are shipped and what you should do when you unpack them. If this information isn't available, consider buying elsewhere.

➤ **What's the return and warranty policy?** The live flowering plant you ordered arrived looking like the victim of a herbicide attack. What to do? Be sure that you can return plants—and find out whether the site guarantees that its plants will live longer than a phase of the moon.

Best Gardening Sites on the Internet

When it's time to buy bulbs, seeds, plants, or anything else for your garden, here's where to buy online.

Burpee

http://www.burpee.com

When you think flower and vegetable seeds, you most likely think Burpee. Good news: You can order seeds online. In addition, you can browse through a library of information about gardening and even get an email answer to your specific question about gardening. There's a recipe area as well.

garden.com

http://www.garden.com

Here it is—the gardening mother lode. You can buy just about anything you want, from bulbs to seeds to herbs; plants; garden furniture, ornaments, and tools—even exotic fish if you happen to have a water garden in your backyard. In other words, everything. There's also extremely useful gardening information, including advice on gardening in your specific area, and helpful message boards as well. But you'll want to come here to buy—over 12,000 products last time I counted. garden.com is the best place for buying gardening products on the Internet.

From plain gardening to exotic fish to water gardening—you'll find information about it all at garden.com.

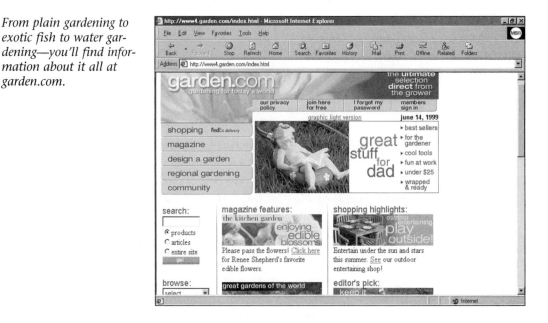

Home and Garden Section of Excite Shopping

http://www.excite.com/

(Click **Shopping**, followed by **Home and Garden**.)

Before buying any gardening-related goods, check here. You'll be able to search the Internet for reviews of gardening-related products, which will help in your search for the perfect tulip bulb or whatever else you're interested in for your garden. Another good feature is the product finder, where you type in what you want to buy and get back a list of suggested products.

Everything's Coming Up Roses: Buying Flowers Online

It's 10 o'clock in the morning, you're at work, and all of a sudden you remember with a sinking feeling that it's your mother's birthday and you haven't bought her a present—and your mother is not one to forgive and forget. You've got a lot of explaining to do. Think forgiveness around the year 2007.

Ah, but you suddenly remember that you can buy flowers over the Internet and even have them delivered the same day. Problem solved. Your mother gets a dozen long-stemmed roses, you earn kudos as the perfect child, and all is well on the family front.

It's a breeze to order flowers online. Your best bet is to buy at one of the many Internet florists (check later in this chapter for specific sites). Before you buy, though, here's what to look for:

➤ **Can you see pictures of the flowers you're sending?** Sounds obvious, I know, but make sure that you can see what you're buying: the bigger the picture, the better—and you'd also like clear, descriptive text of what the flower arrangement looks like.

➤ **What's the delivery schedule?** Not all sites deliver the same day. Check if you need same-day delivery. And check on delivery prices as well because they vary a great deal from site to site.

➤ **Does the site offer advice on which flowers to buy?** Maybe you know the difference between delphiniums and nasturtiums, and you don't need help choosing a bouquet or flowers to send as gifts—but many people could use some help. Some sites, such as the popular 1-800-Flowers at www.1800flowers.com, help you choose the right kind of flowers for the occasion.

➤ **Does the site guarantee the freshness of the flowers?** Picture this scenario: You send your sweetheart a dozen sweetheart roses. Sigh—how

Check This Out

Use Excite's Shopping Agent to Comparison Shop for Flowers

Many Internet sites sell flowers, so you'll want to comparison shop before you buy. Instead of hitting each site yourself, head to the Excite shopping area at www.excite.com/shopping and then click **Flowers & Cards**, and then click **Florists**. You'll be able to search many flower sites to find the best deal.

romantic. Next day they all die. Sigh—there goes your sweetheart as well as the roses. Some sites guarantee that the flowers will stay fresh, for a week, for example. Be sure the site guarantees the freshness and hardiness of its flowers.

➤ **Does the site have a reminder service?**   You don't want to forget your mother's birthday or your anniversary or other special occasions. At some flower sites, you can sign up for email reminders.

➤ **Does the site have a good selection of flowers?**   If all you care about is sending a dozen roses, most any site will do. But if you want to send something more unusual, you could be out of luck. Spend time checking out the site to see what kind of selection it has because some flower sites don't offer many choices.

What a Bloomin' Idea! Best Florist Sites Online

So you're ready to buy flowers online. Here are the best florist sites online.

1-800-Flowers

```
http://www.1800flowers.com
```

This site is one of the most popular—if not the most popular—flower site on the Internet, and with good reason. It has everything you could want: same-day delivery, advice, notification of upcoming occasions (reminders sent via email), and a large selection of flowers and floral arrangements. Check out the following figure to see what the site is like.

You want flowers? They have flowers. The premier flower-ordering site on the Internet is 1-800-Flowers.

ftd.com

```
http://www.ftd.com
```

The national florist has an online site, and it's a good one. Gifts such as fruit and gourmet baskets are also available. The exotic flower section is particularly nice because it has flowers you won't normally find on most Web sites.

Internetflorist.com

```
http://www.internetflorist.com
```

This is another good flower site with plants, food and gift baskets, and gift balloons for sale as well as flowers. It offers same-day service, but not much advice on what to buy. Still, it's a good site.

PC Flowers and Gifts

```
http://www.pcflowers.com
```

You'll find more than flowers at this site; it also sells plants, balloons, gift baskets, sweets, meats—hold on a minute, here, meat? Yes, meat. For that special occasion, get your loved one a boneless rib-eye roast. There's a good selection of flowers here, though, so next time you want to send someone roses and rib steak, you'll know where to go.

Send a Virtual Bouquet over the Internet—Free

Know someone who's allergic to flowers—or maybe you just like the idea of sending a virtual bouquet, rather than the real thing? Head to `http://www.flowernetwork.com/`, go to the virtual bouquet page and follow the instructions to send a picture postcard of flowers or a bouquet over the Internet. The recipient gets an email from you with a link to a Web page that holds the virtual bouquet. As you might guess, you can send a real bouquet from the site as well, if you're interested in sending the real thing—and you're sure there'll be no sneezes on the receiving end. You can also send virtual bouquets from the `www.virtualflorist.com` site.

It's a Gift to Be Simple: Buying Gifts Online

What should you buy for your best friend this Hanukkah or Christmas? And what are you going to buy your wife on her next birthday or anniversary? For some people (present company included), the thought of gift buying inspires anxiety, rather than the spirit of good cheer.

If just the thought of going into a store and trying to decide on a gift makes you break out into a cold sweat, consider going online instead. Here's what to keep in mind when buying gifts:

➤ **Does the site do gift wrapping?**   Sounds like a minor point, but if you're like me and your gift wrapping could pass for a suit that's been slept in, it becomes a major point. Most general shopping sites won't gift wrap; some gift sites will.

➤ **Does the site have a "personal shopper"?**   Shopping online doesn't necessary make it easier to find the right gift. Fortunately, some sites provide personal-shopper services that offer advice on what to buy. If you have trouble making up your mind, head to one of these sites.

➤ **Does the site have a reminder service?**   I'm the world's worst person when it comes to remembering birthdays, anniversaries, and other important dates—as my parents can unfortunately testify. If you tend to forget when it's time to buy a gift, look for a site that offers reminders.

➤ **Does the site ship orders immediately?**   Not all sites ship your goods as soon as they take your order. If you're buying a gift at the last minute, like about 90% of the world, immediate shipping is important.

Best Gift-Buying Sites on the Internet

If you're ready to buy, here's where to go. The following sites specialize in gifts. (Of course, you can also buy gifts at any general buying site or mall, covered earlier in this book.) In addition to gift-buying sites, I've included sites that specialize in offering advice for buying gifts and sites whose primary purpose is to remind you of important upcoming dates.

911Gifts

    http://www.911gifts.com

Possibly the best gift-buying site online. It has everything you need: a huge selection of gifts, help in choosing gifts, a reminder service to let you know of upcoming events, next-day delivery service for many items, and a whole lot more. From gadgets to sweets to fruit baskets, wines, beauty products, and more, you'll be able to find something here.

Cybershop.com

http://www.cybershop.com

Here's a very good gift site. Although Cybershop sells a wide range of products, it is a particularly good site for buying gifts. In addition to an excellent selection, Cybershop ships within 24 hours—an important requirement for people like me who often buy gifts at the last minute.

Gifts & Gadgets Section of America Online

On America Online, KEYWORD GIFTS

Here's the central site on America Online for buying gifts. You'll find links to many gift-buying sites on the Internet and on America Online itself. It's also a good place for finding out about specials and deals.

La Patisserie

http://www.1800gifts.com

If someone in your life loves cookies, cakes, fruit baskets, and other baked goodies, check here. It specializes in bakery gift items—just be sure your loved one isn't on a diet because just *looking* at some of these items can add a few pounds.

Personalize.com

http://www.personalize.com

Some people love getting personalized gifts—it might be jewelry or a teddy bear, a sweatshirt, or a golf ball set. This site personalizes just about anything—from coffee mugs to tote bags to afghans.

PresentPicker

http://www.presentpicker.com

Tired of buying your dad yet another tie for Father's Day? Just having a plain hard time figuring out what to buy your secretary for his or her birthday? Then head here. The site offers advice on what to buy and organizes its merchandise into categories such as Secret Love. So finding just the right gift for someone is easy. The site usually offers very suitable gifts, but sometimes...well, I'll let you be the judge. For example, one time, when I chose Secret Love, the list of gifts was what you would expect: lingerie, chocolates, perfume, a teddy bear. But what to make of this item: "1-inch, snap-lock adjustable nylon collar, fits pets' 18- to 26-inch necks. A matching 4-foot lead is available. Red or Black." Don't ask what it's for, because I don't want to know. Let's just hope that it's this site's way of saying it has gifts for your favorite furry friend.

Buy Unique Gifts Online at New York's Metropolitan Museum of Art and at National Geographic

Are you looking for a special item that's perfectly in tune with the recipient's personality. One great place to shop is New York's Metropolitan Museum of Art gift shop at `http://metmuseum.netcart.com/`. Whether you want to buy a hieroglyph charm, a reproduction of classical Greek sculpture, art prints and books, or many other beautiful items, you'll find them here. Also worth a visit is the National Geographic store (go to `www.nationalgeographic.com` and click **Store**); you'll find great items such as maps, science kits, interesting greeting cards, and binoculars.

NeverForget.com

`http://www.neverforget.com`

The name says it all. You can download software to remind you of important events (free to download and try; $19.95 to buy), or you can sign up for free email alerts.

The Least You Need to Know

➤ When buying big-ticket or big-cost items such as furniture, check out the warranty and return policies—and be sure you can return the goods for cash, not just for credit or exchange.

➤ When buying an appliance, be sure that it's new (not used or refurbished) and that it carries a full warranty.

➤ When ordering live plants, be sure that they're shipped in a way to ensure their safety and longevity.

➤ When buying flowers or plants, look for a guarantee that they'll live for a certain amount of time after delivery.

➤ Look for gift-buying sites that offer personal-shopper and reminder services.

Chapter 25

Where to Buy Clothing, Grooming, Beauty, and Jewelry Products

> ### In This Chapter
>
> ➤ Kinds of sites that sell clothing, beauty, and jewelry products
>
> ➤ Consumer advice for buying clothing, beauty, and jewelry products
>
> ➤ How to get online advice on buying clothing and jewelry
>
> ➤ The best clothing, grooming, beauty, and jewelry sites on the Internet

Daaahling! You look mahvelous, just mahvelous! Here, I must kiss you. (Move closer for air kiss. Kiss, kiss, kiss.) When you look good, you *feel* good, dahling; haven't I always told you that?

No, you don't have to talk like that or be head over heels in love with fashion to use the Internet to get clothing, grooming, beauty, and jewelry products. In fact, you don't even need good taste. All you need is a credit card, tips on how to shop, and information on where to go. So read on, dear one, whether you're a high-fashion maven or your tastes run to cutoffs and T-shirts. Along the way, you'll learn how and where to look for grooming, beauty, and jewelry products as well.

What Kinds of Sites Sell Clothing, Grooming, Beauty, and Jewelry Products?

You can find clothing and related products all over the Web, in all different kinds of stores. Here's the lowdown on where to hunt for the goods:

➤ **Department stores**   No great surprise. You'll find tons of clothes, grooming, beauty, and jewelry products at the online sites of department stores such as Macy's at www.macys.com and J.C. Penney at www.jcpenney.com. Head to Chapter 15, "Mall Fever: Department Stores, Malls, Closeouts, and Bargain Hunting," for help in shopping at them and a guide on where to shop. Figure that you'll find mostly mainstream products at these sites and nothing particularly "edgy" or eccentric and unusual. But you might often get good discounts—and of course, if you shop at these sites, you can rest assured that you'll probably never become a fashion victim.

➤ **Online malls**   Again, you'll find a huge selection of this stuff at online malls. Head to Chapter 15 for help in shopping at them and a guide on where to shop. The America Online Shopping Channel (KEYWORD SHOPPING) has a particularly good selection, as does the IQVC Shopping Network at www.iqvc.com—which is the online site of the well-known TV shopping network. As with department stores, you won't find anything eccentric or unusual at these sites. Again, though, you might well find good discounts on popular, mainstream fashion and related products.

How to Find the Online Site of a Clothing Store

Finding the online site of your favorite clothing store couldn't be easier. Just put www. in front of the store name and .com after it, such as www.jcrew.com. If the store has an online site, that's where it'll be.

➤ **Online sites of clothing, grooming, beauty, and jewelry product stores**   These days, many stores have Internet sites. So if you live in one of the few places on the planet that doesn't have a local Gap store, fear not—you can head there on the Internet at, you guessed it, www.gap.com. Most other major stores also have online sites as well. Check the listings later in this chapter on where to go. If you've shopped at these stores in the real world, you'll know ahead of time what to expect. And shopping online is often a good way to check the merchandise in the real-world store—so you might do some Internet window shopping before spending the time driving across town or to the local mall.

➤ **Internet-only clothing, grooming, beauty, and jewelry product sites** You'll find a number of sites online that specialize in these kinds of products— stores that exist only in cyberspace. Shown in the following figure is one of the more popular ones: www.fashionmall.com. Check the listings later in this chapter for more suggestions.

➤ **Online sites of mail-order companies**   Many mail-order clothing companies, such as Land's End (www.landsend.com) and L.L. Bean (www.llbean.com), have established outposts in cyberspace. After all, selling online and selling over the telephone aren't all that different. These sites are often among the better presented and designed clothing sites you'll find. They're especially good at handling returns and similar issues. They also often offer good discounts.

One of the more popular clothing sites on the Internet: www.fashionmall. com.

Get Great Bargains by Buying Overstocked Items

Some online sites, such as Land's End at www.landsend.com, have special areas in which they sell overstocks—items that they've manufactured or bought too many of. They mark them down big-time, which means that you get big savings. Check out any site for the overstock area—but keep in mind that not all sites have them. Land's End has an excellent one, with a huge selection of overstocked goods. You can even subscribe to an overstock newsletter there, which lets you know by email what products are available at overstock prices. You'll find it's a great way to get bargains delivered straight to your email inbox.

➤ **Bargain search robots**   One of the few sites that will search through cloth-ing sites and find the best deal for you is the HotBot shopping area at www.shop.hotbot.com. Head over to the site, click **Clothing**, and you'll be able to search many different sites for the best deals on clothing. Don't expect to find oddball or eccentric clothing—but you might well find good bargains on products such as jeans and shirts.

What You Should Know Before Buying Clothing, Grooming, Beauty, and Jewelry Products

All online sites that sell these products are not created equal. So how do you know where to shop and how to buy? Check out the following advice and then turn to the end of the chapter for the best sites on the net.

> ➤ **Does the clothing site offer size charts and similar advice?**   Clothes can be cut idiosyncratically; shoe sizes might vary; and in general, it can be hard to correctly gauge what size clothing you should buy. Sites that offer size charts and similar sizing advice are a good bet. That way, you won't have to return merchandise.

Use a Reminder Service

Some sites, such as Avon at www.avon.com, will send you an email alert whenever someone you're buying a gift for has a birthday, anniversary, or similar important date. That way, you'll have plenty of time to buy your gift before the date comes up. For more information about reminder services and gift buying, turn to Chapter 24, "Home Sweet Home: Home, Garden, Flowers, and Gifts."

> ➤ **What is the return policy?**   Because you can't really know how clothing will look on you until you buy it, be sure the site lets you return clothing for any reason. If it doesn't, don't buy there. Also, keep in mind that most times, when you buy a product at an online outpost of a retail store, you won't be able to return the goods to the retail store—you'll have to send it back to the online site via mail.

The Gap Online Lets You Return Goods to Its Retail Store

Most times, when you buy products at an online site that also has a retail presence, you won't be able to return goods to the physical store. The Gap Online at www.gap.com is that rarest of exceptions: If you buy something online that you want to return, just bring it to your nearest Gap store, whether or not it carries the goods you bought.

➤ **Look for sites that let you preview clothes.** Believe it or not, not all clothing sites show detailed pictures of their merchandise. Be sure you see a good picture before buying. Look for sites that let you "dress" a model in clothes you like or let you mix and match clothes to see how they go together. Shown here is the way that the Gap at www.gap.com lets you see how separate pieces will look together.

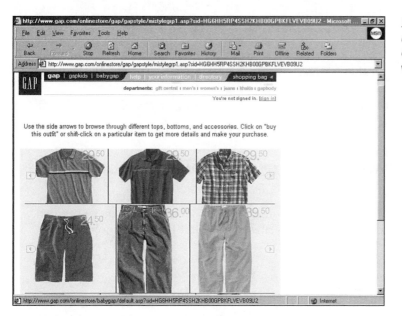

Mix and match clothes at the Instant Style area of Gap Online at www.gap.com.

➤ **Be wary of buying jewelry or other similar goods from auction sites and classified sites.** Yes, auction sites and classified sites offer great deals on all kinds of goods. But be very careful when buying jewelry at them. Because you're buying from an individual rather than the site itself, you could easily get burned.

Mix and match clothes with the virtual style feature at the Gap Online at www.gap.com.

➤ **Find out whether that bargain is irregular or slightly damaged goods.** That bargain you find online might not be as great a bargain as you had thought. When some clothing stores offer great prices, they're selling irregulars or slightly damaged clothing. Be sure to check before buying.

➤ **Buy jewelry only from a well-known site.** How do you know whether that 24-carat gold ring is really solid gold or whether that diamond is really a diamond? Unless a respected jeweler or company runs the site, be leery of buying there.

Learn About Diamonds Before You Buy

Buying a diamond can be a frightening experience—how do you know that you're buying the real thing? And how can you tell a good diamond from a bad one? Head over to the Diamond Information Center at www.adiamondisforever.com for a complete guide to buying diamonds.

Best Sites for Buying Clothing, Grooming, Beauty, and Jewelry Products

So it's time to buy clothing or beauty products or that jewelry that you've been craving. Where to go? Head to the following sites for the best in online shopping.

Avon

http://www.avon.com

Ding Dong! Avon calling. No need anymore to have to answer the door for the Avon lady. She's on the Internet. You'll be able to buy online what you can buy in real life, so if you like Avon products, head here.

Bluefly

http://www.bluefly.com

Here's one of the best clothing sites you'll find online. Great clothes for men, women, and children, great clothing lines such as Ralph Lauren, Calvin Klein, and others, and a well-designed, easy-to-use site. Fashion mavens will want to head to the Flypaper area, which gives the inside scoop on fashion and fashion tips.

Clothes and Beauty Section of Excite Shopping

http://www.excite.com/shopping

(Click **Clothing and Accessories**.)

Here's a great place to find links to dozens of clothing and beauty product sites on the Internet. The sites are organized by category, such as Activeware, Bridal, Hair Care, Jeans, and Jewelry, so you can easily get to the buying site you want.

Designers Direct

http://www.designersdirect.com

Don't be fooled by the name of this site: It's not a high-fashion site where you won't be able to buy even a shirt button. Instead, it's stocked with clothes, sneakers, fragrances, and more from Calvin Klein, Levi Strauss, DKNY, and similar designers.

Delia's

http://www.delias.com

If you have a pre-teen or teenaged daughter, you no doubt are familiar with the Delia's clothing catalog, a favorite among girls of that age (and among parents as well, because the clothes are well-made and well-priced). Delia's has an online site, and in addition to offering clothing from the catalog, there are also contests, links to kid-related sites, and discounts.

Fashion Mall

http://www.fashionmall.com

If the names Armani, Bob Mackie, and Charles Jourdan get your blood running, then run to Fashion Mall. This isn't the place to get a pair of sneakers, but it *is* the place to buy slinky high heels. The main complaint I have about this site (other than the fact that I'm a jeans kind of guy and won't ever buy anything here) is that it has an over-abundance of sunglasses, for reasons I can't fathom.

Check This Out

Get Makeup and Beauty Advice Online

Need help choosing the right color blush or lipstick? Do you want any other kind of makeup advice? Head to the Avon site at www.avon.com and click the **Virtual Beauty Adviser**. You'll get all the help you need, and it's free.

Check Out Fashion Mall Guides for Fashion Tips

When it comes to buying a new suit or other piece of clothing, do you break out in hives? Is your fashion sense somewhere between nonexistent and never-never land? Have no fear; there's a guide to help you. Head to the Fashion Mall at www.fashionmall.com, click **Media**, and then scroll until you find **Guides**. You'll find online advice to help you buy clothing; in a few minutes, you'll consider yourself a fashion horse.

Deals on Fragrances Are at www.fragrancecounter.com

A huge selection of fragrances for men and women can be found at www.fragrancecounter.com. Better yet, it regularly offers deals such as buy-one-get-one-free fragrance specials.

Fragrance Counter

http://www.fragrancecounter.com

Perfumes, colognes, toilet water, aftershave…if it smells and it's in a bottle, you'll probably find it here. This site also features a "fragrance adviser," which guides you to the best fragrance for you, depending on your gender, the occasion, and the time of year.

Gap Online

http://www.gap.com

So you don't have time to get to the mall to hit your local Gap? No problem. At Gap Online, you can buy pretty much anything you can buy at the mall. Gap also uses technology better than any other clothing site I've seen on the Internet. You can mix and match to see how different clothes go together, for example.

GemsandJewels.com

`http://www.gemsandjewels.com`

The IQVC Web shopping site, which is run by the QVC TV shopping network, runs this site. So you'll find the same kind of jewelry sold on the network sold here, a big selection, and good prices.

Land's End

`http://www.landsend.com`

The popular mail-order firm also sells online, and its site is excellent. Everything from the mail-order catalog is available here, and there's more as well. You'll find a huge section of overstocked goods, which offer some of the best deals online. Monogramming and engraving are available. And for those who have a difficult time finding the right size, a size chart index helps you choose the right size and provides information about ordering clothes with the right inseam.

L.L. Bean

`http://www.llbean.com`

Here's another popular mail-order firm with an excellent Web site. What you see in the catalog, you can order here. And if you actually wear your outdoor clothing in the outdoors, instead of for driving to the local mall, the site is also just about the best place to go online for information about U.S. National Parks, including camping information.

Zales

`http://www.zales.com`

This jewelry site specializes in diamonds, although it carries other kinds of jewelry as well. It's a helpful, well-organized site, with useful information about jewelry and an excellent return policy.

Check This Out

Subscribe to Email Alerts

Many sites let you sign up for special email alerts that will let you know when clothing, beauty, or grooming products that you're interested are up for sale. Just sign up, tell the site what you're interested in, and you'll get regular email alerts.

The Least You Need to Know

➤ Look for clothing sites that offer sizing charts and similar information.

➤ Be wary of buying jewelry from auction sites, classified sites, and sites you've never heard of.

➤ Look for sites that offer overstocked items as a way to save money on buying clothing.

➤ Some clothing sites offer a preview feature that lets you "dress" models in the clothes you're planning to buy.

➤ Check out return policies at clothing sites before buying.

Chapter 26

More Than Child's Play: Buying Games and Toys

> ## In This Chapter
>
> ➤ Getting the lowdown on the different kinds of sites where you can buy toys and games
>
> ➤ What you should know before buying toys and games on the Internet
>
> ➤ Where to find the best sites online for getting consumer advice on the best toys and games
>
> ➤ The best sites you'll find on the Internet for buying toys and games

Barbies, Teletubbies, Monopoly, educational games, chemistry sets, action figures, grow-a-frog sets, Davy Crockett coonskin caps (oops, that's not around anymore—I must be showing my age)…ah, to be a kid again when the whole world was a vast playpen and everything in it a toy or a game.

The Internet can't make you young again, but it can make it easier for you to find and buy the right toy or game for a child. You'll be able to get advice on which toys to buy, find the right toy at the right price, and maybe even have fun along the way. Even if you don't want to buy toys and games online, you should head to the Internet. It's a great place to get no-holds-barred consumer advice on which toys and games are worth the money—and which you should avoid. So as you'll see in this chapter, buying games and toys online needn't be child's play.

What Kinds of Toy- and Game-Buying Sites Are There?

Before you head out to the Internet to buy games and toys, you'll first need to know what kinds of sites you can buy at. So before you buy your kids Teletubbies (God forbid!), Lego Bricks, Monopoly, or anything else their little hearts desire (or, admit it, that your big heart desires), read on. Here are the kinds of places you'll be heading to on your next toy-and-game shopping expedition and what you should know about each:

➤ **Online sites of department stores** Any self-respecting real-world department store sells toys. However, not all department stores online sell toys, and those that do have fairly limited selections. You generally won't find unusual or out-of-the way toys at these stores; you'll mainly find well-known, brand-name products. On the upside, however, you can find good deals and discounts.

➤ **Online sites of manufacturers or brands** Some companies that have their own line of games and toys also have a site where they sell goods in cyberspace, such as Disney at www.disneystore.com. In fact, some toys and games, such as Monopoly at www.monopoly.com, Legos at www.legoworldshop.com, and Barbie at www.barbie.com, have their own sites. Some manufacturers use their sites only as marketing tools to promote their products, whereas others use them to sell toys and games as well. And then there's Hasbro, which has jumped into the Web with both feet: One site promotes its products at www.hasbro.com, and another site, among other things, sells its products at www. hasbro-interactive.com. The upside of these dedicated sites is that if you like a specific game, toy, or manufacturer, you'll get the latest, the greatest, and the most in-depth products when you visit. The downside is that you usually won't get any kind of discount, or if you do, it's likely to be very small. And, of course, the selection of toys and games will be much more limited than when you buy at a more general site. You can also use some search engines, such as AltaVista at www.altavista.com, to find manufacturers and brands. But check the fine print when you arrive to be sure that you're really getting to the site you want.

➤ **Online malls** Many online malls sell toys and games, and they're very good places to shop if you're looking for mainstream products. For example, Shopping.com at www.shopping.com has an excellent selection of toys, often at significant discounts. Online malls often offer good discounts, and they're good places to check for specials as well. But as with online department stores, you generally won't find unusual or out-of-the way toys and games here.

➤ **Online versions of bricks-and-mortar retail toy stores** Some toy stores and chains such as Toys "R" Us at www.toysrus.com have gone onto the Internet in a big way. Most anything you can buy in the store, you can buy online. Some sites, notably Toys "R" Us, also have special features such as email alerts and baby registries.

➤ **Online stores that specialize in toys and games**   An increasing number of stores that specialize in selling toys and games exist only in cyberspace. One example, eToys at www.etoys.com, is shown in the following figure. These sites are often tricked out with all the kinds of features you'd look for in a toy-buying site: They're often easy to browse, have gift advisers to help you buy the right gift for a particular kid, and offer discounts. In general, you'll find two kinds of sites: those that specialize in educational products and those that don't. Which type of site you visit and buy from depends on the kid you're buying for.

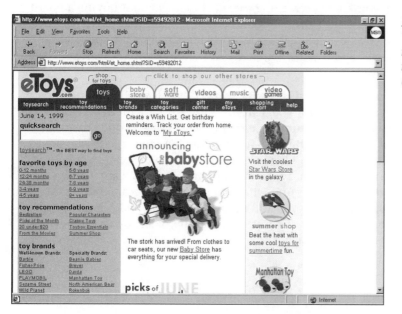

From dolls to software to Teletubbies (Ahhh! Spare me!) and beyond, there's much to buy at eToys (www.etoys.com).

➤ **Bargain shopping agents**   Some sites, or portions of sites, such as Bottom Dollar at www.bottomdollar.com, search the Internet for you, looking for the best deal on specific toys. Sounds great—but when it comes to toys, shopping agents don't do that great a job, because they don't search a huge number of sites. Still, after you decide on a toy or game, it's worth a visit to one of these sites, just in case it can find a good deal.

➤ **Classified and auction sites**   If you're looking for deals on used toys and games, classified and auction sites are great places to go. But be careful: At these sites—especially at classified sites—you'll often be buying from individuals rather than from companies, and you want to be sure that you don't get burned. Often collectible toys and Beanie Babies are sold at these sites as well. I'd stay away from buying Beanie Babies (sure, tell my kids that!) because lots of counterfeit Beanies are being sold—especially high-priced ones. For information about buying at these sites, check out Chapter 10, "Classified Information: Getting the Most Out of Classified Ads on the Internet," and Chapter 11, "Sold American! Buying Through Online Auctions."

➤ **Used toy and game sites**   You might come across an occasional site that sells used toys and games. Be very careful; you really have no way to know the condition of the toys and games. Be careful about warranties and return policies.

Don't Play Games with Your Money: What to Know Before Buying at Toy and Game Sites

So you probably think you know everything there is to know about buying a board game, a Barbie, a Super Nintendo, or Teletubbies (ahhhh! I said that word again! Stop already!). Well, maybe you do—in a real-world store. But there's a lot you need to know about buying games and toys on the Internet. Before playing roulette with your money, ask these questions:

➤ **Does the site have any kind of "gift wizard?"**   If you're buying a toy or game for your own child (or for yourself—nothing wrong with being young at heart; just stay away from Teletubbies), you probably have a good sense of what to buy. But if you don't have children—or if you're buying for kids who are of a different age than your own children—knowing what to buy can be tough. Do 7-year-olds like board games, and if so, which ones? Do kids want Teenage Mutant Ninja Turtles anymore? And which educational toy can you buy that doesn't seem, well, too educational and that will be fun as well? Some sites have a gift wizard, an area on the site that offers advice on what toy or game to buy for the kid you're trying to please.

Head to the Consumer Product Safety Commission Site for Information About Toys and Children's Products That Have Been Recalled

Sometimes a toy manufacturer recalls a toy or other product because it's potentially dangerous or is defective in some way. But how can a parent keep track of recalls? Easy. Head to the Consumer Products Safety Commission site at www.cpsc.gov and go to the **Recalls** section. You'll find a list of product recalls, along with complete information about why each product was recalled and details about the recall.

➤ **Does the site have a reminder service?**   Your 8-year-old niece's birthday was last week, and your sister calls to ask why you never sent a present—and to inform you how downhearted the little girl was because she didn't receive a gift from you. "The dog ate the present" won't work as an excuse (you don't have a dog), and you fear that if you utter the simple truth, "I forgot," you'll be revealed as the self-centered dolt that your sister always said you were. So you mumble something unintelligible that gets you through the uncomfortable moment, feeling all the while like…well, like a self-centered dolt. Next time, don't forget a child's birthday or other important event—buy from a site with a reminder service. You sign up at a toy and game site for a reminder service, filling in children's birthdays, and then some time before the birthday, you get an email reminder of the upcoming event. That way, you'll always remember a birthday. Just be sure that you remember the child's name—don't send a present to 9-year-old Jessica when it's really 13-year-old Jason's birthday (who really didn't appreciate the American Doll present you sent last year).

➤ **Does the site offer toy reviews—and are they honest, unbiased reviews instead of sales pitches?** Which toys and games are worthwhile and which ones are useless schlock that will end up broken and in the trash within two weeks' time? A few sites, notably RedRocket at www.redrocket.com, offer toy reviews that can help you distinguish the good from the bad and the ugly. Be careful, though, to be sure that the reviews are honest and unbiased, and aren't merely glorified sales pitches. At the RedRocket site, for example, all the articles are taken from the Oppenheim Toy portfolio, an independent site that accepts no advertising or money from toy or game manufacturers.

Turn Old Video Games and Systems into Quick Cash

Do you (or your family) have a video game system and video games that you no longer use—such as a Super Nintendo system and game cartridges that you abandoned in favor of Nintendo 64? Don't let your discards gather dust—instead turn them into cash. You can try selling them at auction and classified sites, but a quicker way to get money for your old stuff is to head to the Games For Less site at www.games4less.com. That site buys used video game systems and video games. It posts its prices, so you know up-front how much you'll get. Games For Less sells used systems as well.

➤ **What are the shipping costs?** The site you're buying from might offer a discount, but how much will the toy really cost? You won't really know until you factor in the shipping cost of the toy or game. Be sure to know the shipping costs up-front, before buying.

➤ **How long will the toy or game take to reach you?** If you're ordering a toy as a gift (and most often you will be unless you play with toys yourself), it's especially important that it arrive in enough time so that it can be wrapped and given to the child. Find out when the toy or game will reach you. Many toy sites use United Parcel Service ground service, which can mean a wait as long as several weeks, especially if the package has to travel across the country.

➤ **What are the site's return policies?** You buy your 8-year-old niece a Dentist Barbie, only to discover that she already has the white-suited, anatomically impossible little plastic figurine, crouched menacingly over a little blue dentist chair. (And, yes, for those of you who aren't parents of young girls, Dentist Barbie is alive and well—"Let's brush!" she says chirpily. Dental instruments are included.) What to do? The little girl isn't interested in having a Dentist Barbie convention (How exciting! Let's talk molars!), so you're going to have to return the gift that you so thoughtfully picked out. I hope you checked the return policy—otherwise, you might be stuck with a little Dentist Barbie of your own ("Let's brush!"). Before buying at a site, check its return policy. Find out whether the toy or game can be returned, whether it can be returned for cash, or whether you will have to settle for a store credit or exchange.

➤ **What kind of warranty does the toy or game carry?** Okay, so 7-year-old Jared tugged just a little too hard on Spiderman's right arm 10 minutes after receiving the plastic hero as a birthday gift; actually, Jared tugged the arm right off and is now the owner of a one-armed Spiderman. But he wants a two-armed Spiderman, the way it was in the brightly colored box. You try telling Jared that there's nothing wrong with a one-armed superhero. But it's no go. How can "Spidey" climb up the sides of buildings with only one arm? (He has a point there, you have to admit.) And he's not budging. What kind of warranty do you have? Be sure before buying that you know the warranty, especially given the rough use that most toys and games get, particularly from younger children.

Some Sites Let Kids Shop for Themselves

The sites covered in this chapter all require that parents do the shopping. But some sites let kids do shopping for themselves—parents first allot a certain amount of money that can be spent, and then kids can spend that money on several places on the Internet. For more information about these sites, turn to Chapter 27, "How to Help Your Kids and Teens Buy Online."

Where to Get Consumer Advice Online for Buying Toys and Games

The Internet is a great place not just to buy toys and games, but to get advice on the best toys and games to buy. In fact, even if you don't buy toys and games online, you'd do well to head to the Internet to check out sites that review and give consumer advice about toys and games. Although some buying sites also offer reviews, sites that specialize in reviews give much better, unbiased advice.

So where should you head when you want to find out the best crafts kits, chemistry sets, board games, and other toys and games? The following sites will lead you in the right direction.

Dr. Toy

        http://www.drtoy.com

If you're looking for the cream of the crop, for the very best toys and games for your kids or for someone else's, start here. Dr. Toy compiles lists of the top toys of the year in a number of different categories (Best 100 Toys for the Year; Best Vacation Products; Best Classic Toys). For each toy on the list, there's a picture and a review, including the appropriate age group for the toy. An especially good feature allows you to browse the best toys by age category, as well as by type, such as toys, educational products, and games. Other excellent sections give advice on buying the right toy for a child, and advice on toy safety. And there's a lot more here as well. In short, before buying a toy for a child, head here.

Action Figure Fans, Check Out This Site

Are you (or is your child) a big fan of action figures—anything from Batman figures to Lost in Space figures to Star Wars figures to X-Men figures and everything in between? Then check out the Action Figure Times at www.aftimes.com. You'll find the latest news, views, and rumors about everything to do with action figures.

Oppenheim Toy Portfolio

```
http://zippy.tradenet.net/toyportfolio/
```

This excellent site offers advice, articles, and reviews about the best toys and games to buy for your children. The individual reviews are good, but even more helpful are the longer articles, such as "Crafts Kits for Kids," which is a roundup of the best crafts kits and which kids they're best for. Also very helpful are the issue articles, such as "Girls Software: Hype or Heroine," which delve into the issue of whether software written specifically for girls is good. The following figure shows the Oppenheim Toy Portfolio site on the Internet.

Looking for advice on which toys and games to buy? You won't go wrong at the Oppenheim Toy Portfolio at `http://zippy.tradenet.net/toyportfolio/`.

Best Sites on the Internet for Buying Games and Toys

So it's finally time to put your money on the line and buy that action figure or doll or piece of software or board game. Where to buy? Check out these great toy- and game-buying sites. Note that most online malls and department stores also have a lot of games. When you're buying toys, check out those sites as well, especially because they often have very good specials. Turn to Chapter 15, "Mall Fever: Department Stores, Malls, Closeouts, and Bargain Hunting," for a list of the best online malls and department stores.

BottomDollar Toys Area

    http://www.bottomdollar.com

(Then select **Toys**.)

If you've already decided on a toy or game and are ready to go bargain hunting, this is a good site to check. It's a bargain-shopping agent that searches several sites for a product you're interested in and shows you where to find the best deals. But it doesn't search a huge number of sites, so if you're a dedicated bargain hunter, be sure to check some sites on your own as well.

eToys

    http://www.etoys.com

This huge toy site sells just about every toy and game you can name—and then some, and then more as well. You can browse by age group, by category of toy and game, by bestsellers, by toy brands, and more. This site has excellent recommendations, a gift wizard, a reminder service, and much more. It's a great site for toy buying and for toy lovers as well.

Head to the FamilyPC Site for Advice on the Best Software and Hardware for Kids

FamilyPC magazine at www.familypc.com offers parents advice on the best hardware and software to buy—everything from educational software to games to printers and computers. If you want to buy hardware or software for a child, be sure to check this site first.

Buy Great Halloween Goods Online

For my son Gabriel and my daughter Mia, only one holiday is worth approaching with any kind of religious fervor—Halloween. Bizarre costumes, plastic pumpkins, flying witches, rubber rats—they all haunt my house that time of year. So imagine the joy in my house when I found the Nightmare Factory at www.nightmarefactory.com. It has everything for Halloween, from masks to costumes, makeup, fake blood, aliens...well, you get the point. Scary times ahead for the Gralla household after we discovered this site.

K.B. Toys

    http://www.kbtoys.com

K.B. Toys has toy stores in shopping malls across America—and they've come to the Internet. There's a good selection of toys, and when I checked, free shipping as well. And there are always special deals to be had. When I last checked, for example, you could buy five packs of Pokemon cards for $19.95—a steal, considering that it was almost impossible to find the cards for sale anywhere, and if you could, they were commonly selling for up to $9 for a single pack.

GameCave.com

    http://www.gamecave.com

If you want to buy video games, here's the place. You can buy video games for all the major game platforms, as well as PC games. The listing is huge, the site is easy to use and navigate, and you can preorder hot new titles so that they'll be shipped to you as soon as they're released. You can buy video game hardware at this site as well.

SmarterKids.com

    http://www.smarterkids.com

Here's a great site for educational games, toys, books, and software. There are great educational products, great ways to get advice on what to buy, and a super Parents Center that offers educational and fun activities that parents can do with children—whether or not they buy a product from it.

ToySmart

    http://www.toysmart.com

Here's my favorite site on the Internet for buying educational games and toys. It offers a great selection of educational games and toys, good discounts, and great advice on which toys to buy. Consumers who have bought the toy or game write the product reviews; a product wizard helps you choose the best toy or game for a child; and there's a huge selection of toys that you'll feel good about buying for your kids or other kids.

Toys "R" Us

    http://www.toysrus.com

Let me admit this up-front: I started writing this chapter with a bias against Toys "R" Us. I hate visiting the monster toy chain in person, I hate its grating TV commercials;

heck, I even hate its logo. So imagine my surprise when I visited its Web site and found that it's a very good toy-buying site. It's easy to browse and search, and it offers extra services, such as a Toy Finder, a reminder service, and a baby registry. So my advice is to visit this site when you are toy shopping, even if you hate the real-life store.

RedRocket

```
http://www.redrocket.com
```

Here's another excellent toy and game site. The site specializes in educational and high-quality toys and games, such as construction and science kits. If the selection sounds dry, it isn't; when checking out this site, I found many of my kids' favorites and many more that I suspect will become their favorites. (I have to admit it; I'm a pushover for this stuff.) There's great help here for finding toys as well. You can see RedRocket in the following figure. The site has a relationship with Nickelodeon, so you'll also find toys associated with that cable channel here.

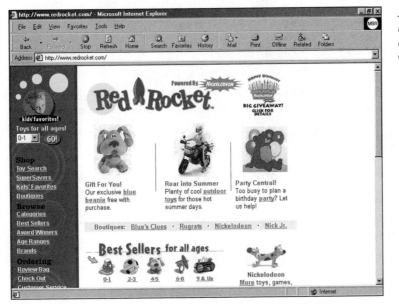

A site for high-quality and educational games and toys: RedRocket at www.redrocket.com.

Head to Internet Newsgroups for Advice on Buying Toys

If you want to ask others to recommend toys and if you are interested in buying used toys, check out Internet newsgroups. Two excellent ones are `alt.toys` and `rec.toys.misc`. Use your newsgroup reader to read them or go to the Web site Deja.com at `www.dejacom.com` and read the newsgroups there. Turn to Chapter 8, "Have I Got a Deal for You!" for more information about using Internet newsgroups.

The Least You Need to Know

➤ If you need help choosing a toy or game, look for a site that has a gift wizard.

➤ Reminder services at toy sites will send you email in advance of a child's birthday or other important event so you won't forget to buy a present.

➤ If you're buying a toy or game as a present, check the shipping time to be sure that you'll have enough time to wrap and deliver it.

➤ Toy review sites are a good source of advice on which toys to buy—and which to avoid.

➤ To buy used toys and games, head to classified sites, auction sites, and Internet newsgroups.

How to Help Your Kids and Teens Buy Online

In This Chapter

➤ How you can set up online shopping accounts for your kids

➤ Why it's a good idea to use online shopping accounts

➤ What to ask before setting up a shopping account for your children

➤ The best kid shopping account sites online

Anyone with a pre-teen or a teenager knows the magnetic attraction that seems to hold between kids and shopping. Music, clothes, makeup, sports equipment, movies, toys, electronics…the list can go on (and very often, does).

That love of shopping extends to the online world, not just the real world. But you're probably uncomfortable handing over your credit cards to your kids to shop with online. (And if you're not, maybe you should be—a teenage girl and a credit card can be a very combustible mix.) Well, there are ways where your kids can shop online—but you'll be able to control their spending, they'll be able to spend only at stores you approve of, and you'll be able to limit their spending. And yes, you can do all this without having to step into that most horrific of places for many parents of kids and teens—the local mall. You'll get just a Net connection and you're ready to go. Read on to see how.

How You Can Let Your Kids Shop Online Without Breaking the Bank

Is it really possible? Is there really a way to let your kids shop online without having to use your credit card, and without breaking the bank? Yes, it's possible, yes it's easy, and as you'll see later in this chapter, it's also a very good idea. Here's how it can be done.

You do it by setting up an account at a site that lets parents create shopping accounts for their kids. They generally all work similarly. At the site, you register yourself and your kids, and for each child, you can set up a separate account. You can give them each a lump sum of money (it's usually a minimum of $25) using your credit card or some other means of payment, although a credit card is the most common. And you can also every week or month give them a shopping "allowance"—you can have a certain amount of money automatically taken from your credit card and put into their accounts.

It's Best to Use Only Credit Cards to Start Kids' Accounts

When setting up and maintaining kids' spending accounts, never use any method other than a credit card. That's because you get consumer protections with a credit card that you don't get if you use checks or some other method. If, for example, the kid shopping site goes out of business, if you've paid by credit card, you get the normal consumer protections that credit cards offer. But if you've paid by check or a similar method, you're out of luck—those consumer protections don't hold.

After the money is in your kids' accounts, they can spend it at a variety of online stores—only those stores that have signed up with the specific buying site. Typically, the stores that sign up are well-known clothing, toys, music, entertainment, and similar sites. Often, you'll be able to determine which of those stores your kids can shop from, so if you want them buying clothing and books but not CDs, for example, you'll be able to limit their spending to clothing and book sites.

Your kids will never be able to overdraw their accounts. If the money isn't in it, they can't buy. It's that simple. And as any parent knows, very few things are simple when it comes to kids.

So Why Bother? What's the Big Deal About These Sites?

In some ways, having your kids spend their money at these sites is superior to having them spend it in real-world stores. These are some of the benefits that these sites offer:

➤ **It allows you to more easily monitor their spending.** You'll get a complete list of things they've bought through their accounts. Some sites even let you veto any purchases before your kids make them.

➤ **You can teach your children the virtues of giving to charities.** Several of these sites include programs that allow your children to give some of their money to charity. It's never too early to teach the importance of giving.

➤ **You won't have to go to a mall.** For many parents (including yours truly), there is no worse fate than going to a mall, especially with a child in tow. Open up online buying accounts, and you'll spend less time in your local food court.

Beware of Letting Your Kids Use Your Auction Account

Kids, just like adults, love to buy things at online auctions. But beware: Don't ever let your kids use your auction account to buy. If you give them your login information, they'll be able to bid as if they were you, and you could find yourself out big bucks. In fact, a teenager used his parents' credit card to run up a bill of over a million dollars on the popular eBay auction site. eBay let the parents off the hook. But you don't want to find yourself bankrupted because your kids absolutely had to buy Elvis's solid gold Las Vegas jumpsuit.

What to Ask Before Registering at Kids' Buying Sites

There are a number of these kids buying sites on the Internet, so you'll want to be smart about which one to use. Before you sign up and hand over your credit card, here's what to ask:

➤ **What are the site's privacy rules?** You don't want marketers and sleazy salesmen drawing up dossiers on your kids and what their buying habits are. Before signing up, find out the site's privacy rules. They should adhere to strict privacy standards, such as guidelines put together by the TRUSTe site at www.etrust.com. Turn to Chapter 5, "How to Check Out a Site and Products Before Buying," for more information about privacy issues.

➤ **What stores have signed up with the site?**   Let's say you sign up at one of these sites, and the only places your kids can buy is from the "World of Pickles" and "DrainSpouts Unlimited." Not good. Make sure that there are sites that your kids want to buy from—and that *you* want them to buy from.

➤ **Does the site let you open savings accounts?**   You'd like to teach your kids to save, not just spend. Some of these sites let you optionally open up savings accounts for kids as well as spending accounts.

➤ **Can your kids use it to give to charity?**   As I mentioned before, it's never too early to teach your kids that everyone has a responsibility to give to the needy. So see whether the site lets your kids use their money to give to charities.

➤ **Can you decide at which sites your kids can buy—and at which they can't?** Some sites let you customize your kids' accounts, and so let them buy at some stores and block them buying at others. If you want to control your kids' spending, this is a good idea.

Look for Special Offers

The kinds of sites covered in this chapter are a relatively new phenomenon, and so they'll give you special offers when you sign up. When I checked in at one, for example, I was offered $30 just to open up a $100 savings account for my child online.

➤ **Do you have "veto power" over what your kids buy?**   At some sites, after your kids have decided what they want to buy, they have to first get your permission. If you want to have veto power over what your kids can buy, be sure the site has this feature.

➤ **Is it easy to track what your kids are spending?** You want an account that will show you in detail what your kids spend and where they spend it.

➤ **Can you change permissions whenever you want?**   Maybe you've decided that your kids are spending too much money on CDs, and now you'd like to limit their purchases there. You'd like a site that makes it easy to change your permissions whenever you want.

The Best Kids' Buying Sites Online

So at which sites should you register? Head to these and you won't go wrong.

DoughNET

http://www.doughnet.com

There's some good and some bad about this site. Let's start off with the good. It lets your kids donate money to charity—and it'll also let them know how they can give their time as well. And if you want your kids to learn about investing, they can play online investing games. The actual sites where your kids can buy are good—there's the exceedingly popular Delia's girls' clothing site, for example, as well as CD sites, and the Barnes & Noble store. But just try figuring out what this site is about or how to use it—it's tough to find even the most basic rules and information.

ICanBuy

http://www.icanbuy.com

This one's an excellent site. There's a nice selection of places where your kids can buy, you can open up a savings account here, your kids can give to charity, and there are even extra features, such as chat areas and the like. The policies are stated clearly, including its excellent privacy rules. (They follow TRUSTe.) And it's easy to get started. You can see the site pictured below.

As you can see, ICanBuy has some of the stuff kids and teens love most—Star Wars stuff.

RocketCash

http://www.rocketcash.com

For my money (and after all, it *is* my money that my kids are spending), this is the best of these kids' sites. Your kids will find great stores such as Delia's, the Amazon bookseller, the excellent Fogdog sports site, CD sites, game sites, and more. They'll be protected by good privacy guidelines—the kids' guidelines put together by TRUSTe. The rules are easy to follow, and there are many specials. And it's the most kid-centric site as well. All in all, it's the best place to go.

RocketCash—the best of the sites where you can set up spending accounts for your kids.

The Least You Need to Know

➤ Look for a site that lets your kids give money to charity and that lets them start savings accounts.

➤ Set up accounts only at sites that protect your kids' privacy.

➤ Find a site that lets you review what your kids buy—and will even let you veto it if you want.

➤ Be sure that the site you sign up with has products that your kids want to buy.

➤ Sign up only at a site that allows you to set rules for the sites from which your kids can buy.

Speak Like a Geek: The Complete Archive

agent   No, this is not 007 we're talking about here. An agent is a piece of software or a Web site that goes out and does a job for you, such as searching the Internet for the lowest price on something you want to buy, such as a book. See *bargain-hunting agent*.

auction site   An online site where you bid to buy goods.

audio file   A file that you can download or play from the Internet that has music or sounds in it.

bargain-hunting agent   An agent that searches the Web for the lowest price on something you want to buy, such as a book. See *agent*.

cable modem   A device that hooks up your computer to your cable system and gets you onto the Internet via a very high-speed connection.

cookies   No, it's not Oreos we're talking about. Cookies are little bits of data that a Web site puts on your computer.

demo program   A program you can get from the Internet that is a version of a commercial piece of software that you can try out for free, but that most likely will expire after a certain amount of time unless you pay for it. See *freeware* and *shareware*.

digital cash   Money that is stored on your computer as bits of data. You purchase digital cash using your computer and your credit card or bank account. Then, when you go to a Web site that accepts digital cash and buy something, the amount is automatically subtracted from the amount of digital cash on your computer.

digital certificate   A "certificate" on your computer that is actually bits of data. This certificate guarantees that you are actually the person you say you are. You could, for example, use a digital certificate when sending email to someone so that they know the message is really from you and not from an imposter. Digital certificates can also be used in financial transactions on the Web. See *digital signature*.

digital signature   A "signature" on your computer that is bits of data and that is unique to you. Digital signatures are a component of digital certificates. See *digital certificate*.

download   To transfer something from the Internet to your computer. You can download software to your computer and then run that software on your own computer. Whenever you visit a Web page, you download the pictures and files that make up that Web page to your computer.

electronic wallet   Software on a computer that stores credit card information, making it easy to shop at a variety of online sites.

email   Messages that can be sent from computer to computer over the Internet, online services, or a company network. It's short for *electronic mail*. See *email alert* and *email reader*.

email alert   An email message that is sent to someone to alert them of something of interest. For example, you can sign up for email alerts to tell you when a given stock hits a certain price, or when a book by a particular author becomes available. See *email*.

email reader   Software that lets you send, receive, and read email. See *email*.

freeware   Software that you can download from the Internet, and use for free. See *demo program* and *shareware*.

home page   A Web page on the World Wide Web. A collection of Web pages at one site is referred to as a Web Site. See *Web site*.

hyperlink   A spot on a Web page that by clicking on it lets you jump to another location on the Web.

icon   A small picture on your computer screen that you click on to run a program. It can also refer to a picture on a Web page that you click on.

Internet Explorer   See *Microsoft Internet Explorer*.

Internet mall   A site on the Internet made up of many different kinds of stores or that has many different kinds of products for sale.

Internet service provider (ISP)   A company that provides services for letting you dial into the Internet.

keyword   A word you type into a search box on a site, such as a shopping site, that describes the product or information you're looking to find.

link   Another term for hyperlink. See *hyperlink*.

Microsoft Internet Explorer   The Web browser made by Microsoft that enables you to get onto the World Wide Web. See *Web browser*.

MP3 file   A special music format that's of almost CD quality, but that produces files that aren't very large, and so don't take a long time to download.

Netscape Navigator   The Web browser made by Netscape that enables you to get onto the World Wide Web. Navigator is part of a package of Internet tools from Netscape known collectively as Communicator. See *Web browser*.

newsgroup   A global discussion group or message board on the Internet in which people post and read public messages. There are many thousands of newsgroups about every topic imaginable, including many about shopping and buying and selling products. Sometimes, you'll hear people refer to these as Usenet groups, too.

newsgroup reader   A piece of software that lets you participate in newsgroups by letting you read and post messages.

online   Being connected to the Internet or to a service such as America Online.

online service   A service such as America Online that you connect to that has information, sites, and services you can access through your computer.

online transaction   A financial transaction conducted over the Internet or online service. When you pay for something using a credit card on a Web site, you've conducted an online transaction.

opt-out policy   A policy that lets you say that you don't want to receive certain services or messages from a Web site. For example, when you fill out a form online and you're asked whether you want to be sent email from that site, if there's an option you can check saying you don't want to receive email, that's an opt-out policy.

password   A unique combination of characters and numbers that you type into a form on a Web page, and that identifies you as the person you say you are. Passwords are used to ensure that when you go to a site that has any kind of personal identifying information, that you're the only person who can access that information. See *username*.

plug-in   A piece of software that works in concert with your Web browser to enable you to view a specific piece of content on the Web, such as music, pictures, or animations.

portal   A Web site such as Yahoo! that is used as a way to navigate through the Web and find information on the Web.

RealAudio   A popular plug-in that lets you play audio files from the Internet and listen to them on your computer. This is an older version of the technology; the newest versions, RealSystem and RealSystem G2, enable you to also view video files. See *RealPlayer, RealSystem G2,* and *streaming media*.

RealPlayer   A popular plug-in that lets you play audio and video files from the Internet and see them and listen to them on your computer. See *RealAudio, RealSystem G2,* and *streaming media*.

RealSystem G2   The most recent version of a popular plug-in that lets you play audio and video files from the Internet and see them and listen to them on your computer. See *RealAudio, RealPlayer,* and *streaming media*.

351

safe site   See *secure site*.

search site   A site such as AltaVista that searches the Web and tells you where to find the information you're searching for. This is also known as a search engine.

secure site   A site that uses powerful encryption technology or a standard such as SSL so that any confidential information you put into a form there is kept confidential. See *Secure Sockets Layer (SSL)*.

Secure Sockets Layer (SSL)   The main standard used today on the Web that ensures that confidential data sent over the Internet, such as credit card information, is kept private.

SET (secure electronic transaction)   A behind-the-scenes standard that ensures that confidential data sent over the Internet such as credit card information is kept private, and that guarantees that the person who uses the credit card really is who he says he is.

shareware   Software that you download from the Internet or an online service to your computer, and that you can try out for free. If after using it you decide you want to buy it, you're supposed to pay the author for it. The fee you pay is called a registration fee. See *freeware* and *demo program*.

site   Another name for Web site. See *Web site*.

streaming audio   See *streaming media*.

streaming media   A technique that enables you to view and listen to audio and video files from the Internet while they're still downloading to your computer. With streaming media, you can view and listen to audio and video files only a few seconds after you click them. Without streaming media, you would have to wait until the entire file downloads before you could listen to or view the file, which could take far longer—depending on your connection speed and the size of the file, it could otherwise easily take a half hour or more. See *RealAudio, RealPlayer,* and *RealSystem G2*.

streaming video   See *streaming media*.

surfing   The act of travelling from site to site on the World Wide Web.

TRUSTe   An organization that sets voluntary rules (that some Web sites follow) having to do with the privacy of the information they gather from you when you visit sites on the Web.

Usenet newsgroup   Another name for newsgroup. See *newsgroup*.

username   A unique name that identifies you to a Web site. Usernames and passwords are often used together to ensure that when you sign into a Web page, you're really who you say you are. This is also known as User ID and/or Login. See *password*.

video file   A file that you can download or play from the Internet that has video in it.

virtual shopping cart   A service you can use when shopping on Web sites that lets you keep a list of all the things you're considering buying. When you're ready to buy, you can then discard things from your shopping cart, pay for them, or keep them there for your next visit to the Web site.

Web   Another name for the World Wide Web. See *World Wide Web*.

Web browser   A piece of software that lets you get onto the World Wide Web, view Web pages, and go from site to site. See *Microsoft Internet Explorer* and *Netscape Navigator*.

Web page   A single page on the World Wide Web. Usually Web pages are put together to form a larger, more complicated Web site. See *Web site*.

Web site   A location on the World Wide Web that lets you get information, view audio or video, shop, or do many other activities. A Web site is made up of many Web pages put together. See *Web page* and *home page*.

Web surfing   Another name for surfing. See *surfing*.

WinZip   The most popular program for Windows that lets you "unzip" compressed files. See *Zip file*.

World Wide Web   The most popular part of the Internet, made up of Web sites and pages that are all hyperlinked together so that you can jump from page to page and site to site.

Zip file   A file that has been compressed using the Zip format so that it's small in size and can be more quickly downloaded to your computer. You'll have to "unzip" the file to use it after it's on your PC. See *WinZip*.

Index

Y-Z